Library Furnishings

Library Furnishings

A Planning Guide

Tish Murphy

McFarland & Company, Inc., Publishers
Jefferson, North Carolina, and London

Photographs are by Tish Murphy
unless otherwise credited.

LIBRARY OF CONGRESS CATALOGUING-IN-PUBLICATION DATA

Murphy, Tish, 1951–
Library furnishings : a planning guide / Tish Murphy.
  p.   cm.
Includes bibliographical references and index.

ISBN-13: 978-0-7864-2871-7 (softcover : 50# alkaline paper) ∞

1. Library buildings — Design and construction.   2. Libraries — Space utilization.
3. Public libraries — Planning.   4. Library architecture — United States.
5. Library buildings — United States — Design and contruction.
6. Public libraries — United States.   I. Title.
Z679.5.M87   2007   022'.9 — dc22   2007007788

British Library cataloguing data are available

©2007 Tish Murphy. All rights reserved

*No part of this book may be reproduced or transmitted in any form
or by any means, electronic or mechanical, including photocopying
or recording, or by any information storage and retrieval system,
without permission in writing from the publisher.*

Cover photograph ©2007 Photodisc

Manufactured in the United States of America

*McFarland & Company, Inc., Publishers
Box 611, Jefferson, North Carolina 28640
www.mcfarlandpub.com*

Merlene Rayford, 1946–2001

In memory of my sister, who taught me that what you experience is the combination of all the choices that you have made and to "always remember to have joy in your life."

Acknowledgments

Words are things and a small drop of ink,
Falling like dew upon a thought, produces
That which makes thousands, maybe millions, think.
— Byron Don Juan, Canto iii, stanza 88

I want to acknowledge my husband, Barry Stuecker, who allows me to look at everything in a different way and who is always there for me. I want to thank my late cousin Bill Garlitz, former principal of Ringgold High School in Monongahela, Pennsylvania, for his tenacious nature, and who relentlessly checked on my progress. I want to acknowledge all my friends for their support and patience, especially Keri Means, who continued to assist me and reminded me that I could accomplish this.

Ellen Altman, formerly the feature editor for *Public Libraries*, opened this window of opportunity for me to have this experience of becoming an author; she shared her opinion with me that "librarians needed to learn more about library furniture" and asked me to write an article in *Public Libraries* magazine. I have developed a new appreciation for the task of writing and I thank her for this opportunity to learn.

I gratefully acknowledge each and every librarian that I have come in contact over the years, as they each have provided me with valuable feedback through their own experiences and my experience with them. It has been a pleasure and I honor the time of working with them in their chosen and worthy profession. My heartfelt thanks go to the specifiers and end users that I have worked with who held true to the product and design that they started with, standing up for the product they wanted even when it wasn't the least expensive, and to the manufacturers that I have worked with who have taught me so much about library furniture and how I can serve in the furniture industry.

Contents

Acknowledgments	vii
Introduction: Anticipate and Facilitate Change	1
1. Laying Out the Library	9
2. Bringing Electrical into Furniture	40
3. Specifications to Installation	53
4. Shelving: Will It Stand the Test of Time?	74
5. ADA: The Primary Rule Is to Exceed Minimums	97
6. Seating: Types, Performance Testing and Use	110
7. Children's Areas: (Quietly?) Entertain while Encouraging Learning	124
8. Teen Spaces: Created from *Their* Input	136
9. Lessons Learned From the Past to Embrace Technologies of the Future	143
10. Using Wayfinding: Signs for Identification and Information	155
11. Green Libraries That Work	165
12. Forward Thinking	175

APPENDICES: CHECKLISTS FOR A SMOOTHER PROJECT

Appendix A: Defining Tasks and Responsibilities of the Development Team	183
Appendix B: Evaluation of Work Station Seating	185
Appendix C: Survey 26 ADA with Diagrams	188
Appendix D: Electronic Planning Table	190
Appendix E: "Watt" Amperage Is Required?	192
Appendix F: Sources of Information	193
Chapter Notes	195
Bibliography	199
Index	203

Introduction: Anticipate and Facilitate Change

Nothing endures but change.
— Heraclitus, c540–c480BC

Planning a new or remodeled library brings both opportunity and challenge. The opportunity is to improve the things that could look and function better and the challenge is to keep these improvements within budget. There are so many details! We begin by planning the spaces of the library. All areas of the library have their advocates who are all correct in knowing their importance to the whole. The quiet area is something that patrons tend to expect. An enticing and active children's area is paramount to a child's future, which ultimately benefits our planet and our life as we know it. Which is more important? Should more seating for public use be in the plan or should that space be used to shelve a collection that has already reached capacity? These are some of the hard questions that decision makers must address.

Will the shelving and furniture selection be in the architectural contract? Will the furniture be wood or metal or a combination? What colors will be used? Often, designated staff will leave their primary duties of librarian behind and serve as coordinator for the project. I think the librarian who is the project manager during the term of the construction might as well consider himself on leave from his librarian work, as his involvement will easily be a part-time job. When the project gets into full swing, it may feel more like a full-time position.

There is a set of choices the planner makes; how will the shelving, tables, seating, carrels and lounge seating be arranged? The library has been called an intellectual marketplace and is moving toward self sufficiency. The furniture designs need to respond to that need. Change never ends and it comes faster and faster in both library functions and in technology. Take study carrels as an example. Once they were desirable, but now are obsolete, as people prefer to lounge as they use their computers or use tables that are more open and let them spread out their materials.

As library functions change, the furniture must be adaptable to different uses — libraries are vastly different facilities than they were twenty years ago, and choosing furniture requires more sophisticated planning. Libraries used to be simpler places. The furniture appeared utilitarian and institutional, and many facilities were without design. Today planners of libraries have a choice as to whether they want the library to look like a library of the past or if they want the library to integrate architectural design elements of the building or bring in elements mirroring the interests and the culture of the users in the location. Libraries have to compete with bookstores and other places where an individual might spend his time.

Change Happens

The only certainty is that there *will* be change. Equipment gets smaller; monitors get larger, the newer flat screens require less depth in the furniture, and so on. There are more peripheral devices and accessories to occupy the work surface and the area under the work surface. There is the CPU that needs to be housed, a mouse with mouse pad, earphones for the sites that have sound — and this doesn't take into account the personal items that public library users bring with them. As the equipment configuration layout changes, the furniture components change, while the library continually appraises space for its greatest potential.

When a librarian stepped into her library in the past, returning books to the stacks followed turning on the lights, checking the temperature in the building and arranging the chairs under the tables. Today the librarian enters a world of technology where computers have been programmed for operating utilities for the facility and are at work monitoring the environment. In the library of the past, library furniture was used for one purpose. Long tables and chairs placed end to end were used for study and remained in one arrangement in reading rooms. Tables are now designed to be multifunctional; a study table or carrel becomes a computer area when a patron brings a laptop to the library. As technological advances are made in the next fifty years, it is hard to imagine how furniture needs will change.

"Powerful" Change

There were few power requirements in the past, but now there are many. Libraries built years ago did not have electrical outlets and data ports dotting their walls. There wasn't electrical lighting in libraries until sometime after 1897, when the Library of Congress became one of the first buildings to use the electrical lighting that followed candlelight and gas lamps. The floor monuments form outlets hidden under the carpet's surface, arising from a trough under the floor which is used to house all the electrical and communication cables. Tables contain electrical outlets to recharge the laptop battery or to save the battery of a portable computer, cell phone or other equipment that the patron brings. Tables and lounge seating also provide electrical access and data ports. The libraries are going wireless ("Wi-Fi").

At the turn of the nineteenth century and into the 1900s, whether books should be open to public access was still being debated. Library books were kept in shelving behind a wall that had an opening, much like our bank teller windows today, for the patron to speak to a librarian who had access to the books. At this time only about one quarter of 67 public libraries in *Architectural Review*'s 1902 pick of the best modern library designs had complete open access to their book collections. Over half of the sample maintained completely closed stacks, while another fifteen percent provided open access to only a small portion of their collections; other types of rooms catering to uses not associated with the book collection (room for group study, exhibition rooms, lecture halls and club rooms) appeared in less than a third of the libraries.[1] At some point the book shelving moved out from behind the wall for public access, but still left the past periodicals closed to the public. In the mid-sixties this began to change in that more of the past issues of subscriptions were brought out in the open where the public could obtain them and read them in an area that eventually grew into the periodicals reading room.

Even the philosophy of the library has changed. The library today is abuzz with activity; though patron voices are still encouraged to remain at a low decibel level, there is a definite hum of activity. Library users of the past were segregated, adults separate from children which perhaps seems quaint today. All of these changes influence the furniture in a library as well as the changing role of the librarian.

Navigating Change

The librarian is an organizer of knowledge. Not only does she know the locations of texts and recorded information, but she has become a navigator of the computer search engines in order to educate patrons on new ways of finding answers to their questions. The librarian's primary task is to serve the community of users effectively. Well studied furnishings will contribute toward accomplishing that goal.

People of today are learning to work together in a different way. Patrons who previously worked in isolation are now encouraged to work together, perhaps using a computer carrel where they and others can gather as a group to view the screen.

Ideally tables are adaptable enough to be used by individuals in classroom style situations and then reconfigured into pods for lively exchanges within small groups. At a public library facility, especially in a rural setting where the library is a multi-use building, the librarian might check his or her calendar to find that certain rooms serve one night as the town meeting place. The next afternoon the same room may be used for an author reading and book signing. Meeting rooms and study areas are welcome additions in public libraries and necessary components of an academic library. "Campus Commons" is a new name for an area that is used for information and student gatherings in academic libraries. This area is computer intensive and should be in relatively close proximity to technical assistance so that librarians can be there to help computer users.

Changes in Everyday Tasks

The tasks being performed in the library are changing. As reference catalogs and card catalogs gave way to online searches, the index tables were replaced with computers that required different types of furniture that included power requirements *through* the furniture to that equipment.

Furnishings support the needs of the library user and the service the library provides. The way books are displayed on the shelving facilitates the ease of locating, storing and reshelving material into circulation and is useful for the patron as well as the staff. Shelving furnishings perform various functions. While regular shelving stores to a maximum advantage, some libraries display books or other items to market them in ways that will encourage circulation. As the number of books on tape and DVDs increase, another storage challenge emerges. Compact shelving, though rarely used in public libraries, fulfills the need for more books in less area for university applications. Safety measures are engineered into compact shelving to make them more user-friendly, as the comfort and safety of patrons are important factors in planning the modern library.

A few years ago it was thought that the book might "go away" and be replaced by e-books. The talk now is of machines replacing the human element of the library staff's task of checking out books and returning them to the collection. Some of the larger academic libraries require the help of robots because of the sheer size of volumes moving within their collections. Nevada's University Lied Library in Las Vegas is one example of automated systems to access books and is evidence that the book is not going away.

When libraries went online with computers it opened up a new world for those users who didn't own computers at home yet. To find a book became faster and easier once it was done electronically rather than through a card system search to learn if the collection included the desired material. Libraries were able to provide their patrons data with an ease and efficiency that was not possible before computer searching on the Internet became so commonplace. And they taught many of us the means of retrieving data on the computer. Being able to try out a computer in the library probably led to a greater comfort level for some people to purchase a computer for home. This goes against the idea that as the Internet brings online research to the person's home, and that the library will become a thing of the past and no longer a place to spend time researching a subject. Many people still would rather work with someone helping them.

The depth of information in the library's collection coupled with the technical expertise of librarians whose business is information-gathering provides an invaluable service to a library's users. Just ask the people where communities are in danger of losing their libraries due to funding cuts. These library users, knowing the part a library plays in the community, are appalled that these types of services would be discontinued.

Reference is now also known as Research and Information, especially in academic settings. Historically, books were checked out, which required more manual and repetitive movements while maintaining a specific place in what was called the charging desks. Now librarians move about the library assisting, locating, reshelving; their physical mobility has increased. Specialized furniture is needed for the self-check units and for the information kiosks that patrons use without the personal assistance of a librarian. Electrical and sophisticated data requirements incorporated into the furniture will increase until wireless capabilities become integrated into all areas of the library and our culture.

Manufacturers must keep up with the trends to satisfy the changing needs of the library. They read trade journals to learn of new materials and constantly change their manufacturing equipment and fabricating methods to keep up with the demands that will be placed on the furniture. Exhibitors participating at the regional and national library conferences not only show support for the library associations by exhibiting but are there to encourage feedback on what kinds of products the librarians need. By the manufacturers willingness to listen to their customers and learn of changes in the library, everyone wins; the users of the furniture and the manufacturers of the furniture become a team whose goal is to make the library a smoother working facility.

Changes in Spaces for People

Children's sections of libraries are becoming larger and more creatively designed, as studies have proven that children learn more in an environment that is mentally stimulating. The size of the furniture is expanding, allowing adults to occupy the seating as easily as the small patrons do. An adult only needs to sit in a child's chair with arms one time to learn that it is not a good idea to specify all the child-size seating *have* arms. It leaves a definite impression on the adult posterior (no pun intended).

Spaces that invite the public to use them should be created with safety and convenience as an integral part of the design. The ease with which a patron can rise from a chair or be drawn to want to sit in it in the first place depends on such factors as appropriate seat height and whether the chair has arms to provide aid in rising from it. These are topics that are acknowledged as making a difference in the traffic a library experiences. Some libraries plan a specialty coffee bar to simulate the bookstore "stay and sit awhile" environment.

Included in the building program is a philosophical statement concerning the library's role within the community or university. Richard Bazillion says in his book *Academic Libraries as High-Tech Gateways* that the planners might decide that the new library should be primarily a book warehouse rather than a "people place" or they may offer just the opposite conception. In the end the structure will reflect its designers' underlying philosophy."[2]

ADA Changes

Time changes things. Since early 1991 the public sector has addressed the Americans with Disabilities Act's laws and found that many of the regulations passed made a more comfortable and usable interior for all of us, not just the handicapped. The mandatory 36-inch minimum aisle width and the placement of the levels of books between 48 inches high and 15 inches at the lowest point for reaching to the front is helpful for persons who have a full range of movement and imperative for those who do not.

A Guide to Decisions

The purpose of this book is to help librarians and library planners make better informed decisions. I trust that this manual will become an easy reference for now and through the changes to come, a reference that will be handy as decision makers evaluate various types of furnishings. I will share experiences of those who have analyzed the areas for library functions; talk about the importance of basic planning and getting specifications written that will assure the desired quality level; and supply a checklist for a successful project. This book will lead planners through the process by explaining the terminology used by manufacturers and installers, explaining the conventions used for measurements such as actual versus nominal and identifying elements for installing stable shelving. Joinery methods of construction in seating and of tables and carrels are an important durability and ease of change consideration. After reading this book planners will understand some of the differences in furniture construction relative to a library that will work for twenty or more years. The outcome is a library that accommodates a variety of information users — a library that works. I'm sure that everyone has seen libraries that are outdated, have not stood the test of time, and are not ready for the electronic age that is here today and the technology that is certain to increase as we are at the beginning of a new century. The services of a technologically outdated facility will find it difficult to compete with a well-planned facility that is able to *flex*.

Having a new or remodeled library presents both opportunity and challenge. To improve and fix things to work properly or more effectively is the opportunity, while the challenge remains to stay within budget. Part of the challenge lies in the decisions, more decisions, and still more decisions to be made. We need to know what purchasing guidelines dictate our buying, whether certain levels of purchasing require going through the bid process and writing formal specifications for our needs rather than estimating our costs and purchasing from a quote. Then there is space utilization, questions of gauge of steel for shelving, paint finishes, other finishes; and don't forget the comfort of the chairs. To furnish the library in a way that makes the community proud and at the same time shows taxpayers that their hard-earned money was well spent are goals to strive for. Sometimes a library wants to showcase the technological changes in a high-tech way and the inner workings are exposed, as in the Burton Barr Phoenix Main Public Library in which "flexible steel electrical conduits for lighting computer stations and electrical outlets simply drop from the ceilings where needed."[3] They wind downward (or upward?) connecting the high ceilings to where the electrical is required whether it be to the book stacks or the unique backlit service desks. The materials are what they are; not adorned with paint or other treatments. The furniture is sculptural, while pure in its materials. The building was designed around book storage, the public's need for information and the means of retrieving it.

Anticipating Change: Keeping "U" in the Future

Some ideas of things to come in the future will be discussed as we explore the ideal environment for a book and compare that with the creature comforts of a person who uses a library. Universities have begun experimenting with the virtual library and the University of Texas–Austin, for instance, took a radical step by removing all 90,000 books from the undergraduate library to make room for a Wi-

Fi (wireless fidelity) powered learning space. The building, open 24 hours a day and packed with computers, has retained five digital librarians, who help students navigate the vast world of electronic media. The library Website has a virtual reference desk with a chat function, and librarians are augmenting course Web pages with recommended e-books, journals and databases.[4]

With all of the technology, hardware and equipment, the challenge is not only to humanize an area but to make it a space in which people of all sizes, ages and interests can find information that they desire. The importance of the users having a pleasant experience of the library will determine continued use over their lifetimes.

1

Laying Out the Library

The books must be near the readers; the readers near the librarian and the librarian near the books.
 — Rolf Myller, *The Design of the Small Public Library* (1966)

Architecture and Function

Thinking more about how the building is situated on the land, the architect uses the building to create something that the interior planners can work with to bring the outside inside or to create engaging areas. The architect calls this concept "transparency" when one has the ability to look inside from the outside, making libraries and their services seem more accessible.[1] If the entry or the interior of the library can be viewed from the road, the activity inside will welcome more users to experience the library. With available woods, metals, laminates, stone and other materials, color and textures of fabrics and finishes can be brought to the furniture and shelving for replicating nature and familiar forms.

Architectural involvement with layout is helpful in every part of the library design. In Farmington, New Mexico, the goal was to bring the outside in through the use of materials like sandstone on the walls, rocks as seating perches throughout the entry area and glass etched with symbols of the Native American culture of the region. In Ketchikan, Alaska, the outside is brought inside by the use of a large picture window revealing the creek that runs alongside the building. In the downtown Las Vegas/Clark County Library the entry feels as though you are still outside because of the use of concrete, rock and hard surfaces found in the city. A riparian area with a lake is viewed from the reading area at SE Regional Public Library in Gilbert, Arizona, while natural tree trunks serve as occasional tables near the entry. Many of these types of ideas will be explored by the architect and interior planners of the building, but it is important to be sure that there is involvement by the users of the library building as well as the staff who will be "living" in the surroundings.

This array of plasma screens is situated in the lobby of the Farmington, New Mexico, Public Library and has the capacity to display nine different videos for information and educational purposes.

The three functional elements that a library provides are reading, book storage and staff working areas, and the normal cycle of uses they house are location, retrieval and communication of information as well as its return to storage.[2]

The circulation desk as we have known it will not be around much longer. Radio Frequency Identification (RFID) equipment is making the contact between patron and library staff less frequent, at least for the functions of transactions and handling items. By using this RFID system at the libraries, inventory can be kept of the book as it is checked out and tracked again when it is returned. This is the same kind of mechanism in place at the do-it-yourself check-out lines in grocery and hardware stores; those RFID also include tracking the unit cost and product number. The most interesting use of RFID that I have seen recently has been an RFID embedded in children's pajamas, so that once they go outside a perimeter their whereabouts could be monitored. As always, as technology advances, our lives become easier but we need to continually adapt the environment to make technology work efficiently.

The Library Entrance

The entrance of a library announces the intention of the library to serve its clientele. Well placed and easily read signs guide the user to find the material or the service desk that they are looking for without frustration.

Consult a knowledgeable sign manufacturer to learn the requirements applicable to public places. When making the choices for signs consider the benefit for Americans with Disabilities Act (ADA) compliant signs and the size of the lettering so that patrons with low vision will have the opportunity to use them as well. (See Chapter on Wayfinding.)

Some people will be more comfortable asking for help from a librarian, so an information/customer service desk as well as the main circulation desk should be a part of what they see upon entering. Some people will pass the assistance center because they are familiar with the general layout of a library and at ease with their choice of browsing and the use of the self-check machines. Like bank machines and grocery check-outs, a patron might no longer require the help of an individual in their visit to the library.

Large multimedia display beacons located near the information desk allow customers to make new and unplanned connections, as interesting facts, quotations, library events, services and resources are shown on a plasma screen. Since people have become familiar with seeing monitors everywhere (in department stores, in sports complexes and in their home and work environments) they are drawn to them, and the monitors then can inform and educate. The benefit of using a mobile display is that it can be used in many areas of the library.

LIBRARY FURNISHINGS

Not only is this book display kiosk at the Farmington Public Library easily changeable, it has castors that can move it for use anywhere in the library.

1. Laying Out the Library

In a larger library, a waiting/meeting area outside the library might be added inside an acclimatized area to protect patrons from the elements.

Entries with hard surface floors, glass and high ceilings may be noisy; the book trucks rolling through the library moving books, the voice helping a customer, the cell phone user — all these sounds will be louder if they have no soft surfaces to absorb them.

Between the entry and the information desk is the ideal place to have the racks for brochures. Displays can act as baffles for quieter areas, control traffic patterns and make an entrance inviting, colorful and interesting. This area is used to arrange informational brochures on wall displays or tables concerning upcoming events. Tables or display units would be helpful to hold seasonal conveniences like IRS forms. Displaying information about community events or performances in a local theatre or posters highlighting what this month celebrates will provide information for your patrons and help the community get information to the public.

It is also common in the larger libraries to place a bookstore, gift shop or used

An information kiosk is conveniently placed near the entry at the Oxon Hill Branch of Prince George's County, Maryland.

book store near the entry to catch the eye of customers. Rental videos are not uncommon and educational videos are often free from the rental video area. You may want to use shelving or display in this area that is different that the standard shelving in order to call attention to the video area. Cafes and coffee shops are conveniently placed in this entry area, which allows them to compete with the larger bookstore's trends. Finally, it appears that more art is being displayed in this portion of the library, whether it is owned by the library or provided by using an on-loan rotating art exhibit. Music piped through over a sound system might be an option for an area like this. Neighborhood gatherings for music, art or poetry fit well with the café ambiance.

The Service Desk

Public service areas such as reference and circulation, which the new language calls "customer service," should be in easy view from the pivotal points of the library. Upon entering, the user reads a space by coming inside the building to have a look and decides first where they want to go and second whether they need help or not. If they decide they do need help, who would be the best person to approach?

A desk with a book drop within the counter near the entry or a book drop located in the parking lot provides a convenience to return books. A descending book truck or another method of book storage and retrieval is housed under the desk, creating an open box where books are held to reshelf. If a book is popular and likely to be a book that will be immediately checked out, a display unit near the desk will provide the convenience for staff of not needing to reshelf the book as well as being handy for patrons to pick up. Kiosks are also being discussed that require another piece of furniture designed around the requirements of a functional book drop that houses a self check-in unit (RFID).

Reference areas near a desk for staff service hold catalogs (both automated and printed bound material) and direct the user to information that he is searching. This desk will involve the use of at least one computer, a telephone, a printer and a surface to spread out books when the librarian has taken on a project for a library patron. This is one of the areas in the building plan that will benefit from early planning because of the necessary tools and the wiring requirements within service desks. The size of this desk is dependent on the size of the library and the number of people who will most likely occupy this space. It could be as simple as a straight desk and would create less of a barrier than the L- or U-shaped desk which would also require a larger footprint of space.

The circulation desk size varies with the size and type of library but some of the same duties of the desk are applicable to the space regardless of type of library:

1. Laying Out the Library

This photograph taken at the Farmington, New Mexico, Public Library illustrates two service desks; on the right is an ADA compliant service desk and on the left is the standard height desk.

health, law, public or academic. Think about curved versus linear layout of the desk. Curves are friendlier to the eye but sometimes costlier to produce. The desk will be planned for staff seated or standing and usually a combination of both. Modular desks may have adjustability built into the design, with adjustable work surfaces that will raise and lower with minimal disruption and use of tools.

A chair to work with a patron encourages in-depth help from the reference staff. If chairs are provided in other professionals' office, why are they not provided for clients who wish to speak with librarians? The absence of chairs at the reference desk sends a very negative message to clients, that is, 'Don't stay too long!' Is this the message librarians want to send in today's climate of client oriented service?

Is it possible for the staff to show the patron the screen in the current placement of the computer or do you need a rotating mechanism to allow the computer to swivel? Can this be supplied by the furniture manufacturer or is it available from the computer supplier? The back of the computer can also be shielded by adding a design detail to the desk or as part of the swivel. This works in two ways: aesthetically (no ugly cords show to the outside) as well as a safety factor that the cords aren't accessible for accidental unplugging.

The space planner can't ask too many questions of the library staff who will use the space. Is the person left or right handed? Will the area work for both or is the placement of the computer only good for the right-handed user? It is widely accepted that ten percent of the world's population is left handed so the impact is significant if an area is planned for a right-handed user.

Will the seated librarians at the service desks use a desk-height (29–30 inches work surface) or a counter-height chair (approximately 39 inches)? If counter height, choose a stool with a footrest (platform or ring) for the legs to rest, alleviating the pressure which is sure to cause circulation problems over time. I have noticed that many times a two-step stool is used in this manner to comfortably rest the feet at the proper level. If this is the way you choose to eliminate the feet dangling, be sure that the stool has enough space for the feet to move. If the person who uses the chair has to sit in one position, it causes stress to the body, so you want to be sure they are able to change positions comfortably while seated. Does the chair adjust in height to fit various users? (See more on choosing a chair in the Seating chapter).

An area with computer catalogs and online access are usually grouped not far from a service desk for patron check-in and assignment to a computer that is numbered or identified in some way. This section intensive with electrical equipment is another area to be designed early in planning so that it is "cable ready" and flexible for future needs. In the future, computers may be interspersed into more areas of the library as we rely even more on computer technology.

One of the first decisions is whether to use desks that consist of standard modules for the circulation desk or to design the functions within a built-in (attached to the floor and built on site) unit that is known as "millwork." A subcontractor that your construction company has chosen to work with builds the service centers according to a plan that is drawn by the architect. When the service desks are designed by the architect and built by the contractor, the library will want to see the plans and discuss the details as to how the desk will be built (how it will look and function). The question and answer dialogue will become most important to assure that the area works for the librarian as well as fitting the look and feel of the building. Be sure to include the information technology (IT) communications specialist in this planning as this person will be knowledgeable on the specific types of wiring that will be brought into the area.

Transaction counters much like a bank teller line will direct patrons to the area

This "postal counter" design provides support for patrons as they wait their turn at the Anne Arundel County Annapolis Area Public Library in Maryland. It was designed and fabricated with the staff's input as to what would work for them.

for service when staff is ready to help them. If a countertop is chosen be sure that there is at least one area along the countertop that a wheelchair user could use to communicate with staff easily. (Refer to ADA chapter for more information on dimensioning.) In the Anne Arundel County Public Library in Annapolis, Maryland, a "postal counter" was carefully designed by staff with their local fabricator's help to provide a narrow but substantially built piece of furniture for patrons to rest their books or other media on while they wait in the line to checkout at the counter. This counter satisfied the library and its patrons on several counts: it gave its users some support if they wanted to use it to lean against and it provided much needed direction as to the area of assistance. The branch manager, Gloria Davis, believed that it was a much better solution than the velvet ropes that were previously used, as children played on the ropes and people knocked the stanchions over as they gave a false sense of stability. The wood counter was designed with rounded edges and a size that wouldn't obstruct the path of strollers or someone using a walker.

Visual Control of Space: How Librarians Interact with Users

It is important to the library staff that the access to the collection is good and that there remains a visual line of sight through the stacks. Windows, doors and traffic flow from main entrance throughout the library dictate efficient placement of staff for points of assistance and for monitoring library use.

The architectural details of a building are another source of security issues. Any alcoves or areas that provide privacy for the library patron (examples: window seat or isolated study carrel or lounge seating area) are problem areas for the staff at closing time and defeat their goal to observe the areas during open hours. A security and safety issue for patrons arises when there are blind corners and niches and other physical obstructions that will complicate visual control of space.

In an academic and public library this line of sight is important to the staff, as the line of sight is always a concern for the safety of patrons as well as easy access when someone needs help from staff. Tables and chairs will be placed in the areas among stacks but in plain view of at least one service desk, which is convenient for the patron and allows staff to monitor security concerns. Internet service computer areas are located near the service centers or staff desks for the same reasons, and the time limits and rules for use are easier to administer.

Grouping Related Areas

Doing an analysis of the work flow in the furniture design process may eliminate problems in the area when it is completed. Ask questions of the people who will use the area. Make rough drawings and diagram the areas with "bubbles" (to define what will occur in these spaces and how it differs from another area). Putting pencil to paper will help get the creative juices flowing and put you in that space, imagining what it will feel like to work in the area that you are designing. Some libraries will have the funding to work with an architect or designer from the beginning but, if you don't, the best way to begin drafting the layout is to use a copy of the architect's drawing and then create templates for the furniture pieces (if they are not available from the manufacturer) that are cutout to the same scale. It is important to be working with a floor plan that is to scale and using templates that are to the same scale.

Creating areas that are in "bubbles" (rough areas of placement) at this point are helpful to use in translating what the library sees as a layout that will be functional. "C Schemes" [Figures 1 and 2] show an architect's conceptual "bubble" of the zones of the library. A more detailed plan of this small rural library followed as more detailed thought was given to what would occur within each zone.

1. Laying Out the Library

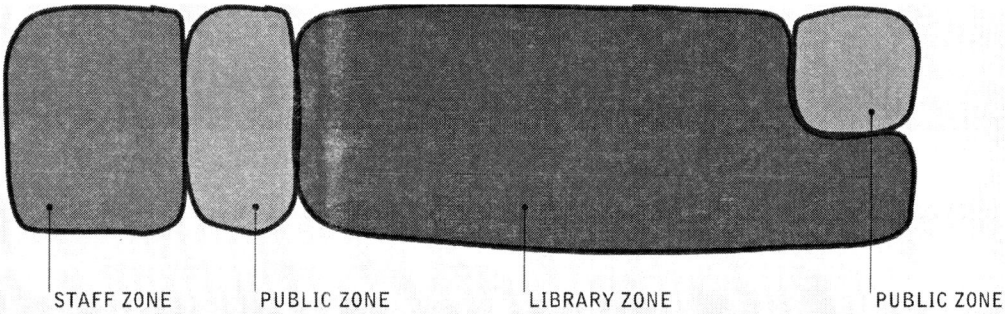

Figure 1: Preliminary schematic plan used to lay out the generalized areas by zones and function.

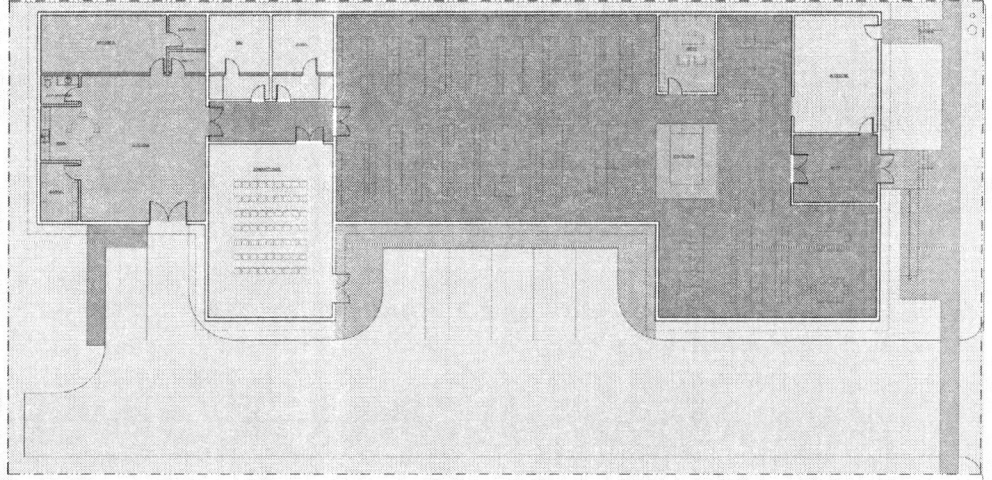

Figure 2: Floor plan showing actual divisions and specific furniture layout within each area by using the schematic plan Figure 1 (both figures courtesy of Robertson, Merryman, Barnes Architects, Inc., Portland, Oregon).

As a librarian, no question is unimportant for you to ask concerning your library and what you expect your new area to look like. It is quicker and easier for staff to work on ideas placing furniture on paper than to begin by using a computer. After the layout is done by hand in a preliminary way, a professional can lay out the preferences of the staff on the computer, having some rough ideas to work from.

In looking at these areas, think about how the various functions relate. Some areas need to have close proximity to each other and some need to overlap. Still others operate better when they have no interaction at all.

The front desk is a part of the entry where the attendant maximizes the control of the entrances and exits while minimizing the interference with traffic patterns and easy access to the workroom. The librarian communicates through the entry to the public by use of the displays and the informational brochures found there. The desk's close proximity to the reference area, which is now the computer intensive area, is important. Each desk is designed to meet the functional services rendered at that desk. In addition to charging patrons, taking money for fines and any fees due, issuing new library cards, storing books on reserve on shelving, answering questions or redirecting calls, volunteers and other assistants will be working at this desk.

The stacks should be convenient to the research/computer area. Traffic through the adult readers and young adult areas are defined by low shelving or by using the periodical lounge area to separate the two. Freestanding bookcases can be used to define reader areas or, if the reading room is large, occasional low shelving will serve to break up the area. Low shelving can also be used to designate areas for new books, "best picks" by the staff, or for display of books that have such a high circulation rate that they never get returned to the stacks but go to this shelving for checkout again.

The children's area should also be visible from the entry but not cross over the traffic toward the other areas of the library. The story room is located in the back of the children's area since it is likely to be the noisiest area. Children ideally should be able to go to the bathroom in close proximity and sometimes their bathrooms, labeled for children only, are located within the area for convenience and safety. In any case, washrooms should be in a direct path for children without crossing the adult area. The children's desk (if there is one) should be in visual contact with the front desk which serves primarily as a customer greeting point.

The traditional circulation desk was rounded and located somewhere near the center of the great room so that the librarian could monitor any direction. There weren't as many rooms or as many functions required of the library of the past as is found in the library of today. The planners held fast to the idea that the library was a series of functionally specialized rooms: a delivery room (for books to be delivered), an information desk, access to toilet and cloak rooms, a catalogue room, book rooms, children's room with open shelves, a reference room and librarians office, all in close proximity to one another. In addition, there were to be resting rooms for assistants, classrooms, mending and binding rooms and periodical and newspaper rooms. Although these rooms could be situated further from the delivery room, they were to be located near the reference room.[3]

The desks of the past were simplified, having some smaller dividers for paper and the processing of the former handwritten and date stamped library card. The insides of desks held open shelves for the librarians to organize for their use. Now

1. Laying Out the Library

These two examples (one curved, one straight) show two libraries that have used low book shelving to divide areas and create pathways.

there are more functions that go on at this front desk than checking out books, although this remains the primary function. There are circulation desks designed for reconfiguration as needs change with adjustable work surfaces: reconfigurable modules. The contents of those modules — doors, drawers and shelves — are designed to be interchangeable.

Storage

What types of storage requirements are needed? Are hanging file folders needed? What about covered storage versus closed storage? When the circulation desk is viewed from the back will it appear cluttered and disorganized? By using information gathered from the librarians about their ideal way of working, filing and ways of assisting the patron, a useable and highly functional design can be accomplished. Librarians have helped manufacturers design standard components that store and organize.

A modular service desk is one in which components can be removed, the placement changed or the work surfaces adjusted. One of the standard modules is open, providing an area for a descending book truck on castors to easily roll inside the desk module when it is empty and rolled out to unload for shelving books. The desk module that includes card catalog components within the drawers is still available although most libraries are automated and no longer use the card system.

Some of the questions you need to ask yourself about storage issues include: Is something to be stored for infrequent use or is it needed at arm's length so that it is easily retrieved without opening and closing cabinets or drawers? Is something valuable enough (i.e., master set of keys or cash) to be under lock and key? When you are ordering locks on your furniture, you should be aware that you have a choice in whether the locks are keyed alike or each lock is different, requiring separate keys.

Different forms of media require appropriate and functional storage in shelving. Also needed are methods of displaying media and the furniture to sit in while using the information. At the end of the stacks there are opportunities to display materials through means of attaching a shelf or transparent Plexiglas holder. This is an area in which to consider additional seating (one carefully chosen chair that is equal to the depth of the shelving). It is also an area where computer access could be planned by placing a table to use at the end of the stack for convenient access to the patron.

Study Areas

Windows in the early libraries were characteristically placed evenly along a wall so that the stacks could be placed perpendicular to the windows and the light streaming in the windows would throw light on the books in the stacks. Carrels were placed in the alcoves where the windows were arched, and the windows were larger for more light to show directly in the carrel to assist the reader in their studies. Today, carrels are available with various levels of privacy. The most private carrel has panels on all three sides with an opening for the seated user. It can be equipped with a shelf and a task light under the shelf. Rounded and angled panels on the furniture can set a completely different mood for the area. There are variations on design which allow light to come into the carrel, due to being open on both sides, and in doing so allow the user to feel a bit more open to the outside world.

There is also a table carrel that is no more than a table with a rail along the outside edges (3 to 4 inches high) which provides a means of keeping the materials on the carrel and allows the user more visual interaction with their surroundings. Panels can continue down the sides and to the floor of the carrel, providing a modesty panel. This type of carrel visually hides wires under the carrel, but wire management is still recommended for safety of the patron. The trend in libraries is toward fewer study carrels and more study tables. Also, individual study carrels seem to be more popular than the banks of carrels that previously were being used. Either the researcher wants to have their own space separate from others or join in a collaborative effort in an area designed for group study.

The mix of smaller study areas to meeting rooms will be determined by the type of library; academic libraries require a greater number of study and meeting areas and larger tables to spread out research projects. The library patron is no longer isolated in their work in that so much of what is being done is group activity. Meeting rooms are planned for all types of libraries for private research and for areas where groups can converge for discussions that need to be confined to that room.

A step down or a shallow ramp creates a definable space without a need for walls. Defining this space, separating the quiet rooms from the rooms that are likely to be noisy, is one of the most difficult challenges that the planner has to accomplish in a library. The open lab in an academic environment can get quite loud, especially in a school environment. An individual or study group will search out study rooms that will accommodate a group, sometimes as many as ten people. Librarians and patrons always need a greater number of private study areas than originally planned.

Sometimes study areas that are built to feel private feel more like a "fishbowl" with floor to ceiling glass. The dynamics of designing a space with mostly hard surfaces has the disadvantage of not having anything to absorb sound, especially if there is no upholstery used on the seating. I've seen study areas that are partial walls allowing the noise to spill over the top of the walls and I have been told that there is a balance between providing enough privacy but not too much privacy, which may become a safety/security issue for patrons.

Leg styled tables will allow more users to gather around the table, while panel styles prevent this but create clean aisles in the library, as people cannot sit on the sides that have full panels. As collaborative study becomes more popular the need for tables that can be moved or reconfigured to provide spaces for grouping individuals is needed. This is a need that has changed from the early days of libraries when a library building was known as a quiet place to study or reflect.

Work and Staff Break Rooms

The service area that contains workrooms, office and staff space should be in easy proximity to the front desk and close to restrooms. The office space should contain enough space for the staff members to have the privacy to concentrate on a project and for them to secure personal items. Contract furniture, also known as office furniture, has its place in library planning. The modularity of the furniture works for staff responsibilities in that when there are changes the area can be reconfigured. Systems furniture or some type of modular configuration is often used because of its features of privacy (enclosure by panels) and the ability to hang storage from the walls, thus saving work space by getting things up and off the work surface and onto shelves or into cabinet storage. Each station can be redesigned over time, adding or reducing the amount of work space and storage requirements. Modular furniture also offers shaped work surfaces, providing the advantage of doing a lot in a smaller amount of space than possible with traditional case goods (desks, credenza units and bookcases).

Lockers or some type of lockable storage is a popular addition to the office space or break room. The staff area's plan might include a counter under a mailbox system with pigeonholes sized to accept interoffice memos, include a bulletin board for postings and are open underneath for storage. The larger libraries may have a computer program on which the interoffice correspondence is based, while smaller libraries still operate in a manual mode. The staff's break room should have a table and chairs for eating and enough counter space for food preparation, along with a microwave and refrigerator. Lounge seating and an area to stretch out in or at least raise the feet off the floor are helpful.

The offices are sometimes located within the larger function of technical services. This area receives books, periodicals and other media for the purpose of preparing them for circulation. Decisions of mending or discarding materials require a good-size table and shelving with cabinets and drawers holding supplies for processing the materials. Mailing of materials is also conducted in this area. A work table on wheels or one that is capable of adding additional working space is handy in this area. There never seems to be enough work space.

If the nonpublic spaces such as the workroom, offices and the staff room as well as the public washrooms are planned as the basic core of the building, this may hamper flexibility but is most functional for staff relationships and sound control.

Building in Flexibility

The less permanent the walls the better, as things are likely to change over time, and what a benefit to be able to change with them! Flexibility is mandatory for adaptability to the unknown requirements of the future. The Burton Barr Library in Phoenix, Arizona, is among the libraries that have been built with complete flexibility in mind, as the only things that cannot be changed are the mechanical spaces and the washrooms.

The basement is a great area to keep flexible. If there is a basement or back area it can be used for the storage of "retired books" until they are donated to another library or sold in a book sale. The basement could store extra furniture and surplus shelving inventory. It could also serve as an area for future expansion or meeting rooms that do not need library staff supervision, assuming it meets with your city or county codes for use.

Different types of users dictate an adjustment in the types of furniture chosen. While public libraries serve all ages, infant to mature adults, a school library serves students, teachers, parents and administrators, and all have staffing needs that are unique. University libraries support research and learning and as a result have a heavier emphasis on teaching and furniture that supports the means of instruction and learning. Tutoring and group study calls for at least two seating positions at a computer station. Large print and special needs equipment to read books, and sections of the library to serve the languages of the locality, will determine how predominate they are in the library layout and the furniture requirements.

Users should be offered all kinds of study options. For some users that means a comfortable chair off by itself, either with a table or carrel or a lounge chair. For others it is a larger table to spread out paperwork, and for some it is a meeting place designed for a group and the surrounds to make it okay to interact and make noise in the process. Booths and seating like a restaurant are used on the first floor of the University of Las Vegas Lied Library and they seem to be fairly well used.

The basic rule is to keep the quiet areas separated from the noisy areas and to create a buffer between them. A browsing area can act as a sound buffer between activity and more quiet areas. There are only two ways to lower sound waves. One is by absorbing them and the other is by scattering them. This can be accomplished through the use of fabric and other porous materials. As computer use become more prominent throughout libraries, "the soft clicking of keyboards will distract few library users from the task at hand; consequently there will be less need to provide physical separation between people using traditional printed materials and those using keyboards, printers and other things that click or whir."[6]

Quiet Areas and Activity-Based Areas

When laying out a library, dialogues between the librarian and the planners are necessary to determine which users make up the majority, as well as which segment of the population is the target market. The general population's ethnicity, income distribution, level of formal education and extent of parent involvement (if

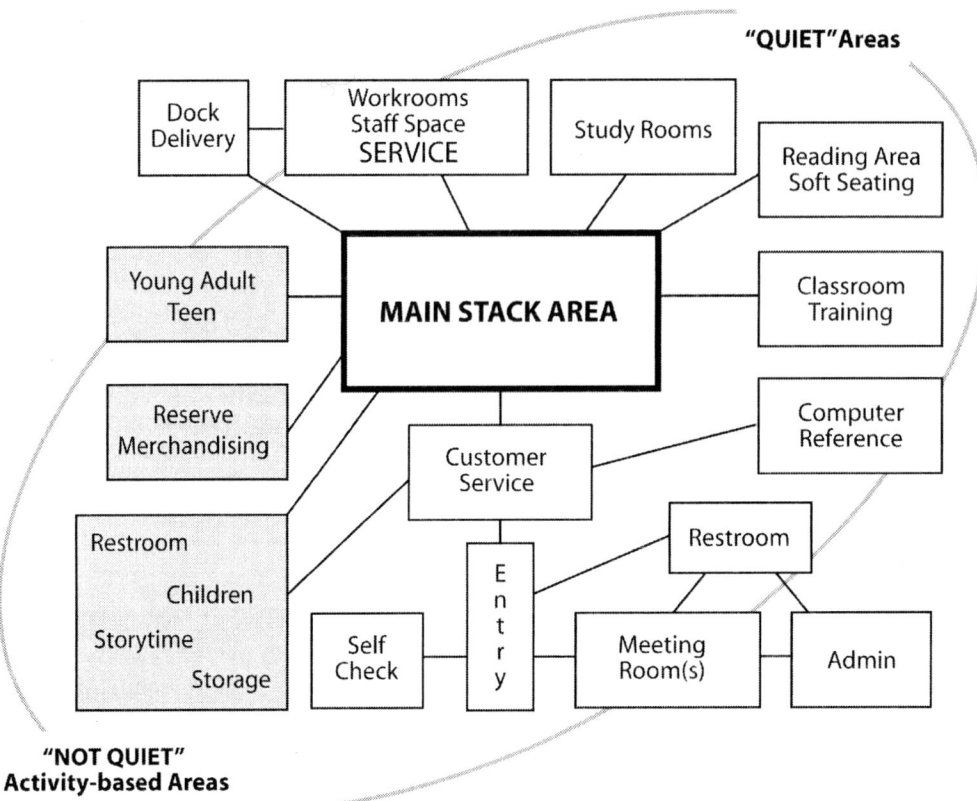

The overlaying oval area in this chart depicts the area that can mutually be decided on to function as a "quiet area" or a "non-quiet/activity based area." If the oval shaped area is designated as a quiet area then sound buffers must be established between the block shaped areas and the quiet area (illustration by Anish Adalja).

K-12 school age) are all a part of the demographics of the area. The planners may not live in the same area and most likely are not familiar with the clientele that the library serves, so they may need to spend some time with the librarians to learn the demographics of the area. For instance, if the library is located in an area that is populated by retirees and it is a shared-use facility, areas that may be used by the public might need some privacy from the study tables or computer learning labs so that the patrons don't feel as if they are attending school as well. The public library supports recreational interests and is responsive to overall community needs, while the school library supports coursework materials and the needs of faculty and staff.

Types of shelving are chosen to house the types of materials most suited to the library. In public libraries, the tone will be more that of a bookstore. Stacks of best sellers will be displayed on tables or display racks resembling a local bookshop in a way to catch the eye of the patrons and subconsciously relay the message that a supply of books is available for loan. In academic libraries the collection will house multiple copies of texts that support the curriculum, so it will be more research driven and more research books are needed for writing papers.

Meeting rooms for small groups and auditoriums for larger gatherings are often located on the outside border of the library with convenient restrooms so that this area can operate independently when the library is not open. Entry issues must also be addressed to satisfy the need for safety of all types of users.

The architect will evaluate the parking issue to serve the needs of the patrons as the library becomes a place to arrange gatherings for authors as well as public interest lectures, various club meetings and activities.

Computer furniture for quick browsing of the catalog doesn't require any seating at all. Neither do the computers for short-term use. Where a longer time at the computer is reserved (usually longer than fifteen minutes) seating will be offered. Users should be able to use one of the stations in each area easily with their wheelchair, so the minimum height of carrels and tables for ADA is a consideration. Computer equipment is now a part of the resources housed within the stacks. If this is envisioned in the scope of use, electrical and data lines to those areas must be planned very early in the project. In preliminary planning stages for all areas of the library architects need to be informed of the need for electrical outlets and data ports.

Concession Amenities: Coffee, Chai and Books?

Beginning in 2000, the trend of including a bookstore atmosphere in the library appeared as "a new library in Howard County, Maryland, borrowed a page from the corporate booksellers' manual: 'Give the customers convenience, comfy furniture and cappuccino.'[7] When designing their Glenwood Library, planners decided to try it. The library reported that as much as fifteen percent of the traffic is from customers for the coffee shop.

Since the coffee bar was located inside the locked doors and open only during library hours, various vendors trying to make a business and not being profitable led to replacing the manned coffee area with vending machines that dispensed coffee. An exterior door for the coffee shop would have enabled the library to provide a much needed service to this rural community that doesn't have the plethora of coffee bars prevalent in a more urban setting. If libraries desire to bring the coffee aroma-filled hubbub of a retail bookstore to mind the population who will use the coffee bar must exist to support this type of addition to a library.

With the use of coffee shops comes a need for a different type of furniture. It is more of a bistro style that conjures up the neighborhood feel of sitting around small tables and conversing with friends or leisurely reading a book or magazine while enjoying a beverage and maybe even a snack. Sometimes the furniture is restaurant or outdoor type furniture. The staffs of libraries that offered this service explain that it provided a place for relaxation, and on campuses it was a place that students could visit as a stress reducer between classes. In Davidson North Carolina, the university provided a coffee hour and then added poetry readings and musical performances, and as patrons learned of these services patronage increased.

There is much debate about bringing food and drink into the area of library materials. "Ninety-six public library directors were surveyed about perceived and actual problems and benefits associated with the consumption of food and drink in their libraries. Approximately three-quarters (74 percent) of the surveyed libraries have policies that forbid food and drink, while one-quarter (26 percent) either serve or permit food or drink. Directors of the libraries with restrictive food and drink polices (no food or drink served or permitted) expected to encounter, on average, nearly five times the problems experienced by directors of libraries with permissive policies." Eighty-seven percent of those surveyed were concerned with damage of the books and computers if food was brought into the areas.[8] Damage to the finish on the furniture would likely be a concern as well. Having trash receptacles that were strategically placed throughout the library was favored as a deterrent to leaving empty beverage and food wrappers for staff to clean up.

Nearly half of the libraries (48 percent) serve food and drinks in a separate indoor café or dining area, while four percent serve in an outdoor café or dining area and eight percent limit their service to vending machines.[9] Outdoor reading areas are becoming more popular as well. If an area of the country is not suited for outdoor areas the next best concept is to bring the outdoors inside by supplying natural light when possible. There are various materials that can create a mood of an outdoor space through the use of design and lighting. This idea worked well in a thriving coffee shop setting in the entry of Tigart Public Library, located in a suburb of Portland, Oregon, that opened in the past three years. The area has the feel of being outdoors although it is protected from the elements. It is a wooded park-like area and the floor to ceiling glass windows allows a feeling of green to surround the area. It has easy-to-maintain concrete floors and bistro seating. It opens before the library opens and the only requirement is to use a lid on your beverage when bringing it into the library.

Light and Power

Lighting and electrical access are important parts of the preliminary planning of the building design. When more lighting is needed than the ceiling lights will provide it must be determined whether additional task lighting will be needed in the study carrels, on the study tables, on occasional tables or as part of the stacks. The vertical member of the steel shelving is a perfect place to contain electrical that can "snake" up the channel to light the aisles. Is this electrical planned into the draft of the building's structure? Electrical planning is crucial to a well planned building. The Electronic Planning Table illustrates one way of supplying this information to your architect and electrical contractor. This table is found in Appendix D. The equipment's

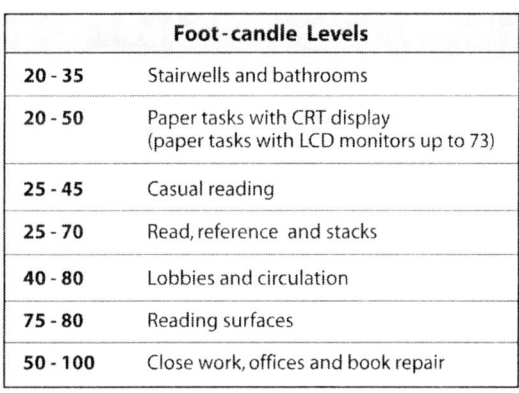

Foot-candle Levels	
20 - 35	Stairwells and bathrooms
20 - 50	Paper tasks with CRT display (paper tasks with LCD monitors up to 73)
25 - 45	Casual reading
25 - 70	Read, reference and stacks
40 - 80	Lobbies and circulation
75 - 80	Reading surfaces
50 - 100	Close work, offices and book repair

Foot-candle = how much light is generated one foot away from its source

Lumen = one foot-candle falling on one square foot of area

Lux = measurement of actual light available at a given distance

One foot-candle = about 11 lux

Lighting requirement chart compiled by Tish Murphy (illustration by Anish Adalja).

electrical and ventilation needs must be taken into consideration and will help determine the size and shape of furniture needed as well as the placement of the outlets on the walls and in the floors.

Office lighting should be at a level of 20 to 50 foot-candles of light for paper tasks with CRT displays.[10] Paper tasks with LCD monitors will require up to 70 foot-candles of light.[11] The monitor screen must be kept free of dust to eliminate glare since the dust contributes to it. The monitor should have the capability to tilt to eliminate glare. To alleviate light from a window that is causing glare, the OSHA workstation Website suggests that vertical blinds be used for an east or west exposure while horizontal blinds are better for a north or south window. Keeping the window at a right angle to the screen or using a desk lamp directed from above eliminates the glare that can cost the user health problems such as headaches and eyestrain. This is a cost to the employer as well since they lose the productivity of the worker. Ventilation or lack of good air circulation, such as air blowing directly on a person's work space, can cause the same type of problems.[12] This type of planning early in the project can save dollars in minimizing change orders to the building contractor and costs from electricians to supply electrical to those areas at a later date. If lighting is well-planned, it will also save additional costs in the future.

Will there be raised floors, sometimes called cellular floors, that will allow circuits to be brought up at a desired point? Wireless access for computers will eliminate some of the planning for data cables but will do nothing to eliminate the need for the appropriate types of electrical. Access to technology needs to be everywhere as technology becomes more prevalent in our libraries. Lounge seating and tables are now being equipped with plug-ins for convenient access. Sometimes these are a pull-out feature from the side of the seating, and there are various ways of bringing electrical to the work surface. (There is a complete discussion of electrical options found in the chapter on "Bringing Electrical through the Furniture").

In the Library of Medicine at Brigham Young University, it was suggested that shelving near the circulation desk be reduced in height from the original plans to provide a functional work space on top of some of the shelving. This opened up the area around the circulation desk and provided the bonus of allowing more light to flow into the area and more pleasant surroundings when compared with the closed-in feeling for its users as well as those working in the library.

Planning natural light in the reading and studying areas is popular with patrons and will reserve the heavier use of artificial lighting for the evening hours of operation. "Up" lighting, also known as indirect lighting, and perforated shielding of down lighting is comfortable and nonintrusive, while more direct lighting provides an essential amount of light required for reading. There is a computer program called "Visual" that is user-friendly and has the ability to determine light levels in a space.

Lighting consultants may use a program called "Lightscape"[13] which is a photometric program that creates a graphical presentation of how a room will look with a proposed lighting system. Some libraries, like the City of Phoenix Public Libraries in Arizona, design buildings using nature's light and awnings that adjust in order to shield the windows with the optimum amount of natural light. The Lied Library at the University of Nevada, Las Vegas, uses cooling towers shaded from the sun to economize on utilities. Will you plan your building with computerized lighting that will operate on electrical timers? What about special baseboards allowing cable installers a slot to run cabling? At what expense does your budget allow these conveniences or a means toward long term cost savings?

Natural daylight is good provided that the library materials are not exposed to ultraviolet radiation. All light destroys paper and fabric, and damage is irreversible. It is always a balancing act to be sure that there is enough light to be able to read but not too much, resulting in deterioration of the materials.

Modern window glass filters up to 98 percent of UV-A, and UV-B low E-coatings help with insulation and some reflectivity that reduces glare of the interior.[14] Research window glass specifications and insist on functional window products.

Task lights mounted on tables are a solution to having enough light where you need it while not subjecting the books stored on the shelving to additional light. Table fixtures can be easily attached to the table to secure their position on the table. There are all levels of pricing for lighting. Do not choose residential lighting as there will be problems in public areas with the type of use and abuse it gets. Purchasing from a commercial fixture company will be a step in assuring that the fixture is built to withstand public use. Check the warranty on the fixtures. A good warranty may save you money.

At a trolley stop in New York City, Baruch College uses motion-detecting lights over the stack aisles with low ceilings to be energy efficient and provides lighting as needed in an area that is not as frequently used. It sounds like a really good idea but when you experience it the downside is that the area is dark and not welcoming to the user when seen from a distance. Natural light is desirable in a library but the disadvantages must be taken into consideration, such as when the glare of light would be problematic in viewing the computer screen. North face windows provide good lighting that is kinder than that of a west wall but the geographical location must be taken into account to see how much of a detriment a west exposure really is. Reflective walls improve this issue because the light bounces off the wall.

The Construction Timeline

The building program compiled by the library committee or an outside consultant lists equipment required for the operation of the library, moveable furniture and built-in equipment. Once the design stage is in progress, the construction documents for the building are completed and the building goes out to bid. After contracts are awarded for the building, the interiors team is created and at this point the interior planning becomes more of a priority. Most likely by the time you have chosen this book the building contract has been awarded and that portion of the project is behind you. Now, at this point, the suppliers of furniture are able to get involved and work as part of a team with planners who may comprise an individual along with a group whose size is dependent on the size of the library project.

Once the budget is known the library can seek funds for interiors if they are not already in place. Funding sometimes takes the form of donations. Fund drives can be a long drawn out period of time, again dependent on the size of the community and their enthusiasm for the building. Friends and family can be memorialized by the purchase of a chair, a piece of artwork, a room in the library or a plaque to honor them. Assemble focus groups to create themes and provide goals. The community's awareness of the financial needs and the items to be accomplished can work toward getting public involvement in the project.

By this time some kind of *F*, *F* and *E* (Furniture, Fixtures and Equipment) package is budgeted and the dollar amounts become known. Remember, only the first *F* is furniture. The second *F* and the *E* (Fixtures and Equipment) is a fairly large chunk of the FF&E budget. Libraries vary in what items they include in the furniture budgets. Sometimes computers are a part of this budget, which makes the amount for furnishings seem larger than what it actually is. Also the self-check unit that is bringing self-service into the library is being purchased from various fund sources (furnishings budget, furnishings and equipment budget, equipment budget, computer budget or ADA renovation funds). This self-service unit requires specialized furniture to support it.

You might not look into specifics of size, style and colors until after the building's cost is in and the contractor is chosen. After the building budget is determined you will know how much you have to spend on furniture. The point at which the architect lays out the library shelving might be the first time you think about furniture. Now you will get a rough idea of areas, along with the tables, study areas and seating. This is a great time to use the scaled drawings with cutouts of the furniture. When you have developed an accurate and complete layout from an equipment list of all items needed, create a spreadsheet with a guesstimate by area so that you can determine which areas have the greatest financial impact and which unit prices need adjusting to fit your budget. At this time you may be able to adjust the building size, adjust quantities, make a decision to reuse more existing furniture or get more money allocated for the building project.

We've talked about the need for extensive investigation into products. From

1. Laying Out the Library

Rayford University Project
July 2007 - March 2009

July 2007	Jan 2008	June 2008	Aug 2008	Sept 2008	Oct 2008	Feb 2009
					Manufacturing (10-16 weeks)	Transit and install (2-3 weeks)
				Order verification with drawings if needed (2-3 weeks)		
	Choose interiors planner (5 months)	Bid with evaluation and approvals (6-8 weeks)	PO's to successful bidder (2-4 weeks)			
	Develop interiors budget (6 months)					
		Building construction (12-18 months)				
	Collect catalogs Talk to reps	Request demo product				
Visit libraries to get ideas (4-6 months)						

This is an example covering a 1½ year timeline providing the average time estimates that might be used from the beginning process of visiting libraries for the purposes of researching furniture and shelving and showing the average times one might expect to spend planning, purchasing and installing furniture while the library is being built (illustration by Anish Adalja).

the time that you begin looking at manufacturers' binders and installations and begin thinking about what you would like to see at your new or renovated library, two to three years are often involved in your project from start to finish. On large projects such as a new library at a university, it is not unusual to have the project stretch over a ten year period although work is not constant.

Shared Libraries: A Good Partnership?

There is a trend in some areas of the U.S. toward a "joint" or "shared use" library that is shared by the academic sector (community college, high school or mid-school) and opens in the evening as a city branch library. In a program at a state Library Association Conference in November 1997, the director of a large metropolitan city library said the comparison is much like a successful marriage. A panel of library administrators agreed that when sharing a facility works for both parties it is a good match. They continued their discussion by providing examples illustrating that although many carry on a courtship they find it would not grow into a good relationship. At that point they go their separate ways and remain independent. On the other hand, if they merge this joint effort causes change to the library collection as well as the need to satisfy the furniture requirements of both segments within the same space. The challenge to the planner is to have a library for use by the student and community population that does not feel like a school library.

There are two types of dual or joint use libraries: those libraries that join upper level academics (community college) with public libraries and those that join schools (junior high or high school level) with public libraries. Joint-use libraries meld the use of a library by young people and the general public while designing it to look like a public library. These were known as "school-housed libraries" in Canada. Joint use is not a new idea. It was in the 1800s that Dr. James Kay advocated that the village library should be sited in the schoolhouse, and in the 1900s that Henry Morris suggested that public libraries should be established in Cambridgeshire's village colleges.[15] The taxpayers of Carnegie built a new high school, which was completed before the library opened. This new high school was located at the bottom of what would eventually be known as Library Hill. It was built there, to be in close proximity to the library, and special steps were constructed to expedite travel between the high school and the library. In addition to the students' use of the library proper, high school concerts, plays, and other assemblies occurred in the music hall, as the high school did not have an auditorium. In looking at the furniture placement of a joint-use library, collections are sometimes integrated, children's fiction with adults. The primary goal is to intermingle as little as possible, with the public function of story time being far removed from the student study area that tends to be quieter (sometimes) and definitely from the adult and public area that may require less noise. There must be a clear conduct of behavior understood.

Joint libraries are usually built in areas of heavy growth; they have extended hours since they must be available to students and teachers before school hours and then to the public hours after school is out. It is an efficient use of funds since the building is so well used. They will have collections comparable to a public library and then add books appropriate to the academic level that they serve. The site is the key, no more than five miles from another library and public parking and the main entrance visible from the street with a separate entrance to the campus. There should be staff for both the public and an instructional library specialist for the academic services or the appointment of one professional librarian to manage both services offered to both schools and the community. A high school joint library lends itself better to joining a public library because the adult furniture is used in both types of libraries. In the event that the two libraries are designed together and it doesn't work it is helpful to have a "prenuptial" agreement that speaks to who will receive what in the case of dissolution. In many cases the school district supplies the building and anything "built-in," while the city provides furnishings, bookshelves and anything moveable. Most people will agree that the success is better when both the district and the public sides are able to join together to design the library.

Partners must go in looking at this process as "cost effective" versus "cost savings."[16] "The savings is upfront in capital costs,"[17] agrees Scottsdale Public Library's former director, Judy Register, as it has shown to be a cost savings only in the initial phase. A separate entrance and separate bathrooms are essential for the safety of the students and the convenience of the public. Combined libraries should be visible from the street and have a 24 hour book drop. The exterior signage must be large and well-lit and designate that it is a separate entrance for the library distinct from the school entrances. The hours sign on the door should clearly indicate the library hours.

When the library is owned by more than one element (public with academic, city with county, etc.), invite participants from both agencies to plan the facility. The maintenance of the furniture and the collection is a responsibility that needs to be determined. There needs to be an agreement by both parties as to what the physical library space will look like. Public input through town meetings concerning the library is crucial to a library's success. Parameters must be clear as to what type of input is needed from the public so that the process continues to move. Empty storefronts have successfully grown into libraries strategically placed among other necessary services that the customer uses and in the flow of pedestrian traffic.

Combining a library with a multigenerational facility makes sense, as the "senior" today is more active and requires more physical and mental activity than the senior centers of the past offered. Linda Meissner, director of the Boomerang Project in Chandler, Arizona, says that removing the "senior" label from the program's name was integral to the program's success," when speaking about the multi-departmental venture looking to support the needs of future retirees.[18]

Building on the Past

When libraries increase their size they build on the past using the ideas or restoring the pieces of furniture and ideas that work, improving or replacing what is outmoded and adding space to the part of the collection and services that are growing when populations demand it. Each year in April *American Libraries* magazine prints an annual showcase of new and renovated library facilities. It provides a means of taking a visual tour of libraries that are showing the latest in finishes, styles and trends that are surfacing in libraries.

Ventilation in the early days was as easy as opening a window on a pleasant day. Now that it is a more complicated issue, pollution and security concerns no longer make that an option. When a historical library is adapting their facilities to this century or a previously owned building is renovating to be brought up to date with electrical, lighting, plumbing, and heating and ventilation systems, the updates to the building are for our health, safety and access.

The staff will be working in the areas and should have as much input as possible for a well-organized workplace. Collect catalogs from vendors. Get ideas from their literature and Websites and by making visits to libraries that have recently completed a building project. Digital cameras are helpful to bring back good ideas to the planners as well as what won't work for their new building or expansion project. Ask other users what planners they worked with and their experience with suppliers and installers. Librarians who have worked on a library project are usually eager to share their joys as well as their mistakes. Take the opportunity to ask the librarians what they would have done differently.

High ceilings sometimes give a more spacious and uplifting sensation to a space. In the Brigham Young Law Library in Utah, David Armond explained that by using the two- to three-foot dead space in the ceiling and raising the finished ceiling higher, the vaulted ceiling is a much preferred addition. The cost factor of providing the extra height must be weighed against the positive psychological effects that higher ceiling heights can achieve.

Beamed ceilings, multi-story windows, and ceiling lights in areas that are located high above the floor and other areas difficult to maintain continue to be a problem for some libraries I visited. The ability to maintain a library building and its furnishings is a cost savings worth considering when it is spread over the life of the library. Cost of furniture should always be evaluated in the same way; it is not only the original cost but the maintenance costs over the furnishings' life cycle which is the real cost.

Whether a new structure or a historic renovation, the librarian needs to recognize that their own knowledge of the way their library works is the most important key to their interior planning. In the momentum of the construction, do not allow this key to be lost or to be undervalued. I can't recall the times that a conversation about something not working is followed by a sigh of something similar to "no one asked me." The involvement of an experienced and interested librarian as part of the building team is a priceless component. Nancy Cummings, a former librarian in Las Vegas, once said that "All librarians should have one (project) under their belt before they retire." I believe that she says this because it is such a reward knowing that you have been part of something much larger than what you could have ever created alone.

1. Laying Out the Library

The Seattle Public Library has created a dramatic 11 story high window wall that gives an abundance of natural lighting, reducing the average lighting bill while creating large useable areas. The windows were designed with the exterior hardware to tie into the window washer's equipment on a maintenance schedule of two times each year to maintain the building.

Check This Out: Laying Out the Library

• Are public service elements (circulation, online catalogs, copy machines, etc., easily located from the entrance and are the online catalogs accessible from all parts of the library with instructional cards for catalog use?

• Do the Children's, Adults, Reference/ Information, DVD's and CD area, Computer online catalog areas stand out definable by signage, lighting, color or furnishings?

• Are signs easy to see and logical to follow?

• Can the meeting room be used after library hours with an accessible restroom and public telephone?

• Are there provisions for returning books after hours? Is the book drop separate from the building or located in a fireproof area?

- Is there space for distribution of community information, tax forms, flyers and other handouts?
- Are there spaces for quiet study areas and are these areas acoustically controlled?
- If the library has its own staffed security, is that staff in an area that is highly visible to the patrons as a deterrent?
- Can computer monitors be raised or lowered to different viewing heights?
- Is there space provided for book trucks when they are not in use?
- Is the reference desk located where staff can see the patrons who may need assistance and is the reference is sight for patrons and are staff reference materials close to the reference desk?
- Is the noise level controlled around electronic equipment and is the area adequately ventilated?
- Are the circulation staff offices located near the circulation desks?
- Are there adequate numbers and types of drawers and enough desk space for smooth work flow and tasks by staff?
- Is there enough space allocated for staff storage, separate staff restrooms and adequate break room for staff?
- Can staff perform various functions behind the service desks, conveniently come out from behind them to help customers and move freely from one area to another?

Check This Out: With Your Architect

- Is the entrance sheltered from the weather?
- Can patrons gain access into nonpublic areas without notice by staff or places they can stay undetected at closing?
- Is there space designated for receiving operations and a loading dock with storage?
- Have provisions been made for fire safety, emergency exits, area of rescue assistance?
- Will sun control, excessive ultraviolet rays and glare be handled architecturally?
- Is the building easily maintained and energy efficient?
- Is the flooring around the circulation and in the lobby a surface that will minimize noise, and is it easily maintained and safe during all kinds of weather?
- Are the height and the width of the circulation desk appropriate for various functions and accessible to someone in a wheelchair or motorized scooter?

- Is the circulation desk modular so that it may be changed in the future?
- Is there seating for patron/staff consultation and is the reference desk the appropriate height?

Check This Out: Joint or Dual Use Libraries

- Is there adequate signage to designate school entrances from the public entrance?
- Are there study areas that are isolated from the public traffic and activity?
- Is the children's area in a different area of the library than the student classroom and study areas?

2

Bringing Electrical into Furniture

Knowledge is power and enthusiasm pulls the switch.
— Steve Droke

Inventorying Your Requirements: Where Do You Need Power and Data?

"Furnishings, equipment and shelving are conventional occupants of (academic) library space. A less tangible occupant is information technology. The associated equipment occupies three general categories: (1) the library's integrated automated system, (2) networked workstations for staff members and library users, (3) portable computers equipped with Ethernet cards, brought into the library by users. A power grid laid throughout the building offers a simple connection to the campus information network. There are copiers, microform reader/printers, fax machines and scanners. All of these machines occupy space, generate heat and therefore affect interior design layout, air handling systems, electrical power requirements and furniture construction. Existing information technology must be accommodated, along with provisions for future developments. Before the architect can be instructed properly, the electronic terrain has to be scouted and mapped."[1]

Taking an inventory of the data and electrical requirements will turn out to be one of the best investments of time that you spend in your planning. The size, amperage, watt and any requirements of special ventilation or shielding will be useful in planning the furniture that will house the equipment. The planner will need to determine how the furniture will be used, whether it will be a stand alone unit or if it is to become part of a grouping. Computer commons areas and classrooms will be equipment intensive, and once the electrical and communications persons get involved the building's wiring diagram will take form. This planning should occur at the earliest stages of planning the building so the architect/interior designer should meet with the Interior Technology person as soon as possible.

2. Bringing Electrical into Furniture

Although most of the furniture literature that you see will not indicate that stowing electrical and data cabling is an issue, it is. There are rarely wires shown in the photos and this was before wireless was an option. When it comes time to install the equipment on the furniture it will be obvious that it is an issue. I have many times wondered why they don't show the wires in the promotional pieces. Could it be that wires strung all over the top of the furniture and down to the floor are not attractive? Wires do not look good and they are a safety issue.

If the stacks and furniture could be laid out around a three-foot dimension, it could make maximum use of the space and not have the problem of columns becoming an obstruction that you need to work around. If the shelving is planned for 15 to 18 foot runs, it can work around the columns instead of losing the space for shelving. Using a three-foot standard measurement for the center-to-center dimension of a shelving unit, the electrical needs for any lighting or computers in the stacks can be determined. If the measurements and locations of electrical boxes are checked before the concrete pour, discrepancies can be noted before it is "set in concrete." Online access computers at the ends of the stacks will need to be part of early-stage planning. Does the equipment require dedicated or isolated circuits? Can it be plugged into the same area as other machines? Does it require a surge protector? What about wireless capability?

The data ports that were once necessary in carrels, lounge seating and table tilt-up outlet designs aren't as prevalent with libraries and other public areas with the advent of wireless capability. All laptops on the market now will have wireless capability integrated into their computer or with an accessory plug-in of a card or chip. Cellular phones and other personal communications devices are wireless ready as well. But we are not completely wireless yet. Recharging these devices still requires outlets in the furniture.

In study carrels the requirement might be quite different than at a circulation or service desk. The study carrel options include a task light, electrical connections and data ports. Some manufacturers provide electrical systems that are universal to every piece of furniture that is offered while other manufacturers have styles of furniture within their line that have their own electrical system. The physical style and dimensioning of the furniture will determine which electrical components would work for you. For instance a table could have a grommet where the cord disappears from the top of the table to underneath the table where it plugs into a duplex connection, or the cords could be bundled and continue toward the floor to be plugged into an outlet on the floor. The outlet could also be one that is placed on the top of the table and tilts up to be used or lies flat in the top of the table when not in use. Encourage your furniture supplier to build wire management into your furniture.

Nationally Recognized Testing Laboratories

An important consideration is whether your furniture will be equipped to accept all the connections (electrical and data) and house them in a useable and safe manner. There are nine labs in the United States that do independent testing. Underwriter's Laboratory is nearly 100 years old and the best-known nonprofit third party testing product safety certification organization. All the labs create standards by which to test product. Some manufacturers also conduct their own testing in their facility. The manufacturer may conduct in-house testing and upon the passing of the in-house testing go a step further and get an outside or independent lab to issue tests as well. Furniture for commercial use constructed of particleboard can undergo tests at one of the Nationally Recognized Testing Laboratories (NRTL) that test products for "minimum requirements of widely accepted product safety standards as determined though the independent testing."[2] The labs will show how the piece of furniture burns should it be exposed to flame. There are several testing laboratories, like UL, Canadian Standards Association (CSA) and Electrical Testing Laboratories (ETL), in the U.S. and Canada which prove that the product that is labeled with the mark has been tested to take certain abuse at the testing labs that translates to in-the-field use over a period of time. The product is dropped at various angles and struck at particular parts of the piece with an impact that simulates the type of abuse the piece might incur in real life. The Nationally Recognized Testing Laboratory (NRTL) is an independent laboratory recognized by the Occupational Safety and Health Administration (OSHA) to test products to the specifications of applicable safety standards such as those from UL and other standards-writing bodies.

Underwriters Laboratories (UL) has been the most well-known testing laboratory that develops standards and test procedures for materials, components, assemblies, tools, equipment and procedures, chiefly dealing with product safety and utility. You see their marking on many consumer products in the United States. UL does not "approve" any product. Rather it tests product samples and permits acceptable products to carry the UL certification mark, as long as they remain in conformity with the standards and with the samples tested to those standards. Placing the mark on untested products would be a type of trademark infringement and would violate the UL license to the manufacturer. UL maintains a list of over 100,000 products it has tested and that database is available online to the public. The database can be accessed at www.ul.com/consumers under the "certifications" tab. A product with Underwriters Laboratories listing is said to be "UL Listed." Purchasers can identify such products by the distinctive UL mark.

The company's "file number" may be on the label (typically a letter followed by five or six numbers [e.g., E12345]). The "UL File number" can be used to look up a certificate at the UL Web page. A manufacturer of a listed product must demonstrate compliance of its design with the appropriate UL standards, and then demonstrate that it has a program to ensure that each copy of the product will similarly meet the essential criteria. If a product design is modified, a representative example may need to be retested before the UL mark can be attached to the new product or packaging. The organization began testing to aid insurance companies in exerting some control over what they insured. For example if there was a claim against one of their listed products they would defend their own standards and that product as having passed their criteria. Underwriters Laboratory (UL) saves us some of that work, as it functions as a safety engineering consulting firm and recognized for electrical testing although safety testing is done on products that will not be electrified. UL earns its livelihood from manufacturers that pay for its services in detecting what's wrong with their products before they hit the market. The power of UL arises solely from its standards and its long and honorable reputation and it holds 80 percent of the market on testing.

You as a consumer should see on a label two encircled letters: UL. This "listed product" designation means that the particular piece of furniture has been tested and is acceptable for its intended use. This third party testing laboratory conducts unannounced inspections on manufacturers that are listees. There is a cost associated with a manufacturer being UL Listed and maintaining that listing, so you can expect to see that cost reflected in the price of a listed product.

In some cases a component may be "UL recognized," meaning UL has found it acceptable for use *in* a product that will be tested for UL listing. UL has ratings standards for hundreds of types of components and products, even bullet-proof vests. The average householder may be more familiar with UL-rated products such as home electrical appliances. A typical standard for electronic products includes not only requirements for electrical safety, but also fire spread and mechanical hazards (such as sharp or moving parts or tipping over). Just because a product has a UL listing does not mean the product will perform acceptably or that it is safe under all conditions.

A UL mark is a representation but not a guarantee that a marked product conforms to the corresponding UL standard. Installing or selling a product without a UL mark (or equivalent from another recognized lab) may be considered gross negligence in some circles, and may violate insurance requirements or local regulations, meaning the insurance may not have to cover any damages or that the violator may have to pay a fine. A licensed professional may lose his or her license for failure to use materials marked with a UL (or equivalent) label where required.

In the past twenty years great strides have been made in harmonizing international safety standards, and now the UL mark has attained reciprocity with some other national testing laboratories (i.e., the standards are similar and the tests are similar). The label for products certified for both Canada and the USA includes "C" and "UL Listed" below the UL logo.

A moderately famous video clip shows UL researchers demonstrating the risks of certain models of deep-fat turkey fryers. This serves as a suggestion of the importance of this sort of product testing. The European analog of the UL mark is the CE mark.[3]

Office systems furniture, which consists of fabric or wood panels with work surfaces and storage which is designed to hang off specially designed hardware was the first furniture to become UL listed. Office furniture is sometimes used in parts of libraries that are not public areas (tech services, administrative offices). Later some library manufacturers felt that UL listing was an important issue and followed suit providing the same standards of the industry.

In approving electrical devices UL uses three different and distinct terms to describe their listing. "Recognized" represents approval of an electrical component that is not complete as a component but when used *as a part of* a complete product. Light switches and computer power supplies are typical of equipment that can earn recognition. UL-recognized devices are intended to display a special symbol: a slanted letter *U* and a backward *R* (for recognition) combined and shown as the symbol. "Listing" applies to complete product you can buy, an entire appliance, monitor or computer system. Listed product are entitled to use the familiar UL trademark. Although a UL listed trademark often consists of UL listed components, it does not have to be, nor does the use of UL products automatically confer a UL listing on the finished product. The reason is that the UL Listing means the product is safe for use in the form in which it is delivered to you. UL Recognition means only that the component is safe when installed and used properly. The listing shifts the responsibility to you. A UL recognized component might be safe in one use but is not safe, for example, when it is constrained in an area that has improper ventilation or any other way it was not *intended* to be used.

"UL Classified" is the third term that is given for product that applies to commercial or industrial use (compared to consumer use) to verify that they conform to published codes or standards and will not present specific hazards.[4] Some manufacturers provide electrical schematics of their electrical system for the electrical/communications technology person at your library so that the proposed system of supplying electrical and data can be evaluated by someone who understands the needs of the library. There is a vast difference in the emphasis placed on the UL issue by various vendors.

2. Bringing Electrical into Furniture

Planning Electrical and Communication Ports

Some manufacturers will ask for the guru at your library to tell them what is required, while others will work closely with the library planner, architect or interior designer to determine what is needed. Since there are various options for data, patch cords and telephone jacks, blank covers are used and the communication outlets (voice jacks or voice and data jacks) must be ordered separately. Data ports are not required if the client intends to directly connect data cabling or patch cords to the equipment.

Grommets are the most low-tech and low-cost solution to dealing with cords and wires. Grommets consist of a plastic liner that fits in a hole bored into a work surface or panel. A grommet can be any size so that wires and cables can "thread" through the furniture to an outlet. They are various shapes and colors and are available with caps to cover up the hole when it is not in use. The management of these wires is an inevitable challenge with all the technology that is used in a library. Even though wireless technology is growing, there are still many cords that need to be housed in the furniture. Grommets have become a design element in the past few years. They are not the boring (pardon the pun) options that was the grommet of fifteen years ago. There are more questions to ask than the size (1¼ inches or 2¾ inches?) and shape (round or oval?) and the options (with or without cover?). Now the grommet can play a part in calling attention to an area for convenience by using a bold color or shape; it can act as part of the design, contrasting in color from the surface that surrounds it. All shapes, sizes and colors are available.

Some of the ways electrical bundling is handled becomes a part of the overall plan. In the Burton Barr Library in Phoenix, Arizona, conduit is twisted and bundled and is obvious as part of the high tech futuristic connection of the stacks and the furniture to the building's ceiling, which is high above the furniture.

Some of the manufacturers try to bring solutions to their furniture with unique ways of managing cables visually to blend with the styling of the furniture, while others try to hide the cords. There are *S* hooks, stylish shapes of cord managers, desktop wire managers, troughs that guide wires under a desk, along the edge of the desk and through the legs. There are holders that spiral around the cord to give it a different look and hide the fact that the cords are there, and also provide a means of protecting the cords from tampering.

The wire managers that keep the cords together and safely away from someone's reach can be a solid trough or a bracket. The next step "up" in both sophistication and cost is a trough that contains duplex and data boxes that bring the access closer to the equipment than could be done by using wall or floor connections. There are wire molds that carry the wires under a table to the leg, which has been hollowed

Here at the Desert Broom Branch of the Phoenix Public Library in Arizona are reading tables with flexible spines that camouflage the electrical and data cables from the floor to the surface mounted outlets in the table tops.

out to accept the cords, and a cord cover of some type (plastic or wood to match the leg) is used. A more costly solution and sometimes a cleaner one is to use a "power leg" where the electrical is actually built inside the leg and a cord for plugging or a cord that is hard-wired comes out the base of the leg to plug into the floor or wall.

If the styling of the furniture is a panel style rather than the leg style, the electrical can be housed in an accessory that is built as an integral part of the electrical system, with only the cord exposed at the bottom. The length of the hardwired plug is dictated by the National Electrical Codes, usually no longer than two feet.[5] Because this cord can be only as long as the code allows, early planning of the furniture layout to the electrical layout is crucial for a well designed library. The more people on the planning team realize this is significant, the more effective they will be at getting it done. Everyone has experienced libraries where thought has not been taken to assure that this type of planning is done. The library ends up with floor monuments (electrical boxes) at a user's feet that inadvertently get kicked and

2. Bringing Electrical into Furniture

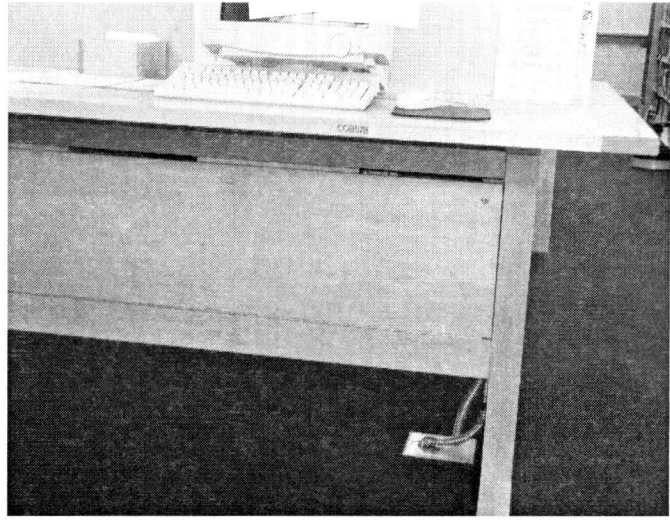

Top: Depicted is a large reading table with the power cables running through a bottom channel that is part of the design of the table and continues up a center leg-style support to a surface mounted outlet in the table top. The inset photograph at top is a close-up of the same table showing power plugged into a floor monument where it is not likely to be disturbed. *Right:* The wiring scheme on this table goes from the tabletop through a central keel that has an access panel locked to discourage tampering; the electrical is hard-wired into its source, the floor monument.

Unfortunately, this is an example of not using proper data and electrical cable management.

disconnected from the machine on the furniture. Another example of poor planning is where cords are stretched to the point that the prongs bend in the plug trying to reach the outlet. Some libraries can't electrify work stations or their task lighting because the electrical didn't end up near enough to the source of the electrical.

A cellular floor, sometimes called a cell deck or Walker Duct, consists of cable trays between floors installed in critical segments creating a high degree of flexibility in changing the location of existing computing clusters or creating new ones by accessing the electrical through the floor or ceiling. The quantity of duplex openings is contingent on the known or anticipated equipment needs of each station. The following are some general guidelines.

Electrical Planning to NEC Codes

For stations that require one PC, plan one receptacle for the computer monitor and one for the CPU. The two (2) receptacles required equal one (1) duplex.

2. Bringing Electrical into Furniture

When planning computers on a 30" × 60" or 36" × 60" panel style table plan for one computer and one printer or two computers. In this case three duplex openings will be required (six receptacles). Depending on how the computer user works — paper or paperless — each person usually needs a minimum of a 30-inch wide space to give them sufficient room. In research areas, the size of the work surface is recommended to be 30 inches deep and 42 inches wide. If users will also have papers or books alongside the computer, they will need more space. Since more research is being done as a collaborative effort, work surface areas have expanded. The National Electric Code (NEC) allows no more than thirteen (13) power columns or duplex outlets per circuit. Canada and New York City allow ten (10) power columns or duplex outlets per circuit. Always check the code that applies to your particular region.

Integrating Electrical Systems into Furniture

There are modular configurations for service desks that are complete with a modular system of wiring that can be changed. In millwork circulation desks that are more of a built-on-site method the wiring is built into the construction. Involve all parts of the team, including staff, (see Appendix A) in this planning as well. Don't rely on the architect and construction company or manufacturer of the "built-ins" to know what will work for you.

Power entries are one component of the modularity that plugs in an outlet or is hardwired into the outlet. The decision to hard wire or plug-in is decided by the type of electrical in the building as well as the conditions to work with and the equipment that will be powered. Any circuit can be provided with an isolated ground. The isolated ground circuit is used for sensitive equipment and is typically used in conjunction with a dedicated circuit; however, there might be an occasion where multiple clean computer circuits are needed and a raw or "dirty" (contaminated by other machines that share the same circuitry) circuit for everything else. Because of the confusion that exists through the evolution of electrical systems by various manufacturers, the term "dedicated" was used not only to describe proper use but everything from "designated" to "isolated ground" circuits. For the sake of clarity many manufacturers are describing "dedicated" circuits as "isolated dedicated" circuits.

One of the "rules" is that if you want the electrical to be convenience receptacles — that is, convenient for the patron — it is placed *above* the work surface. An example of this would be a plug-in of a laptop, calculator or battery recharger. Colorado State University's information commons area has 80 laptops that can be borrowed for use while at the library. One of the solutions in this application is to use a power/data tap. This can be of triangular design and fit into the left back corner vertically as standard in a study carrel (where the side meets the back) and these power taps are not intended for powering stationery equipment like a PC or AV equipment. Some of the models of this power tap have the option of a switch with a pilot light which operates the top receptacle of the power/data tap. This receptacle is intended for plugging in task lights. Interconnecting of power/data taps is not permitted by many municipalities. Each power/data tap must plug directly into a floor outlet or wall outlet.

The horizontal trough, also called a channel, provides duplex outlets attached to the underside of a work surface or mounted to the back panel of the study carrel by brackets. This channel is just a bit shorter than the width of the carrel that holds it.

There is another option for convenience of the patron. Tilt-up power/data

A tilt-up electrical access in the middle of this table has the cabling managed from this access point to the floor monument, which appears near the panel leg in this photograph. This tilt-up access allows for a flush surface on the tabletop when the electrical is not in use.

modules are available to tilt up on the surface of the table when they are being used and recede into the table when not in use. Each tilt-up box must be plugged directly into the floor outlet in many municipalities.

When an area is of a more permanent nature — PCs that should remain plugged in and to discourage the tampering with the connection — the cords fall away from the equipment through a grommet hole, or the design of the work surface allows a gap between the surface and back panel to provide a place for the cords to pass through to the underside of the surface. This recess in the design of the work surface is an advantage in that the allowance for the size of cords is not restricted by grommet size. Under the work surface the cords are handled in one of the previously mentioned ways: trough (with or without outlet capability) or connection to the building (on the floor, from the wall or ceiling). The library equipment (PCs, AV equipment, etc.) qualifies for "stationery" equipment when the equipment can be set in place with cords stowed. The printer is most often located on top of the service desk where payment can be made as copies are picked up.

As wireless becomes more prevalent, fewer troughs will be needed for bundling data and telephone transmission cables. The electronic planning table in Appendix D will assist you in providing information to your furniture fabricators, which will prove helpful for your layout and the size requirements of your furniture.

Cabling Maintenance and Wire Management

Cabling needs to be accessible to the technicians who will be responsible for maintaining and upgrading technology in the library. An OPAC (Online Public Access Computer) station that is designed with panels that remove with a minimal use of tools makes a convenient option. With this option there is full access to change out wiring as technology advances. Any piece of equipment that has need for maintenance should have a means to get to the back or the sides of the machine as needed.

What about ventilation or circulation requirements of the equipment you will purchase? Some electrical/data equipment requires that there be a specified clearance around the actual dimension of the equipment, or a venting requirement for heat dissipation that builds up when the equipment is in use. You want to make sure you check equipment specifications to learn what may be needed.

Other areas that need attention and coordination between the IT people and the supplier of the furniture as it concerns electrical requirements are the self-checkout units, check-in stations and any other station for accessing library services (e.g., reserving a public internet PC). Although these have been in use for a few years it has become clear that they have different requirements than were first thought.

When we first put them in furniture they didn't have enough ventilation. We added vent grommets. Then we added more ventilation slots as we learned that there was not enough circulation for the heat that needed to dissipate. Now we find them on top of a counter so that they are not only at the proper height for us to use but are open where they can "breathe."

Check-in stations, where the library card is swiped as the book is returned, have many of the same requirements: providing adequate ventilation, physical space around the unit to work and at a counter height for comfort. It is helpful to have some extra room to the side of the check-in and check-out machines on which to place books after they are processed.

Rule # 1: If It Gets Plugged In Involve "IT" People

Ross McLachlan, library services administrator for the City of Phoenix Library, says that "If the service you are providing is to be plugged into an outlet the IT people have to be at the table from the beginning." These are the folks who will maintain your network infrastructure, so they should be involved in designing it. Otherwise it is inevitable that the questions will arise as to why something doesn't work as it should. And the shame is that the mistake could have been avoided.

The larger the project the more paramount it is to keep the lines of communication open. When there are so many details and so many people involved in the project, it is helpful to have a plan that designates responsibility and roles of all parties involved in the planning. Appendix A lists of responsibilities broken down by the types of people who may be involved in a project. The larger the project, the more people there are to take care of the responsibilities.

Check This Out: Electrical

- Is wiring and cable easily accessible and designed to accommodate changes in the location of electrical equipment in the future?
- Is there raised flooring to accommodate wiring and cables?
- Are there enough electrical and data outlets in strategic locations and can extra outlets be added easily?
- Is humidity, temperature, natural light and planned lighting appropriate for books and people?
- Is lighting in all areas adequate and free from glare?
- Is there task lighting where appropriate?
- Does lighting allow for flexibility in moving stacks and furniture?

3

Specifications to Installation

A man should keep his little brain attic stocked with all the furniture that he is likely to need, and the rest he can put away in the lumber room of his library, where he can get it if he wants it.
— Sir Arthur Conan Doyle

Decisions, Decisions

Manufacturers make choices based on what works best for them as a company with their equipment and profit margin. Librarians make the decisions concerning the style, colors and quality of furniture and shelving knowing that they will have it in the building for twenty years or longer. The more that colors or finishes date you to an era the less likely it will be appreciated in the future. With this in mind, the moveable and replaceable fixtures (artwork, displays, anything except the furniture and fixtures) should be what provides the pizzazz to an area. This way they can be changed as times and interests change. The more flexible the area for change, the more likely it is to be changed and to be fresh and appealing to users over the years.

A decision based on aesthetics will bring your attention to one manufacturer, but I hope that you will look further to see what the manufacturer will be offering you in the long run. The manufacturer will have standard lines of furniture reflecting a few basic styles in their literature and on their Website to show what is standard. You will also want to inquire as to whether they will deviate from the styles in the literature you have seen. Some manufacturers will offer what they call "modified" that uses the standards and modifies them slightly to fit your need. Some manufacturers will do custom furniture and the cost is determined by the amount of modifications from the standard and the quantity of the item. Once they get set up to run a job there is economy in scale. The more pieces of one item that they manufacture, the less each item will be. There may be also nonstandards or uncataloged items that are still in the line of offering but do not add appreciable costs to the project. For example there could be a panel style that is constructed with one design detail that is good, but if you could change it slightly it would be better, as it could follow a detail that is used throughout the building. Wood or wood accents, paint finishes, and steel shelving colors should be decided in the building program stage. Since the end panels visually take up a large block of space, the decision of what these will look like is a decision to be made early in the process. This should be handed to the designer as a starting point along with the type and nature of the equipment and furniture that is proposed.

Products on the market must be thoroughly evaluated, and no one has more of an interest in the library than the people who work there. The investment of time toward the research, which may include visiting factories, will pay off handsomely in the years after arriving at decisions.

As Richard Bazillion and Connie Braun write:

> The design and furnishings of libraries, with their long life span, require the gift of clairvoyance. No one can know with certainty how the future will unfold, as new technologies emerge and old ones decline. Yet decisions have to be made in the present, and in such a way to place as few constraints as possible on users of the building a generation hence. Durability, utility and timelessness are criteria that apply to all aspects of the building, from its finishes to its furnishings and equipment. These criteria should be kept in mind during discussions with the architect and his or her consultants, and during preparation of the bid documents for shelving, furniture, carpeting and equipment. As a corollary to this advice, cheap solutions to any related questions are very likely the wrong ones. To obtain the best value for any investment, extensive research is absolutely essential.[1]

When writing specifications for furniture and shelving, "Standard of Quality" is defined by writing overall requirements accompanied by drawings and details. This is achieved by the facility staff or an agent employed by the library to put this package together, in conjunction with outside advisors when necessary. There is nothing wrong with collaborating with a vendor because of a favorable ratio of price to quality and citing their product as your standard in the specifications that go out to bid Do not use the terminology of specifying a particular product and then add the qualifier "as equal." This opens the door for an inferior product to bid and merely state that they are equal in craftsmanship. Instead, prequalify bidders who may bid prior to the bid date. Ask for submission of products with documentation that can provide furnishings of equal quality. Those who propose alternates know the level of quality they are expected to match. "Reserve the right to evaluate bidders and determine if they are eligible to bid. Vendors who cannot match the standard are thereby excluded, which sometimes simplifies the process. The point of the whole process, in the end, is to strike a balance between price and quality in line with budget realities."[2]

Furniture Specifications	**Potomac High School**
Issue Date: December 21, 2006	Project No. 9507-705

SECTION 12629 — LIBRARY FURNITURE STANDARD OF QUALITY

PART 1 — GENERAL

1.1 SCOPE OF WORK

All labor, material, equipment, and services necessary to furnish and install standard wood library furniture as indicated or specified.

1.2 PERFORMANCE QUALIFICATION REQUIREMENTS

- A. This specification covers the requirements for standard wood library furniture. The minimum acceptable requirements for manufacturer's extent of product line, design, materials, workmanship, performance, safety, and services are set forth hereafter. Failure to meet the minimum acceptable requirements will result in disqualification of Bid.

- B. All furniture shall be of a design, material, and workmanship to withstand hard daily usage over an extended life with a minimum of maintenance and repair

- C. The manufacturer shall guarantee for a period of five (5) years the product to withstand normal everyday usage in a high traffic, institutional setting. Abuse or deliberate defacing of the furniture is considered the responsibility of the Owner.

- D. Submittal required prior to the Bid for preapproval are proposed alternate products, alternate construction methods, and exceptions to the Specifications.

PART 2 — PRODUCTS

2.1 ACCEPTABLE MANUFACTURERS

Design and arrangement of equipment shown on plan as herein specified has been determined after considerable study and planning. The Contractor will be required to adhere to the requirements shown on the drawings and specifications. The approval of a manufacturer other than specified does not necessarily indicate that the manufacturer's standard products are acceptable. The specifications indicate required design and styling, sizes, arrangements, and detailing. They indicate a minimum standard of materials, methods and workmanship.

Furniture Specifications			**Potomac High School**
Issue Date: December 21, 2006			Project No. 9507-705

Product No.	Plan Code	Quantity	Description
WLEPD48	D48	4	48" high end panels to receive 25¼" deep canopy tops.
WLEPD48	D48P	4	48" high end panels to receive 28¼" deep canopy tops. End panel depth to be 28½"
WLEPD66	D66	4	
WLEPD84	D84	11	**Manufacturer: Big Pond**

Style: Emerson

Double Face End Panel

Specifications: See end panels and canopy tops for steel shelving Section 3.0

All end panels facing interior of library are slot wall for display. All end panels to outside of building (the other end of the range) are HPL (no slot wall display). End panel contractor to coordinate with steel shelving contractor to determine actual dimensions of end panels.

Size:

    Depth: 25½"

    Thickness: 1¼"

    Height: see quantity

Finishes:

    HPL: Wilsonart 7504–60 Wild Cherry

    Frame: Black PVC

When writing a furniture spec, it is better to be too detailed than too vague. Include everything you know about the product. Don't leave bidders to assume anything. If there is a miscommunication in what is desired and product comes in wrong, additional negotiation, not to mention finger pointing as to whose fault it is that the specs were misinterpreted follows. As an extra precaution send all your specs to the representative to double check every detail. Model numbers can be long and confusing and no two manufacturers have the same system. If a number or letter is left out it could mean something different and you could end up with a piece of furniture different from what you thought you ordered. If your representative has a copy of the bid they can also alert you to changes in pricing or product if the project is on hold for a while.

Include a sheet in your specification stating the manufacturer, name, phone number and e-mail of the local rep or contact person. Be sure to include the following items in your specification. The name of the product as the library can easily identify it: "desk chair" and a code that makes sense when you look at the specification ("CH"). The first type of chair would be "-1" and the second type "-2," etc. The third part of the model number "-A" in "CH-2-A" would be the first type of fabric, the second "-B" and so on. You want to be sure to include the factory model number, every option, the dimensions, frame color, castor requirement, fabric, fabric source, fabric rep and client contact and to tag the spec with the location where it will be installed. A photo or line drawing with the specifications is always useful toward identification of products in the future. For examples of specification examples, visit www.libraryfurnishings.com.

Each manufacturer designs their product around their manufacturing capabilities, producing a value engineered result. When working on a project it is to the library's benefit to choose someone to work with based on appreciating what they have to offer in goods and services. Look at things like what has been produced in the way of literature and drawings and at installations that you have seen using the manufacturer you've chosen. At that time you can begin working closely with that manufacturer to develop a style personalized for you, that differentiates your project from another. This will save both time and money. Not only will this be a cost savings but you would have the benefit of the prior testing on the product that has already been paid for by the manufacturer. Using modified product in lieu of designing and producing new product is usually a huge cost savings.

As you have probably imagined, there are and have always been choices at each bend in the road of planning. The more ground that is covered in the initial planning stages, the less it costs in "change orders." A change order is a written addendum to the contract that specifies a change or a group of changes that the owner and the contractor mutually agree upon. Change orders cost in time so this translates into dollars in fees for the reprocessing of information through the chains of people this change impacts and the administrative costs of that change.

Purchasing administrators will often state in their procurement regulations that there will be no "proprietary specification." If you think about it, there are no specifications that are technically proprietary (or owned by only one manufacturer), as all manufacturers could produce product in the desired way (shown in the specs). Rather, it is the case that the manufacturers are able to fabricate product and use their methods for joinery and types of finish because that is the way their system is set up to manufacture.

Purchasing agents issue all prospective suppliers this package of requirements for the purpose of entering into a bid process or RFP (Request for Proposal). In a bid situation the lowest cost is sometimes the determining factor and in other bids the bid amounts are not disclosed and an evaluation is conducted that will decide who is the apparent low bidder — that is, one that has the lowest price meeting all the specifications. When a request for proposal is submitted, a decision is made based on what is best for the library and the submitter may never know what the decision-breaker was. A matrix system is sometimes used where weight is given to such things as design, presentation of mock-ups, etc., as well as the price. In the example that follows I have chosen certain criteria for evaluation. All the information can be overwhelming and this is one method that can be used so that everyone involved in the decision is evaluating the product on the same chosen criteria (the ones that they come up with together).

Having been a manufacturer's representative for over twenty years, I feel strongly that it is important to give the bidders feedback. If you are able to share with the bidders the information as to where their product falls short of meeting your needs it will help them. They can take this information back to the manufacturer and give them the feedback that is needed from the "real world" and the products that are meeting the requirements of the users. There was one time in particular that I was following up on a multimillion dollar bid to supply a local utility company furniture that I represented over a three year contract period. They told me that I was not on the "short list," which meant my manufacturer was out of the running for the contract. I asked for some feedback, knowing that it could not only help the manufacturer I represented but also my job as a representative in the future. That same day they called me back and said that we had received the contract. This taught me that you should always ask what you can do better for the customer.

Price Does Not Necessarily Denote Quality

To make it more confusing, quality isn't always about price. Things don't have to be costly for quality to exist. If a local manufacturer doesn't have high costs (overhead) of factory space, showrooms or promotion in all of its forms, they could

3. Specifications to Installation

Example of Using a Simple Matrix System for Evaluation

COTTONTAIL PUBLIC LIBRARY RENOVATION

	Years in Business	Bid	Cost	Mock-Up	Presentation	References	Total Pts
Steel Company A	20	$78,345.60	2	5	3	4	12
Steel Company B	35	$89,234.78	3	4	4	5	13
Steel Company C	12	$60,479.03	1	5	1	3	9

Point System: 1–5
1=Poor
2=Unsatisfactory
3=Satisfactory
4=Very Good
5=Excellent

Result: The decision is whether this end user wants to spend $10,889.18 more for a one point spread

JACKRABBIT MIDDLE SCHOOL LIBRARY SEATING

	Bid	Comfort*	Warranty	Ease of Adjustments	Total Pts
Library Manufacturer A	$20,934.00	4	5	2	11
Library Manufacturer B	$18,980.00	5	5	4	14
Library Manufacturer C	$24,786.00	3	4	3	10

*Evaluation Form by Staff
SCALE: 1–5

Result: The decision looks clear: the lowest priced product got the best marks-now to look at life cycle costs.

---

be providing a durable product of the same general quality for a cost much less than someone who needs the markup in order to survive in the market they have chosen. With transportation costs as they are, the decision to buy local or pay freight to get it to you is a significant choice.

When you are determining the cost of an item be sure that the maintenance over the life of the item is taken into consideration rather than looking only at the original cost.

Plywood, Lumbercore and Veneer

Specifications indicate a minimum standard of materials, methods and workmanship desired for furniture. There is much controversy over the type of furniture construction that is "best." What is important is the combination of joinery and materials that are used in constructing a product, which needs to be both able to perform in the field and to be a durable product for its anticipated life cycle. Life cycle cost analysis will include the initial expenditure, the maintenance costs and the anticipated useful life of the product. Ask for performance testing, which is testing that is documented because "quality" is a perception and results of testing will enable you to make better comparisons. It seems that once a person is sold on a particular type of construction they perceive that way as being best or the finest quality without pursuing other options. For instance the use of particleboard versus lumbercore is an issue that surfaces when a person has been sold on the idea that one is better than the other. The reality is that each has its own advantages and disadvantages.[3]

A better question is how the product will be used. Lumbercore is stronger than particleboard were all components equal. Lumbercore provides less deflection over length than particleboard; however, it has greater deflection across the grain (width) of the table, and generally has better screwing power. The strength can be enhanced in either lumbercore or particleboard by using metal inserts embedded in the wood. These metal inserts would accept the screws rather than the screw going directly through the wood. In order to prevent warping of particleboard or lumbercore under changing climatic conditions it is imperative that both sides of the material be covered with the same material, be it laminate or veneer. Lumbercore is particularly suited for a long span where additional reinforcement is not possible or would ruin the design if there was additional visual support. Lumbercore is used on four-legged tables with a 90-inch length, tables without aprons and anything subjected to additional load: book trucks, index tables, shelving.

Although wood is the most basic of building materials, the technology and terminology involved with harvesting, sawing and selling it have made it a bit more complicated. All woods are hardwood or softwoods and this is a botanical distinction that has nothing to do with durability. Basically, hardwoods are cut from leaf-bearing trees (deciduous) such as oak, maple and hickory. Softwoods come from evergreens (conifers) such as pine, spruce and redwood. Some soft woods, like redwood, are more weather resistant than some hardwoods and that is why redwood is used for decks and lawn furniture. Woods need to be evaluated on their own merit as to how they will be used.

Hardwood plywood is sold as paneling and for making cabinets and furniture. The veneers may be glued to a solid lumbercore, a veneer core from a different species, or a core of a composite material. The best grade is "sequence matched" which means the veneer panel on the face continues from one panel to the next. Most hardwood plywood is sold in 4 × 8-foot sheets but a few lumberyards sell smaller pieces since it is so much more expensive than standard plywood. Thicknesses range from ¼ inch to ¾ inch thick, but larger size panels are available in greater thicknesses by special order. Birch plywood, with its smooth tight-grained surface (think maple) is popular for furniture that will be stained or painted, and it doesn't cost as much as plywood with more exotic veneers like oak or walnut.

Lumbercore material is random width strips of solid wood glued together. It has 1/16 inch veneer on either side to hold the stability of the wood. Particleboard consists of wood chips bonded together with adhesive. Veneer is a thin skin of solid wood grain bonded by adhesive to the surface of veneer core, which is made up of slices of wood (3-ply or 5-ply being the number of layers) that are stacked at right angles to the grain of adjacent plies and the edges and ends of the panels. The face veneer is graded and the terms "select" and "nonselect" might be used. If the finish that is chosen is one that is a natural, non-hiding stain, your choice should be the select unless you like to see the imperfections that are part of wood's character. If the finish is darker and will hide any imperfections there is no need to incur the additional cost of having the manufacturer select wood that is free of imperfections. What you don't want is to have the surprise of wood on the same chair with different colors at different places. The finish is chosen from manufacturer's standard to coordinate with architectural details like doors and window frames or the finish is presented to the manufacturer so that the finish can be matched to something that exists (other furniture or something in the building's interior).

Plywood is made by gluing thin sheets of wood together and is available in various densities ranging from low to high and in different classes for suitable use in both interior and exterior environments. Strength and screwing power is directly in proportion to the density. For added strength, the sheets or veneers are placed so that the grain of one layer is perpendicular to those above and below it. Because of its construction, plywood has terrific lateral strength.

Another descriptive word that might be used to describe wood is "sound." Sound means that the wood is free of imperfections (called voids, splits or laps) and would be suitable for balanced construction that would be visible when the wood is finished.

In the past, particleboard has suffered a bad reputation from being used in furniture that was poorly made. This underengineering still exists in the ready to assemble furniture available in the retail market today and this is why some people think that particleboard construction indicates that the furniture is inexpensive. The current industry standard is the American National Standards Institute (ANSI) A208.1–1999. ANSI grades include 1MS, 1M2 and 1M3. The first digit describes the resin binder used, the second the board's density and the third its physical properties — e.g., internal bond strength and fastener holding capacity. Particleboard can be faced with hardwood veneers, high- and low-pressure laminates, thin vinyl, decorative plastic film, paper overlays or direct prints. It is used to create tables and countertops, institutional and office furniture, cabinetry, vanities, speakers and bookcases. The boards that have the finest particled surfaces are prime candidates for filling and base coating, ready for painting. Many of the sixteen other construction grades are used for floor underlay, home decking, stair treads and wall sheathing and siding. Since home centers still stock the cheapest particleboard that they can find rather than industrial grade interiors projects require, there are a lot of do-it-yourself jobs out there unwittingly perpetuating particleboard's bad rap. For both custom and ready made furniture the Composite Panel Association, formerly the National Particleboard Association (NPA), located in Gaithersburg, Maryland, recommends that interior designers learn to ask for particleboard "made to 1999 ANSI *industrial standards*."[4] The words refer not only to correct grades but also to compliance with federal regulations regarding formaldehyde emissions.

The part of the specification that speaks to the drying of the wood and moisture content is crucial to the finished product due to the fact that when it is shipped to its destination it will experience a change in humidity. The adhesive and the method used to bond the materials together is important because as the furniture goes out in the field it may experience a wide range of temperature changes that cause the glue to fail. Before the building is ready for occupancy the furniture may be exposed to an extreme range of temperatures. Living in the Southwest area of the U.S., I have known schools to store the furniture in libraries, in the summer, without air conditioning and expect that the materials would not delaminate or warp. It is a harsh test and if the furniture is successful at making it through that test it is great, but if it doesn't, who is responsible for this? Should furniture be subjected to these kinds of conditions? Properly laminated and finished veneers should last many years before there is any noticeable degradation, provided that the furniture is not subjected to extremes in temperature and humidity. If it is subjected to extremes you can expect to see signs of veneer checking and discoloration over time.

Hardwood bullnose edge banding is shown on this plastic laminate tabletop; this type of edge banding can be used to finish the edges of end panels, study carrels, canopy tops and panel leg styles. This edge band detail can be used with any type of surface material such as wood veneers or solid wood panels. Table by the Buckstaff Company.

How the edgebandings are bonded to tables and the framing on the end panels is important as this is an area that can come apart over time if not applied correctly. Maximum gluing surface and quality adhesives will provide a lasting connection. The construction varies by manufacturer, using a combination of wood or mechanical joinery methods and hot glue methods including radio frequency curing.

In the early 1900s hardwoods were plentiful, and antique furniture reveals that solid woods were used much of the time. As wood use increased, lumber core was more prevalent in furniture. As wood continued to be used, veneer core was used. As there was less wood available, particleboard began to become more common in furniture use.

Particleboard was developed in the 1930s and is roughly ten percent binder and ninety percent wood particles rescued from wood shavings, sawdust, trimmings and other wood residues. "We imagine a nosy visitor checking out the backs of cabinets and the underside of furniture and discover that we are harboring 'phony wood'— phony wood that oddly enough, happens to be made of the real thing. Particleboard began its commercial career in the 1930s in Europe after World War II in which homes, businesses and forests were destroyed and went on to form a basis for sophisticated high end designs."[5]

Jeffrey Swiggett, president of Helikon Furniture Company, says that "Wood veneers have been substituted for solid woods for centuries. It was not until better glues and resins were developed in the 1950s that it became the preferred alternative to solid wood."[6] One of the many aesthetic benefits to working with veneers is the beautiful patterns that result from the manner in which that veneer is cut from the log. For example, cherry logs cut in plain slices yield an attractive cathedral pattern, while cherry logs cut in quarter slices result in a veneer with a straight pattern. Mahogany is typically specified as a flat cut, but the quarter slice version yields a beautiful striped pattern known as ribbon. The point is that there are many options available when specifying figured patterns and it behooves designers and their clients to review all the various options with the manufacturer. Swiggett continues that manufacturers have many options available when selecting veneers for their collections. More often than not the wishes of the design community drive these selections. Over time, various species of woods fall out of favor. While the availability of many types of domestic and imported popular hardwoods is good, they can become overused. It is a case of supply and demand. Swiggett says that "An architect or designer that intends to use a popular wood for a job of any magnitude should insist that the manufacturer send samples of the veneer flitch that will be used prior to releasing the production run. In this way, they can be assured that the product will be fabricated with veneers that have the figuring that you expect from high grade architectural veneers."[7]

Manufacturers make choices based on what works best for them as a company with certain manufacturing capabilities. One of these choices is the type of veneers used. Understanding the process that wood goes through from its natural state to the furniture you see begins by understanding grain and veneer. Grain is the pattern in wood that gives it its distinctive appearance. Veneer is a thin layer of finishing wood bonded to each side of a thicker sheet of less refined wood. The grain of the wood is determined by the way it is cut from the log. Logs are cut into sections called a "flitch." A rotary cut will give you a wild grain in the appearance of the wood while the other end of the spectrum (in both look and price) is the sequence matched panel-to-panel where all panels come from the same flitch (log) and the continuity of pattern is matched side-to-side. Half-log or flat-sliced flitches create a flame or cathedral pattern on the veneer. There are half-round, plain sliced and rift cuts. Veneers sliced parallel to the center line of a log produce a plain sawn appearance called flat cut veneer. Two bold patterns of flat cut wood grain are called flame and cathedral descriptive of their grain pattern. Quarter-log flitches are generally flat-sliced or rift cut and produce a narrow-striped pattern veneer. Rift cut gives straight grain and it can be slip matched or book matched. Slip matched is when the pattern is matched

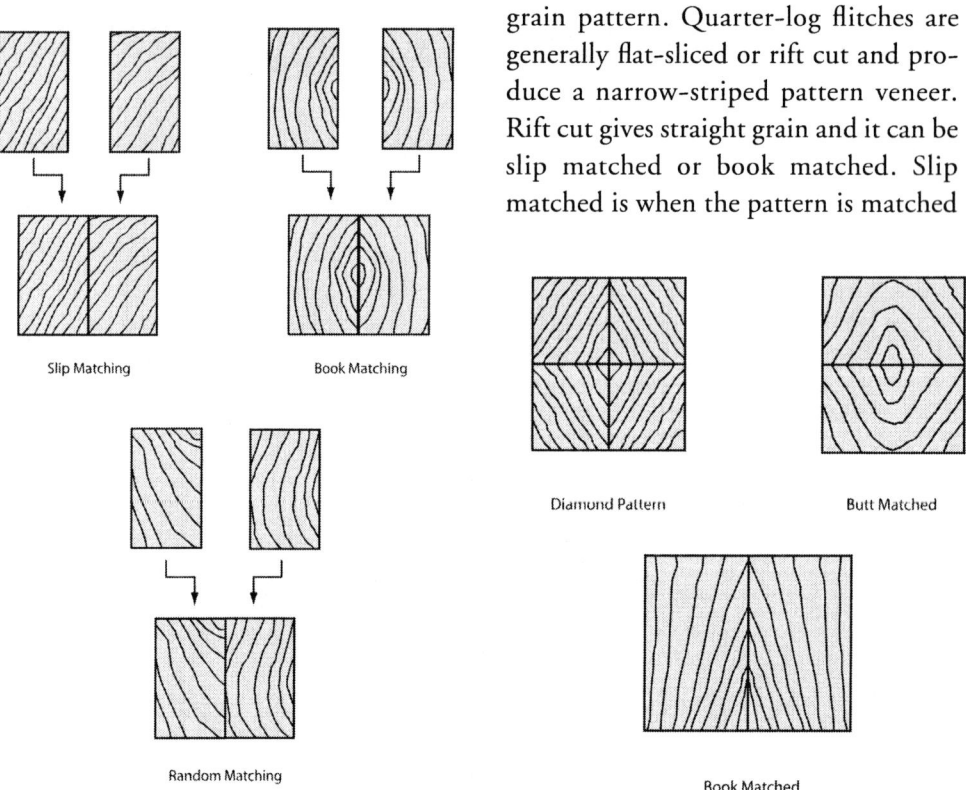

These are examples of veneers and how they can be matched to achieve different pattern effects that may be more or less desirable for the end-user (illustration by Anish Adalja).

side-to-side so that the pattern continues across the grain. Book matched is a pattern that radiates from the center where one veneer mirrors the one laid next to it.

Veneers sliced at right angles to the growth rings produce a quarter sawn appearance and are called quarter cut veneers. Rotary sliced veneers are cut in continuous sheets like a roll of paper. After the veneer sheets have been sliced, they are laid side by side and bonded together to form a veneer face.

The three most common patterns of veneer matching are slip matching, book matching and random matching. Veneered furniture is not cheaply made (compared to using "solid wood") but instead it is known that the veneer gives added strength to furniture construction and helps prevent warpage. Large expanses on furniture can have a consistent pattern or appear as a single piece by the use of veneers. Diamond pattern and butt matched would be decorative laid veneers in patterns that might be used for a conference table or a piece of furniture large enough to appreciate the detail.

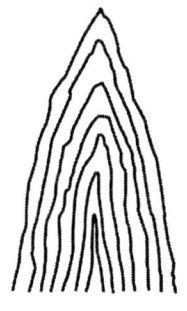 

Cathedral   Flame

Two bold patterns of wood grain called flame and cathedral are shown below. The names are descriptive of the grain pattern. The spire effect is called a cathedral and the other pattern resembles the flame of a candle. Flat cut veneers create their bold design (iIllustration by Anish Adalja).

Another option is to use high-pressure decorative plastic laminate (HPL) on particleboard. Homeowners are familiar with this material as it has been used in bathroom vanities and kitchen counters for many years. It is often referred to generically as Formica, which is a actually a brand of plastic laminate. HPL may be maintained with a damp cloth or ordinary soap and water. HPL gives you solid colors and patterns to meet contemporary design trends, while the wood veneers give the aesthetic benefit of real wood. After a few years of use, natural woodgrain HPL that matched the veneer might have been a better choice for durability. If you can't get beyond the idea of "fake wood" know that there are great colors and textures available on the plastic laminate market. That choice has broadened greatly in the past fifteen years.

There are general-purpose HPL grades where the surfaces must be functional, durable and decorative and vertical surface grades intended for applications that absorb less impact than a comparable horizontal surface. There are also low pressure laminates (melamine is one) and they are only suitable for vertical services where the durability factor is not a concern. Postforming grade of HPL is used on horizontal or vertical surfaces where it is necessary or desirable to roll the laminate on a simple radius over the edge of a substrate. In any case the surface wear, impact resistance and cleanability are important factors.

Steel materials and trims are used in library furniture and shelving as well. All materials used in library furniture by major manufacturers are commercial grade assuring the user a product that will withstand public use.

General Specifications: The Blueprint of Requirements

A "boiler plate" (basic standard description the school district or architect uses on all their documents) may be used for every project that is put out for bid, becoming the minimum standard and grading of materials that will be accepted on the project. The materials that are to be used are then called out in detail with any applicable standards to be followed for the materials.

The quality of the joint connecting hardware or joinery methods should be specified. (See illustration of "Typical Joints" with descriptions that follow.) The hardware used in joining two canopy tops together to provide a seam free appearance is called a tight-joint fastener. An effective specification will speak to the quality intended. This joinery specification should also apply to the joinery and adhesives used in edgebanding. The means of application and the joinery methods can become the "spec lock," meaning that this is a requirement that all suppliers must meet. It can "lock" the spec into one product that meets the expectation of the buyer; anyone that wants to supply pricing needs to adhere to this specification or convince the buyer that the materials and methods that they are supplying are just as good as or better than the written specification.

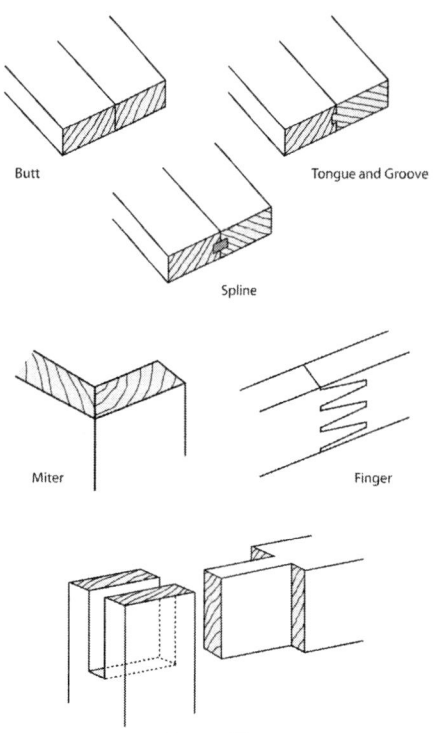

Differing examples of joining solid woods; some of these techniques such as splines or butt joints can be used with particleboard as well (illustration by Anish Adalja).

3. Specifications to Installation

Typical Joints

Butt — A joint formed by square edge surfaces (ends, edges, faces) coming together; end butt joint, edge butt joint

Tongue and Groove — A joint formed by the insertion of the "tongue" of one wood member into the "groove" of the other

Finger — A series of fingered machined on the ends of two pieces of wood to be joined, which mesh together and are securely joined in position

Mortise & Tenon, Slotted — And tenon right angle joint in which the tenon is visible on two edges once the joint is complete

Dovetail — A joint formed by inserting a projecting web-shaped member (dovetail tendon) into a correspondingly shaped cut out member (dovetail mortise)

Mitre — The joining of two members at an angle that bisects the angle of the junction

Spline — A joint formed by the use of a "spline." A spline is a thin narrow strip usually of plywood, inserted into matching grooves which have been machined in abutting edges of panels or lumber to insure a flush alignment and secure joint; customarily runs the entire length of the joint

Doweled — A joint using "dowels" (cylinder-shaped pieces of wood) that fits inside openings of the same shape and length

This is where the evaluation can become tricky, as words imply strength and durability. The only means

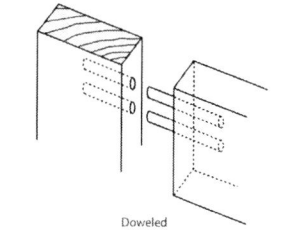

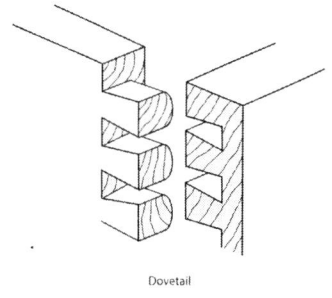

Dowelled joinery is generally used for face frames of cabinets and the dove tail joint is many times used for attaching the drawer face to the sides, or sometimes this joint can be used to accent a joint technique along the edge of two pieces of wood put together at a perpendicular angle (illustration by Anish Adalja).

of comparison are in analyzing written test results of the product. If manufacturers have not performed the same tests, it makes comparison more difficult and the durability claims must be based on trust by visits to installations of the supplier to determine how they are holding up over time. A trip to the factory to see how the furniture is made may prove helpful. Basically it comes down to researching and evaluating a product and then trusting that you are receiving a product that will work for you.

Marilyn Farrow, former president of the Institute of Business Designers, says that "The selection of appropriate contract furnishings is a complex process." She says that we can rely on the client's perception of appropriate utilization and return on investment, each designers training and personal experience and standards developed by ANSI/BIFMA (American National Standards Institute/The Business and Institutional Furniture Manufacturers Association). She adds that we can use research and publications defining the environmental and ergonomic impact of various components of products and the valuable knowledge of sales representatives. She says that a client comes to the table with a concept of what they want to achieve, an opinion of fair pricing (and often a mandate to cut costs) and not always a realistic timeline for installation.[8]

If you have decided on a look from one manufacturer there may be a reason that it is not available from another manufacturer. One of those reasons is that a patent might exist on the design. With modifications they may be able to provide the same overall look with some of the details omitted to make your project with a new design for you and not an infringement on a patent.

In Nancy Lohrer's article on "How To Select Furniture for the Library," she suggests doing a construction analysis to determine what furniture will last the longest. She continues, "In Massachusetts, furniture must last the lifetime of the facility, at least 80 years. For the library furniture project at Plymouth State College in New Hampshire, 22 different stack chairs were tested before making the final decision." She adds, "Look for craftsmanship."[9]

Types of Finishes and Future Availability

Methods of finishes are another choice that the manufacturer makes for their product line and sometimes they are capable of producing more than one type of finish.

The finish and the steps taken to apply the finish are important factors when combined with how well the furniture maintains its appearance over time. If the sanding of the furniture and the finish are not consistent in application, the furniture will show it. If glue is not sanded away from the joining of the parts before the finish is applied that will show as an obvious mistake in the finishing. If the finish involves painting rather than staining the material, the method and type of painting needs to be included in the specs. Part of the submittal package from the interested bidders should include an actual piece of the finish if it has been chosen so that it can be used to make matches for other finish decisions as well as to match against the furniture or shelving shipment. You might ask the manufacturer you are considering for a sample of their finish so that you can conduct your own tests.

Solid wood has the disadvantage of expanding and contracting if it is oiled rather than protected from the elements with a finish. An oil finish is a petroleum based product that is allowed to penetrate the wood, giving it a natural appearance. It is not a film that seals the pores. Easy to apply, easy to repair, but it provides poor protection against reagents, scratches and moisture. Catalyzed lacquer or conversion alkyd-urea varnishes are both durable and easy to maintain. Ask to see the test results to see how they react to various forms of abuse. They are both a multistep finish process and impervious to many chemicals.

Addressing the availability of parts in the future is a smart detail to add to your specification. If a manufacturer cannot or will not produce an item in the future as you need it, you would want to learn this up front. You might include in your specification some parameters concerning the time that the product would be available from the manufacturer. I would think ten years would be a reasonable time to commit to making a product to match the original order. It is an advantage to purchase from a company that will ensure the availability of their parts in the future so that the design you have chosen does not become obsolete.

Detailed Specifications

So far, all of the specifications have been what would be termed "General Specifications" and relevant to the overall product. The specifications can get as detailed as is your preference. You can have a complete breakdown of each type of furniture: tables with their shapes and sizes, seating with its own set of construction specifications, joinery, finishes and upholstery when applicable.

In this case each panel (in the case of a study carrel or panel style table) or component of the piece is detailed by materials and size. The specifications may take at least two different forms. One lists quantity of each item, dimensions and location by individual item. It is a recap of all the furniture in the project categorized under general area identified by room number or location, as it is easier to make changes to the specification when changes occur. The other form provides one page per type of table, carrel or chair and gives it an item number and dimensions with a complete description. In this type of specification format a photo or line drawing is convenient.

This item specification sheet may include complete specifications as to materials, dimensions and any accessories that could be used in the future. If accessories are listed it is best to clarify that "0" quantities of this accessory are used or a term like "not applicable" to this bid, also known as "N/A."

Electrical and data capability will be something that is a part of detailing the specification. You might ask for assistance from the manufacturer's representative by talking with them and letting them know what will be used in each area needing electrical or data and allow them to specify the furniture for you. When they have completed this task, have your Information Technology person take a look at it and see that it has all the components that are needed since they are the experts in the technology field. (Refer to Electronic Planning Table found in Appendix D).

The bid should include a requirement to check field measurements to confirm the actual dimensions when the walls are built and the building is ready. Compare it again with the blueprints and the specified product's dimensions. All the locations of the floor and wall power/data outlets, thermostat, vents, registers and any interference of wall outcropping should be noted on the blueprint. The bidder should be responsible for checking the building's progress and becoming familiar with the unloading facilities and access to the location where the furniture will be installed. The bidder's efforts should be coordinated with the project schedule. This is usually the job of the manufacturer's representative or local distributor.

The designated representative of the library will want to make periodic site visits as the building takes shape. A daily walk-through is even better in that issues can be questioned, addressed and solved. Sometimes minor adjustments can be addressed at this point that will allow the center to function as the staff visualized it. If the electrical is not found to be where it has been planned, time and money will be saved by noting and correcting it early in the project.

Your original specification package, along with all the fabrics used, finishes and any installation instructions, cleaning and warranty instructions, should be kept in a place where staff can use it for future information or purchases. It makes the task so much easier if all this information is available in one place.

Options in Purchasing: Bids vs. Contracts

There are purchasing procedures in municipalities, school districts and the private sector. If you do not have a policy in place you might want to consider options to putting the product out to bid.

If you have put a project out to bid, you know that there is a cost of time and money that goes into this specification process. If the project will go out to bid, the time for the process must be factored in on the front end. If you are able to get all the documentation that is needed to make your decisions and you have the ability to skip the process and time that it requires in publishing the specification, evaluating the specification the time (estimate three to four weeks) for the bidders to put their package together for submission, it is a savings of everyone's time, time that can be spent working on your project. My experience has been that the bid time adds a total of two and a half to three months to the process, and by then you may be running to catch up to make the lead time that the manufacturers need to fabricate the product. Many times it limits the competition rather than encourages it due to the time a supplier has available for lead time once the decision is made to purchase.

Furniture and shelving can be bought from a catalog. This is common for rural areas and libraries that may not be ordering a very large amount. There are fewer styles and finishes available but since they are off-the-shelf items (in stock) the lead time may be faster and more cost effective.

Product can be purchased from a contract. This means that there is a prenegotiated discount taken off a price list that is current at any time, and this discount is good for a negotiated time frame. This way the savings is in going through the evaluation process once per time frame (usually one to five years), and unless the supplier provides unsatisfactory product or service there is no need to constantly renegotiate pricing.

An equipment list that has an itemized breakdown with prices is more realistic than the cost per square foot estimates that a contractor who has no expertise in furniture selection and specification might provide. A manufacturer can supply budgetary prices which will help you determine the furniture portion of the total budget and might assist you in knowing whether you want to bid it or make use of one of the other options. Calculating a cost based on the equipment list along with any allowances for freight, delivery, installation and the best estimates for increases of cost for all of these factors (should the time frame for the facility be later than anticipated) will prepare the library for worst case scenario in budget costs.

Installation Requirements

As a customer of the manufacturer you could inquire as to whether a CD or DVD of installation procedures is available. The DVD is good for the installers to watch prior to installing product. There may be written installation instructions.

Expect an installer or the bidder to ask about available storage and staging areas and the times that are permitted for building access. They will want to learn access issues so that they will know how far they will need to move the furniture and if there is a dock to receive the furniture. If there is no dock what will the route of entry be? If the truck doesn't come equipped with a lift then a piece of equipment will be needed to unload the truck. Is the exterior walkway or driveway finished to the point that a truck can use it? Sometimes, if the concrete has not yet cured, the sidewalk will not be available to take the weight of the equipment that brings the materials into the building. What precautions need to be taken? Will a hand cart need to be used? If elevators are available only during limited times the contractor will know that they must work around this. This will sometimes incur additional cost if the materials must be brought into an area after hours.

The premises on which the installation will take place needs to be free of any obstacles or conditions that could impede the installers during delivery and installation, including other tradespeople still installing ceilings or pulling electrical conduit to the area. In other words, the building needs to be ready for the furniture or shelving. It is also better that the furniture not be delivered until the workmen are out of the area since a table, carrel or chair can make a handy step stool for the tradespeople. Steel shelving can be dinged and scratched by being installed in an area before it is clear of the tradespeople doing their part of the installation. Be aware that if delivery of the furniture is taken at a destination other than the final installation there may be additional costs to store and transfer the goods. Anticipate additional costs if the building is not ready for the furniture on the agreed delivery date. The more times the furniture is moved the more chances of damage or loss of parts and pieces. Part of the receiving party's responsibility is to check for any freight damage and make the freight claim for the client. If you choose to take the responsibility to receive your product and install it as a cost savings, realize that the hassle of dealing with a freight company can be costly in time spent.

Upon installation of the furniture it is expected that the furniture be cleaned to "showroom" condition by the installer and all dusting or sawdust removed from any furniture. Floors should be vacuumed and the furniture set into place according to plan. Instructions should be available for cleaning methods and touch-up of furniture, with proper maintenance and any tips for stowing electrical cords. Touch-up paint or finish might be available to you as well.

In the myriad of details that make up a construction project there are often on-site adjustments that must be addressed to arrive at a solution agreeable to all parties. Blueprints do not always reflect the placement that is functionally optimal until the furniture is installed. Designate one person as the contact at the library with the authority to approve changes. Realizing that some decisions impact more people than others, a good administrator knows who should be involved to reach a conclusion. It isn't so important that there are no problems but rather the importance is in whether they are resolved to everyone's satisfaction.

Check This Out: Specs to Install

- Do you really want to open up your project to all manufacturers, seeing them "as equal"? Or do you want to protect your specifications with prequalification of bidders based on those requirements that are important to your project?
- Address any questions and respond to all bidders in writing so that everyone is working from the same information.

3. Specifications to Installation

- Avoid needless and costly change orders by being thorough in the initial planning stages.
- Evaluate materials and joinery methods used. Ask *how* it is used and consider the material and joint method used.
- Try to stay away from choosing the finishes and styles that are "hot" in today's market; they will be "dated" in the future.
- Evaluate bidding vs. constructing a contract so that it is a winning situation for both the supplier and the buyer.
- If there is a planning committee, choose a project coordinator to act as liaison between the committee and the interior planner.

4

Shelving: Will It Stand the Test of Time?

Speaking to the infrastructure of shelving:
"I have a bookcase which is what
Many much better men have not.
There are no books inside, for books,
I am afraid, might spoil its looks."
— Henry Cuyler Bunner
Longtime editor of the humor magazine *Puck*

Shelving Requirements

This section addresses shelving requirements with the purpose of helping the person who is selecting shelves to become familiar with the type of shelving generally used in libraries, known as bracket type freestanding reinforced book stack, consisting of upright supporting columns placed on modular centers. It has adjustable cantilever style shelves hung on brackets with the ability to attach on either (single-faced) or both sides (double-faced) of the upright. This section also addresses various end panels and canopy top options for the cantilevered shelving.

When determining which library bookstack manufacturer gives you the best value, consider the following: The design and engineering of the shelving as a unit is the key. The method of construction is as important as the gauge of the metal. There are two primary characteristics in considering how the unit is constructed: the gauge of steel and the paint finish. The gauge of steel is measured by a number; the smaller the number the greater the strength (i.e., 14 gauge being stronger than 18 gauge). The uprights of the frame, cross members, and shelves all have individual gauges. The total unit and the way it is designed for stability will complete the evaluation. *Library Technology Reports* publishes testing on the finish of resistance to abrasion and the stability of the units. Is the shelving meeting or exceeding the test requirements? Evaluate paint finish for visual consistency.

4. Shelving

All shelving layouts begin with knowing how much space will be available for books, periodicals and media. Learning the footprint that each unit requires and calculating how many units will be needed to house the collection is one of the first steps. The units that fit into a row, also called a "range," begin to take shape when this calculation is known. Determine how many volumes will fit on each shelf and recognize the breakdown (by type) of the collection. In this analysis of the building it will become apparent that there are areas unuseable for shelving space. These areas can be used for aisles, for clustered lounge seating or study areas due to architectural details in the building. Useable floor space is a concern since windows, doors and other use of wall space reduce the space for book storage. The shape of the area and the traffic flow will also determine the shelving plan. I am hearing more and more that the public does not want to bend or stretch to obtain the books on the shelf. The librarians try to place the bulk of the books on all of the shelving, with the exception of the top and bottom shelf. The only exception is when the shelves are so full that this is no longer possible.

If the planner doesn't know what to look for, all steel shelving will appear to be the same. The quality of construction providing stability, the gauge of steel materials and the thicknesses of paint finish are all factors to be considered. This section addresses the cantilevered steel shelving (starter and adder and welded frame construction) and *not* the four-post type that consists of shelves with vertical uprights that clip or bolt into position and are commonly used in warehouses for industrial or commercial uses. Case-type shelving consisting of full back, top and end panels will not be addressed in this book. Case-type shelving is used in law libraries and other areas that do not need the flexibility of individual shelf movement that other libraries require as their needs change. We will look at wood shelving as an option to other materials and those options will be covered in greater detail in the Materials for Wood Furniture chapter.

Seeing the Difference

The best way you can determine what shelving is best for you is either to view samples of the shelving from the factory or, better yet, see it at existing libraries in use. Talk to existing customers and see how it has held up for them. Some of the things to look for is to examine the steel shelving along the edges and look closely at the bends that make the shelf. Are they sharp with burrs? Do the shelf ends meet adjacent to each other or are there gaps? These ends should meet and have smooth edges to prevent the tearing of books as they are shelved or catching the clothing of patrons who are using them. Look at the shelf end. Is the space at the top of the shelf end consistent with the gap at the bottom of the shelf end?

Look at where the shelf ends meet at the base shelf and then follow along the front of the base shelves. Is it neat and clean in appearance from one unit to the next? Ask the shelving vendor if this alignment is possible before you consider this shelving inferior. It may take a minor adjustment by installers to take care of this problem.

Are the gauges consistent with industry requirements? This is the actual weight or the thickness of the steel material. There are differences in the paint finishes as well which range from one millimeter to three millimeters thick.

Terminology

You need to be aware of the different terms that the shelving manufacturer uses so you can make the best choice for you. A range consists of a continuous row

 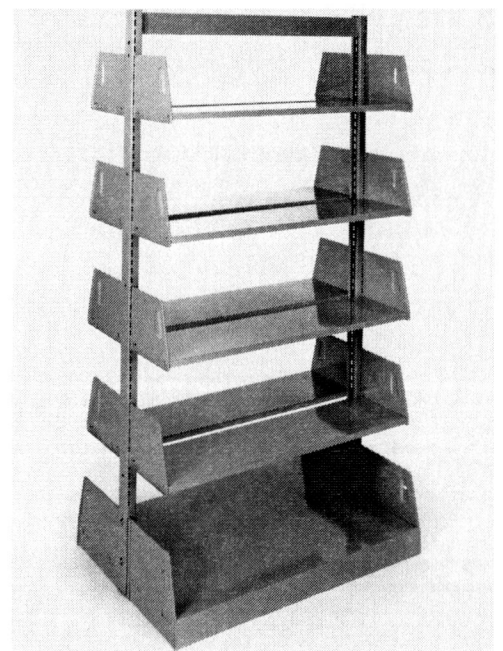

Left: This is a welded frame design that is a single-faced steel shelving unit which is generally fastened to a wall using angle brackets. Shelves are adjustable in one inch increments. This unit can be part of a range or stand alone. ***Right:*** This is a welded frame design that is double-faced and a free-standing steel shelving unit which is accessible from both sides. Shelves on both sides are adjustable independently at one inch increments. This unit can stand alone with or without end panels or grouped in series to create a range (photographs courtesy of MJ Industries, Inc.).

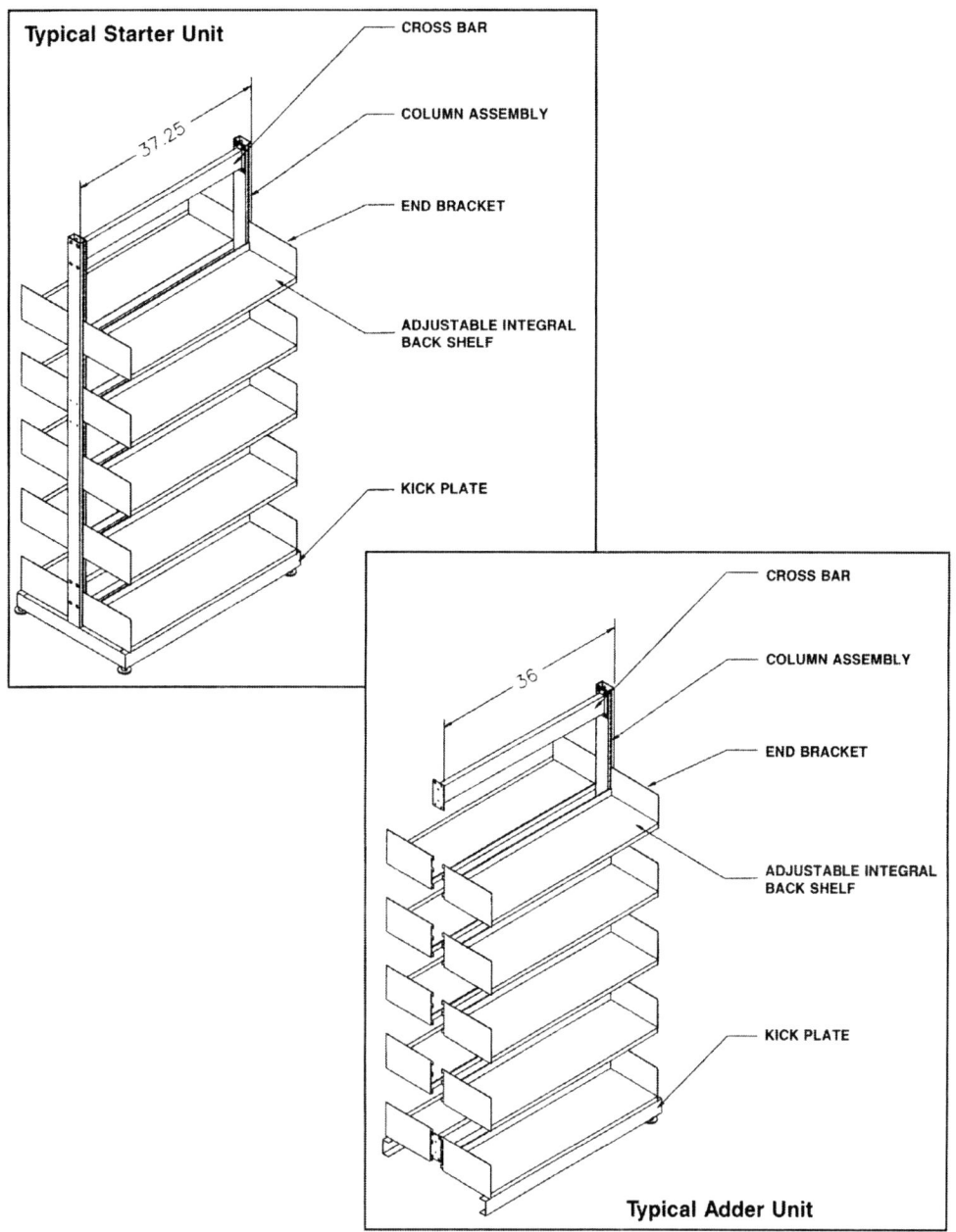

Top: A typical starter, also called an initial unit, is similar to the welded frame system in that it has two upright columns and horizontal spreaders at the top and bottom of the unit, completing the four sided "box" on all sides for stabilization. Unlike the welded frame, this frame is clipped or bolted together in some manner. *Bottom:* A typical adder unit is three sided, sharing the fourth side with the starter that it is attached to the adjacent unit by means of bolting (courtesy of MJ Industries, Inc.).

of connected units. Double-faced units allow books to be stowed on both sides. Single faced units must be attached to a wall for stability or anchored to the floor if the unit is not braced against a wall, with only one face available for use.

Failing to understand the difference between single-faced and double-faced units and the terminology can result in a costly mistake. If each single-sided (or face) is quoted as a unit rather than being designated as the double-sided unit that it may be, the equipment list is incorrect and the cost is nearly double when compared with a single-sided unit. It is a mistake that could easily be avoided if both parties understand the terminology. One double-faced unit is less costly than two single-faced units. Double-faced units cost an estimated 50 percent more than the single-faced, so cost per linear foot is reduced where double-sided units are used. Wherever shelving is back-to-back and using the same frame, the shelving should be expressed as double-faced (or double-sided) since two single-sided would rarely be freestanding using two frames. There are exceptions where additional components such as triangular gussets are used that stabilize the single sided unit to enable it to be freestanding. This is an exception and a design used most commonly for display units.

Welded frame shelving units are independent of each other (non-progressive) whether the first unit or the second attaches to the first. Any one of them can be removed from the middle or one of the ends. Another type of design is known as starter and adder units. This type needs to be ordered as one starter (also known as an initial unit) per range, while all the remaining units are adders and continue the run. Basically the starter unit is complete and able to work independently. On the other hand the adders have only three sides, sharing the fourth side with the starter unit.

Standard Shelving Dimensions

Most steel shelving comes in five standard ranges for height: 42 inches or 48 inches, 60 inches or 62 inches, 66 inches or 72 inches, 78 inches or 84 inches and 90 inches or 93 inches. Standard width of a unit is 36 inches. Heights falling between the manufacturer's standards are available for an extra charge dependent on quantity of each special unit needed.

Actual measurements in height, width or depth are not the same as nominal measurements for steel shelving. For all adjustable shelves, the actual depth is one inch less than the "nominal" depth. For the bottom shelves, called the base shelves, the actual depth of the shelf, as well as the overall depth of the book stack unit, will measure 1⅜ inches greater than the "nominal" depth for single-faced units and 7/16 inches greater than the "nominal" depth for double-faced units. For most cantilever type book stacks the adjustable shelves and base depths are given in "nominal" dimension, which indicates the depth from the front edge of the shelf to the centerline of the frame that is two inches deep. The illustration (at right) will explain the difference between nominal and actual measurements.

Hinged or fixed periodical shelving is an exception to this rule as the shelves are deeper and the lip that keeps the material from falling off the front of the shelving is the deepest point for this type of unit. The example is taken using the welded frame system of MJ Steel Shelving. All shelving has its own measurements that may be different and need to be obtained from the particular shelving manufacturer. Actual widths also become important when calculating the wall space available for shelving from wall to

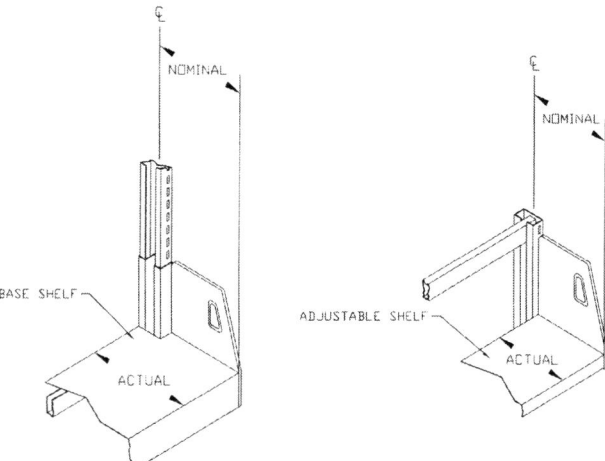

For a cantilever-type bookstack, the adjustable shelves and base depth are given in "nominal" dimension, which indicates the depth from the front edge of the shelf to the centerline of the 2" depth frame. For adjustable shelves, the actual depth is 1" less than the "nominal" depth. For base shelves, the actual depth of the shelf, as well as the overall depth of the bookstack unit, will measure greater than the "nominal" depth for single-faced units (adding the true dimension of the frame). The nominal depth uses the full depth of the frame for the single-faced unit but only half of the depth of the frame for the two-sided unit. The "actual" dimension is the overall true measurement of the space that the unit takes up (courtesy of MJ Industries, Inc.).

wall or wall to door or window (also known as "critical measurement"). To use every linear inch that is available for storage, it is helpful to know that widths other than the 36-inch (offered by all manufacturers as standard) are available. Ask if manufacturers will supply "special" heights to accommodate windows, or special widths to adapt to the space on the wall. Some manufacturers provide 24 or 30 inch widths at the same cost as the standard 36-inch width. This is most advantageous when you are trying to fully utilize every inch to its greatest potential. Ask if the manufacturer will supply "special" heights to accommodate windows, or special widths to adapt to the wall space. For instance, 144 more books can be stored on just one 36-inch wide 78-inch high shelving unit if you have the 36$\frac{1}{16}$ inches linear inches of space on a wall to add one unit. In areas where space is short, a common occurrence, this can be an important option. Make sure that you are being clear by expressing the number of shelves *plus base* on a unit's face or the "x" number of shelves *including base* per face of shelving. Talk about levels or shelf openings to be sure that you and the manufacturer are speaking the same lingo. Also consider the size of the opening between each shelf. Shelves are installed at equal increments unless it is advised otherwise; incremental slots on the vertical frame allow flexibility for change in the future. The standard shelf opening is 14 inches if all the shelves on a unit are used and placed equally. The shelf heights may be adjusted to accommodate large books on any shelf, or as the collection changes the opening size can be adjusted for the change.

Actual measurements are important in calculating the "footprint" (the space allocated for the shelving) so that you don't run out of useable space, which would be the case if your measurement calculates the shelving using the nominal dimension. Each manufacturer must give their actual dimensions because each varies by design. Nominal is the measurement that excludes the dimension of the upright front to back but includes the overall dimension side to side with the exception of any "creep." The creep occurs along the run of shelving and is sometimes expressed as growth of the run. This is a dimension added to each unit (in width) and used to calculate the space it will require. Consult your shelving manufacturer for this factor as well.

Fillers are available for corners and areas that might attract debris or places for books to hide. Fillers are used to fill a void created when two single-faced units are joined at a right angle with a double-faced unit or when two sections meet at right angles to each other. If all these measurements are on the plan and known to be accurate the installation of the shelving should match the layout, thus avoiding unexpected surprises at installation time.

Book stacks should not usually be longer than 24 feet in length. The longer they are, the further a person has to walk to gain access to the next aisle. In estimating the number of linear feet needed allow 25 percent for collection growth. In other words, increase your plan by 25 percent of existing total book storage capacity.

On opening day books should fill no more than 75 percent of the shelving. Crowded shelving makes it hard to find items and detract from the ability to market the collection to customers. Also, shelving filled to capacity makes it harder for older customers to find and retrieve desired materials.

One note of caution in measuring: Be sure that space has been allocated for the end panel dimensions since they will extend into the aisle beyond the shelving. If wood end panels are used (including the use of plastic laminate clad wood) the

Shelf Selection

Type of Volumes	No. of Vols. per Linear Foot of Shelf	Recommended Depth of Shelf
Circulation (Non-Fiction)	8	9–10 in.
Fiction	8	8–9 in.
General Literature	7	9–10 in.
Economics	8	9–10 in.
Reference	6	9–10–12 in.
History	7	9–10 in.
Technical & Scientific	6	10–12 in.
Law	5	10 in.
Medical	5	9–10–12 in.
Bound Periodicals	5	10–12 in.
Art (Folios)	7	10–12 in.
Juvenile (Elementary)	10	9–10 in.
Juvenile (pre-School)	12	10–12 in.
Public Documents	5	9–10 in.
Video Cassettes	34–35	6 in

end panel dimensions (typically ¾ inches to 1¼ inches thick) must be calculated. The end panel depth is calculated with an overage of ¼ inches to 1 inches dependent on the overall design concept that you hope to achieve and the style of the end panel. Make sure you confirm the dimension with the manufacturer. Maintaining the generous aisle dimension that you've planned is an important factor to watch. You will also want to be mindful of meeting or exceeding ADA guidelines for aisle space.

Calculating End Panel and Canopy Top Sizes for Steel Shelving

Take the actual measurement for the depth of the shelving when figuring for the size of the end panel or canopy top that is needed. This would be the measurement from the outside (front to back) of the widest part of the shelving unit. This widest part is most likely to be the shelf base except in the case of hinged periodicals where the front lip of the shelf protrudes to the front of the shelving unit beyond the size of the base. When you are housing the periodical shelves in end panels a decision needs to be made whether to extend the depth to cover this additional dimension. It has a cleaner appearance when the depth of the front lip is included within the end panel dimension.

With this actual depth overall dimension, a half-inch is added to a single-faced end panel. If this shelving is double faced, the additional (overhang or wrap) is twice the overage that is desired. For example, if a single-faced unit is a nominal 36" W × 12" D, it may actually measure (12" + 1⅜") 13⅜ inches That would mean a 14-inch end panel would be required to properly "dress" the end of the shelving range.

On a double-faced unit in which the overall dimension is 24 inches nominal, you might need to add as much as seven-sixteenths of an inch to the nominal dimension to arrive at an actual measurement of 24" + 7/16" = 24 7/16" and since this unit is double-faced (two sided), add the overhang of a half-inch to each side and the total required would be 25½ inch depth for this end panel.

If no canopy top is used, the end panel should be fabricated a half-inch taller than the actual shelving height. Also use this dimension if the canopy will rest within the end panels. If a canopy top is used, add to this dimension the thickness of the canopy top. For example, on 42-inch high shelving without canopy top the new dimension would be 42½ inches. If the canopy top is 1¼ inches thick, the end panel size would increase to (42½" + 1¼") 43¾ inches finished height. The other way of doing this is that the canopy top would rest on top of the end panels. In this case the canopy top length would increase the thickness of the end panel.

Canopy tops are based on the nominal 36-inch width plus one-sixteenth inch per unit of shelving. This one-sixteenth inch dimension is creep. Using as an example a range of six units would require a length of 18 feet ⅜ inch (6 × 3'0") + (6 × 1/16") plus any dimension of the end panel if applicable.

Veneer or high pressure laminate top lengths will be no longer than 12 feet without a seam ("non-spliced"). Longer tops will be spliced in the field with a joint fastener or some other means of drawing them together.

Check the manufacturer of the steel shelving for actual depths. Don't rely on the model number to be the actual depth.

To recap:

(1) End panel size width =

Base size (actual, NOT nominal size) + desired overhang (½"–1" per face)

(2) Height = Steel Frame (actual) height + ½" + Canopy top thickness (if applicable)

Compare the overage to a good fit of a garment. To enhance the wearer (in this example the shelving), the garment (the end panels) dimensions need to be well suited to the person (shelving) or it detracts from the overall appearance.

A rough floor plan showing areas (Fiction, Nonfiction, Reference, etc.) would be helpful in determining the height and depth of shelving to be used by area. At that point, computations of total volumes by type can determine the capacity of the library.

Shelving Capacities at 75 Percent Filled

42" Single-face	65 Volumes
42" Double face	130 Volumes
66" Single face	105 Volumes
66" Double face	210 Volumes
84" Single face	150 Volumes
84" Double face	300 Volumes

Paint Finishes

Paint finish is an important point for comparison. Specifications will list the thickness of the paint finishes. One millimeter thick is the standard in the paint industry. An inconsistent paint finish on the shelves will not endure over time since the sliding of the books in and out with dust particles (that always accumulate no matter how well maintained the library) wear away the paint finish. A uniform paint finish is a benefit because if the thickness varies the thinner areas will wear through, resulting in unsightly appearance and ultimately exposure of the metal to the adverse effects of the environment.

Tests are conducted on the resistance of the finish to abrasion. The most current report by the *Library Technology Reports* is November/December 1998.[1] In this test three shelves are selected at random. On each of the three shelves, six randomly selected areas are used to measure film thickness: three areas on the top and three areas on the front edge. Three locations were selected that have the lowest film thickness that occurs two or more times. The falling sand abrasion test, performed according to American Standard Testing Methods D 968–51, is run on three locations of the shelf. The average number of liters of sand required to expose the specified area ($5/32$-inch diameter) of substratum used in the three tests is compared.[2] The test results prove that a consistent and properly applied finish resists abrasion normally encountered during its service life.

The two types of paint finishes are powder or liquid. The liquid is subdivided into enamels, high solids and water processes. Both enamels and high solids have problems. Enamels historically emitted Volatile Organic Compounds (VOCs) into the atmosphere. VOCs are known to result in the formation of ground level ozone, depleting ingredients that can produce photosynthetic smog in cities and may impact human health and plant life. The high solids were difficult to smooth out in the finishing stage.

The liquid paint process consists of the steel being subjected to an automated, multistage treatment to ensure the best possible enamel adhesion. All parts are first cleaned and rinsed, then coated with a phosphate solution designed to inhibit rust and corrosion and finally given a chromic acid bath which lightly etches the surface and leaves it with a slightly acid pH. An electrostatic reciprocating disc painting system applies the enamel. In this process the paint is drawn to and covers the product evenly. It is then baked for 30 minutes at 300 degrees.[3]

In 1985, when the Environmental Protection Agency (EPA) restricted the number of volatile organic compounds (VOCs) that could be emitted, both types of paint became compliant by government regulatory standards. On June 25, 1996, the EPA proposed a standard to govern the architectural and industrial maintenance coatings sold in the United States.[4] What does VOC really mean? It is the measurement of how much vapors a product gives off. The higher the VOC content, the more a product becomes airborne, increasing potential for exposure. There are environmentally friendly water based finishes and paints becoming more available in the marketplace as consumers become more aware of human health and environmental impact of many construction and household items.

Powder finishes now dominate the market for painting all types of consumer products. Ultimately, the reason is its durability factor. Even when it is used in exterior applications, the powder finish withstands rust and ultraviolet (UV) rays. The powder finish is a painting process where all parts are prepared for coating by passing through a seven stage wash and pretreatment process including the following: cleaning, rinsing, iron phosphate, three rinses and a final sealer. Parts must then pass through a dry-off oven before coating. The powder based epoxy finish is achieved by an electrostatic process using a high-grade powder and then baked at 375 degrees for twenty minutes.[5] Ask for paint finish tests from the manufacturer that you plan on using to determine durability.

The idea of repainting existing shelving is suggested as a way to cut the project cost. With the labor involved in dismantling the shelving, moving it to a vendor for repainting and then transporting it back to the library, the desired savings is seldom realized. Also, you would want to check out the type of finish, its durability factors and any references for the finishers that you employ.

Stability Factors

This begins by determining what is acceptable for your use. The thickness of the steel is one aspect to consider. While gauges of steel vary by manufacturer, the manufacturers' methods of construction ultimately determine each of their component designs. Steel gauge is measured by a number; the smaller the number the greater the strength (i.e., 14 gauge is stronger than 18 gauge). The uprights of the frame, cross members, and shelves all have individual gauges. Weight loads are part of the testing. Most shelving will test to bearing a weight of 50 pounds per foot. Proper gauges and construction provide shelving that will not bow when fully loaded with books. This shelving is not designed to accommodate the weight of computers or overhead projectors, so if that is your use check with the manufacturer as to your best choice. This shelving is designed for the weight of books. Question your shelving supplier if it does bow under the weight of books. Bowing is known as deflection; a maximum 3/16-inch deflection is allowed by load testing.[6] The units are tested for leaning in the process of being loaded or unloaded (even one-sided loading) for two reasons. If the shelving would lean excessively it could cause a shift in the center of gravity of the stacks and provide an unsightly appearance if each stack within a range were to lean at a different angle. It would also create an unsafe condition. Excessive deflections in this test would indicate a weak structure in the shelving. If one side is leaded with reference books with 12 to 14-inch deep shelving and the other side is eight to ten-inch shelving and the shelves are not fully loaded, a solution for better distribution is called for as any shelving could not be expected to work in these circumstances.

Some products have more leveling devices than others. Leveling is a basic requirement of properly installed products. The total design of the product must be considered rather than speculating about whether more levelers on each unit are an advantage over those with fewer levelers. Also, some leveler designs have more adjustment capability than others.

There are various seismic zones in the United States and the zones are determined by the severity of the earthquakes found in that area. The illustration of the Seismic Map of the US shows simplified versions of the most recent U.S. Geological Survey probabilistic seismic hazard maps showing peak ground acceleration for 10 percent probability of exceedance in 50 years. Structural integrity of the steel frame construction is achieved by bolting horizontal cross braces to the upright columns or by welding at the intersection of the upright and the crossbars. This keeps books from falling on the floor unless the frames topple over. Some areas of the country require seismic bracing on the steel shelving. This can be accomplished in a few ways depending on the manufacturer. "Beefing up" the uprights with a thicker gauge steel is one way to become compliant. Other methods are adding a middle spreader or the use of triangular reinforcing gussets. These considerations will become a part of your discussions with the engineer or consultant familiar with your project, the manufacturer you are using and local codes.

Whenever the shelving above the base shelf measures the same as the base shelving depth, additional stabilization may be required on units 78 inches and over. An example of a unit requiring stabilization is one 10-inch shelf on both sides (2" × 10" or 20" overall nominal) over a 20-inch nominal base shelf. Floor anchors or top tie struts or both methods would be used. Hardware for floor anchoring is never included in the cost of bidding but is an installation cost. Top tie struts are channels

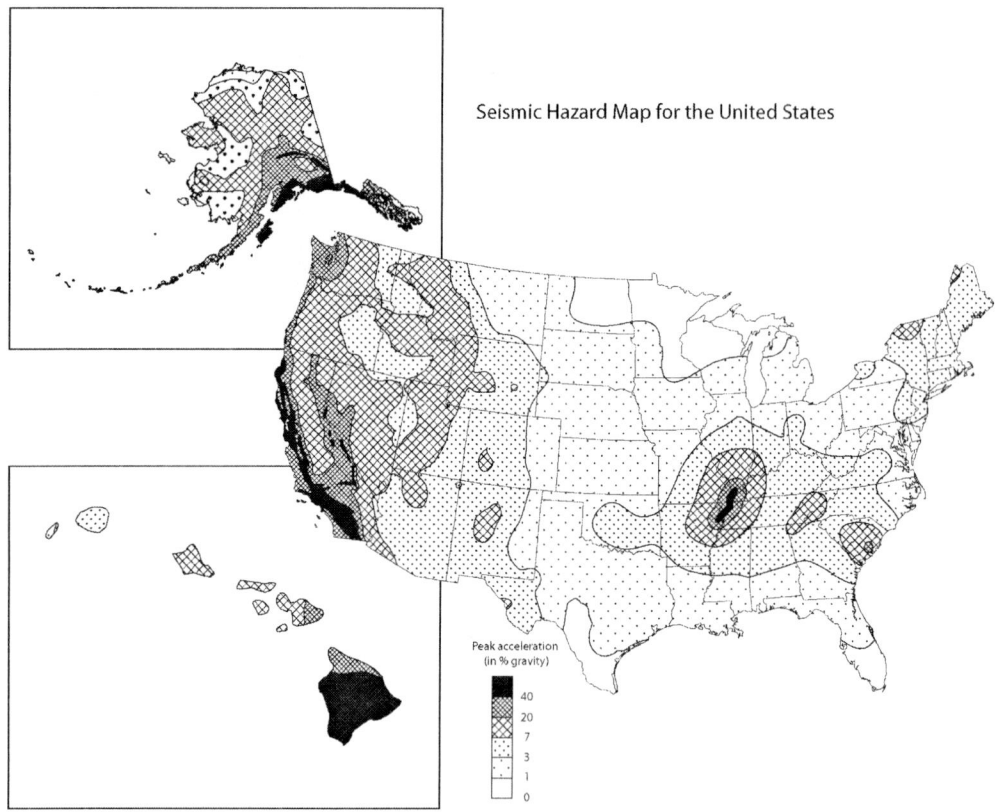

Darker areas of the map delineate regions of higher than expected ground motion from earthquakes. For more information see http://earthquake.usgs.gov/research/hazmaps/ (courtesy of U.S. Geological Survey, Denver Federal Center, Colorado).

that run perpendicular to the shelving and "tie" together or stabilize the shelving. They are long enough to span a few ranges. Another way of making sure that the units are stable and safe is by the use of sway braces. Sway braces form an x across the back of the unit and are visible as you stand at the face of the unit. Sway braces can stabilize a range of steel shelving units, and because these braces are visible and accessible a safety issue arises if the turnbuckles are not kept securely tightened.

If any particular stabilization method is not acceptable, note it in the specifications. Sometimes, because of the ceiling detail, the top tie struts would not be visually pleasing to the architect or the planners. In other cases, floor anchoring is not desirable. Where there are plans for expansion and the shelving layout will change, drilling through the carpet would not be a good choice. The manufacturer and architect can work with you to provide the options to achieve the desired end result.

4. Shelving

Accessories

Adjustable shelves are standard in depths of 8 inches, 9 inches, 10 inches and 12 inches. In flat adjustable shelving a book support is required to prevent books from falling sideways. Some shelves use a rubberized strip affixed to the midline the length of the shelf to keep the books from sliding. Divider-type shelving includes its own dividers, eliminating the need for other book supports. This type of shelving is most commonly used for children's books or other oversized soft books.

Book supports are available in a variety of options and some of the choices are determined by the shelving chosen. Findable book supports allows the foot to slip under the book and may be used on any shelves (see illustration). I would recommend adding cork on the bottom of the support (where the support rests on the shelf under the books) or the purchase of a support with nonskid composition on

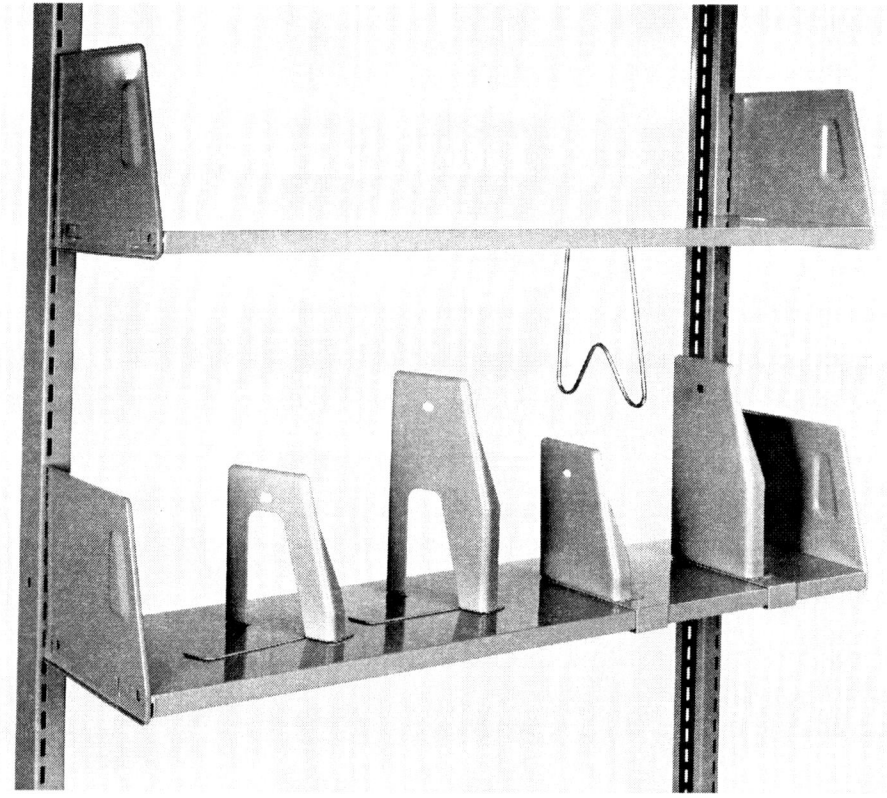

Some common types of book supports available from steel shelving manufacturers. From left to right; Findable book supports 6 inch and 9 inch high, 6 inch hook-on book support, wire book support (from underside of shelf) and 9 inch high hook-on book support (photograph courtesy of MJ Industries, Inc.).

the base for the following two reasons. The first is to protect the paint surface as it slides across the surface of the shelf and the second is to quiet the metal-to-metal sound that is heard without the nonskid composition. Hook-on supports along the front of the shelf can be used, but are not used as often.

One of the most popular supports after the findable is the wire book support. These supports attach under the shelf, but above the one that is using the book support, and are supplied in the same depth as the shelf above. Integral wire book supports can only be used with an integral back shelf that is identical to the basic adjustable shelf, but with an added lip 1¼ inches high across the width of the shelf as part of the shelf. These supports attach to the underside front edge of the integral back shelf. Another type of book support can be used only on the integral back shelf; it attaches to the back edge of the shelf and is called a sliding wire book support.

Components

There is no loss of filing space when a center back stop is used. These are used on double-faced shelving while the adjustable shelf backstop is used on single-faced units to keep materials from falling off the back of the shelf to the floor or to the other side of double-faced shelving. They are both fully adjustable and either backstop moves up or down independently of shelf end brackets. Steel shelving can be specified with closed (steel) backs as a standard accessory or ordered with acoustical surfaces for noise reduction or surfaces that can be used as tack boards. Be aware that these backs will become an obstruction to the line of sight across the library.

Hinged periodical shelves are slanted display type shelving lifting up and exposing recent issues of periodicals and newspapers, while fixed periodicals don't hide the storage shelf, but are placed a few inches below the display shelf. The Sunday edition of larger metropolitan area newspapers may become so large that a Plexiglas shield added to the display shelf will help to keep the paper from sliding out of the display. Other methods of storing the newspapers is in the clear Plexiglas units that are freestanding or on the wooden rods that are supported by a table or shelf unit that has a modified cutout to accept those rods (usually six to ten papers can be hung on this type of unit). Some librarians prefer to stack the newspapers, using no display system at all. If there is a need for oversize display, confirm the actual height of useable display, as it is usually no higher than 14 inches.

A sliding reference shelf slides out on roller glides, providing a temporary work area. It is attached to the underside of standard bookshelves within the stack configuration. These shelves could slide out easily on roller glides and would be placed at counter height for convenient use by a person standing in the aisle. Work

4. Shelving

It is important to provide good lighting for the bottom shelf as well as to contribute to the overall lighting of the library.

shelves constructed of plastic laminate are available if the work surface is needed all the time. As with any dimension that protrudes into the required aisle clearances, you will want to plan for this shelf in advance. Another convenience for the patron and staff is to use one shelf on each side of the range, identifying it with a contrasting paint finish color in the stack area easily noticed for patrons to leave books for staff to reshelf. That shelf would contain a sign notifying library patrons of its special designated use. There are shelf label holders to accept signs that clip onto the shelf front. Sloped base shelves are useful for oversize books but they separate one side of double-faced shelving from the other. If the storage is oversized a flat shelf will provide more space than the sloped shelving on a double-sided unit of shelving.

As more attention is paid to the lighting supplied in the stacks, light brackets suspended over the aisle have been used in libraries. An arched bracket was a popular way of getting the light over the aisles while matching architectural detail of the building. At the end of the arched light holder the bracket attaches to linear lighting at three to four foot intervals. Not only is it important for providing good lighting for the bottom shelf but also the stack lighting is sometimes responsible for contributing to the overall lighting of the library. Another way of using linear lighting is to build the canopy top with a soffit that hides the lighting inside. Also, other types hang within the shelving but don't direct the light over the aisle as well. All of the options will require careful planning as to where the source of the electrical will be placed.

Close-up of a linear light mounted above the top shelf of the unit.

Media Storage

Compact discs (CDs) and audiotapes (books as well as

4. Shelving

music) are growing at a rapid rate. Video collections in libraries also need to be addressed. There are various ways of accessing them and the option for storage is suited to the users of the library. Listening areas hang from the ends of stacks to give the users a chance to try on some new music that they might not otherwise sample. A paperback shelf that can also be used for CD or video storage is six inches deep and the shelf slopes at a seven degree angle for easy viewing of the spines. A zigzag display shelf supports the back of a book or video, while the front is highlighted to get attention.

There is a new type of front display that uses a support that hooks onto the front edge of a shelf and allows a book to lean against it. When books are set apart in this way, it provides the extra exposure needed to get them noticed and circulated. Hang-up bag racks are available for learning tools or other packaged kits housed in clear plastic or knapsacks for easy carrying.

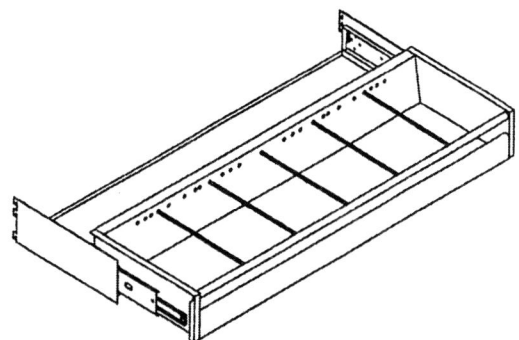

Single Tier Pull-out Browsing Box

Browsing bins are a relatively new way to deal with growth in the "other than text" areas of materials for check out. The capacity for storage and ease of access to the tapes or CDs has made these bins popular. People are familiar with this type of display because they have used it in the past for retail applications. The same bins can be used for videotapes, audiotapes, DVDs or CDs. With a minor change in arrangement of the rods (which separate the items) storage can be organized for a different type of media. It is important to have flexibility and to adapt to different media. Media cabinets are available with lockable storage.

There are freestanding pieces

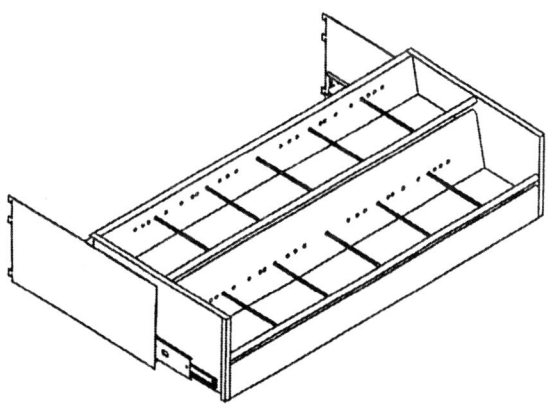

Double Tier Pull-out Browsing Box

This illustrates two versions of browsing bin storage that mount on the steel frame and slide out into the aisle for easier viewing of media such as tapes, CDs and DVDs (courtesy of MJ industries, Inc.).

Wood browsing bin with pull-out shelves for convenient viewing.

of furniture that are browsers, with the option of using this type on steel frames. They are quite often adjustable within the drawers for displaying CDs, DVDs and audio books. The browsing boxes enable a user to easily search through the collection.

Finding adequate display for the barrage of media available for library use is a task (especially with video and DVD collections growing at a staggering rate). I have met with librarians eager to learn of the newest storage choices that will house the vast collections that are currently on order for purchase. There seems to be a lack of types of storage for media, and librarians are always searching for new options. There are choices to be made: to add-on to existing shelving or to allow the media area to draw attention to itself by taking on a newer hi-tech appearance or a look that will create an area of its own.

Steel, Wood or Laminate Shelving?

Steel shelving is repeatedly used in large projects when both wood shelving and laminated plastic shelving are more costly. The steel shelving is chosen in public and university projects, or other large installations that will grow to a size for which wood shelving or laminate would not be economically feasible. Steel shelving is a better option for a public library or university since it receives harder handling and can withstand it. The lower grades (K-8) may choose wood veneers if they have the money in their budget and want the traditional look, while the laminates provide color that is more common for the younger users.

Steel shelving is more economical than wood, especially if steel end panels and canopy tops are used. The cost of steel shelving with steel end panels is approximately half the cost of steel shelving with wood veneer end panels, dependent on the species of the wood and the complexity of the design. Cost of high-pressure laminate panels ranges somewhere between steel and wood. If the shelving design is contemporary and fits the look of the library the ends may be exposed, without the use of end panels, resulting in substantial savings to the library. Plastic laminate or wood veneer end panels are an upgrade in price to the steel, although another option is perforated steel end panels or a design using a combination of materials (laminate with wood edges, wood with steel trim or laminate inlay, etc.) so these variables make it more difficult to create a budget without knowing all the options chosen. Closed metal backs, acoustical or tackable backs are also available if wanted on a project.

Wood shelving is available with backs (to match the veneer finish or a painted solid color) and finished on both sides to allow use in the middle of a room (known as "island shelving"). They could be single faced against the wall and, if used with backs, require no attachment to the wall. Some wood manufacturers fabricate sizes in widths that are field modifiable (by means of using a template ordered from the wood manufacturer) but the standard width is 36 inch nominal.

Canopy Tops and End Panels

Wood or high pressure laminate (HPL) canopy tops are a necessity on 42 inch and 48 inch high shelving, as the visual appearance of looking down on the shelving makes the shelving look unfinished. They can be used as a functional work surface and to display books or other ongoing or changing exhibits. Steel canopy tops are an alternative on taller shelving to achieve an aesthetically pleasing look or as a deterrent to dust settling on the top shelf. The same material choices are available for canopy tops as for end panels. I've seen a design detail on wood end panels where the bottom of the canopy top and the insides of the end panels are finished in a plastic laminate that matches or coordinates with the shelving. Canopy tops are usually no longer than nine feet (nominal) for wood veneer and 12 feet for high pressure laminates (HPL) and these dimensions are based on the standard sheet size of materials. Don't forget to add the creep (found earlier in this chapter under Measuring for Shelving), as that measurement will add to the lengths that are needed for canopy tops or for the footprint that the shelving will occupy.

When canopy tops are used one pair of brackets are used for each section (per face) to attach tops to the shelving. Canopy brackets are inserted into the topmost slots of the upright and secured to the canopy top with metal screws. A wood screw or metal screw ties the bracket into the end panel and the shelving at the end of a run.

Most end panels are attached through the upright by using wood screws into a wood end panel or bolts into a threaded metal insert. The base bracket has a hole punched in it to attach it to the end panel. That is the only place, other than along the upright, that the end panel is attached. This allows the adjustable shelving to remain flexible and to be moved up and down in one-inch increments.

If end panels are steel they are attached to the steel shelving using bolts through the uprights into the flange on the end panel or in some other way unique to each shelving manufacturer. To determine the recommended attachment, contact the manufacturer. If the ends of the steel shelving aren't flush, they may require some special end panel with a cutout on the inside to fit the steel shelving.

A way to provide an area for display of new books is to design the outside of the end panel with a slat wall. These are panels fabricated to accept some type of flat or slanted shelf or a clear holder for display purposes. These are sometimes used on the end panels toward the center of the library and not on the ends that are less visible. Another cost saving measure might place a design or a more intricately designed end panel where it is most visible (from the main entry) and use the basic end panel without the design in an area where it will not be as noticeable.

Writing Specifications

When you have chosen a manufacturer who meets your performance criteria, those specifications can be used as your minimum requirement. One decisive prerequisite that shows stability of a manufacturer is to have had a continuously operating plant. Some plants have had to close down, some have been sold and moved to another state and others have been bought out. Samples are sometimes used as a part of the bid requirement to establish quality of product to be furnished by the successful bidder. When you are overseeing the installation be sure that all shelving has been installed to meet ADA compliance and any applicable seismic requirements and that all the written specifications are followed. The American Library Association has conducted tests that compare one factory's shelving product with another. These tests are a non-biased source to consult for comparison.[7] See Chapter 3,

"Specifications to Installation," for tips on writing specifications, why they are important and how to be sure you get what is important to you.

Installation

Experienced installers are cost efficient in the long run. The steel shelving arrives in parts: welded frames, boxes containing shelves, boxes containing shelf ends and a box with hardware. Even the adjustable levelers need to be installed on the frame. Any framing carpenter should have the skills needed to complete the installation if they learn the basics of the particular shelving manufacturer sometimes called "the tricks of the trade." Contractors and in-house maintenance may save the project money but most times they amplify the installation margin of error. Situations that appear to be a manufacturer problem may actually be an installation problem and some type of stabilization like top tie struts or anchoring to the floor may be needed. It is helpful if the same distributor that sold this shelving is responsible for the installation. If the vendor does not have its own crew of installers, make sure the vendor will take responsibility for the installer's work. Check on how your own installation affects the factory warranty.

Steel shelving installation is usually not difficult, however if the basic instructions aren't followed, the shelving will not be easy to install. One of the most common problems occurs when the shelving is not installed in a straight line. If the shelving looks out of line or a range seems unstable, a minor adjustment by the installers may be in order. Ask the shelving vendor about this alignment "problem" before you consider the shelving inferior. The leveling plays a major part in the appearance and the stability of the finished product.

Single-faced shelving can be hung on wall strips if needed. This type of shelving is great for offices and backroom technical services in libraries. The important part of any wall installation is that the shelving is anchored securely to the wall. Different types of fasteners are used dependent on the material construction of the wall. The manufacturer will provide wall clips (an L shaped special bracket) for any single-faced shelving. It is a good idea in new construction to reinforce the wall with two-by-fours placed horizontally and tied into the studs behind the drywall. If this wall exists already, the wood boards can be placed flush and level on the wall and will be hidden by the shelving. In either case the boards act to diffuse the weight over a span, providing a more secure attachment to the wall.

Units can be welded and bolted and a new type of connection on the market allows the frames to have a snap-on type of application.

Determine the installer's reputation and the manufacturer's standing in the industry. Has the manufacturer been in production continuously for many years?

Ask the manufacturer for a local installation firm that has installed product for them. Ask for a list of references on a number of projects and check them out. Talk to contacts at previous projects to determine that experienced or factory-trained installers are used and ask the users if they were happy with the shelving and the installer's work. The distributors of the product are likely to have the most experience with installation, but there are cases where an installer from another industry (installers specializing in casino partitions, school bleachers, compact shelving) may work well. Basically you want someone, at least in a supervisory position, who will be patient to think through instructions and someone not too proud to call the factory if they need further instruction or if something doesn't seem right. They could possibly be missing some crucial point, or a component that should have been shipped could be missing. The installation situation is different in various areas of the country. Some areas have what are termed as independent installers. These are installers that are hired by a distributor or the manufacturer. Visit installations to see finished product and use the manufacturer's catalog to guide your choices.

One consequence of using inexperienced installers may be that the aisle spacing is not measured accurately. Aisles must be wide enough to meet municipal codes that allow egress from a building as well as to meet the Americans with Disabilities Act. Aisles must be a minimum of 36 inches.[8] It is smart planning to provide a 42-inch aisle when possible, as a 42-inch aisle is preferred. Aisle placement that is tight or uneven is bad enough if the shelving is not secured to the floor (a method known as "anchoring"). If it has been anchored to the floor, this mistake can be a disaster since the anchors, which are huge bolts into the floor, need to be taken out and redrilled into the floor. The carpet may now need repair if that part of the floor is exposed from the original installation.

Choosing an installer is as important as choosing the product. Do your homework beforehand, so the installation is as smooth as possible. Don't be afraid to question.

Check This Out: Steel Shelving

- Is the shelving sturdy and well-built?
- Is the shelving adjustable to changes in the collection?
- Is shelving height and depth adequate for different uses?
- Are there special features that might be needed: pull-out shelving, shelf dividers, book supports, shelving for display material?
- Is furniture used to display and promote merchandise? Is there a space near the entrance for announcements, display case or seasonal display area? Is display securely controlled by a nearby staff station?

5

ADA: The Primary Rule Is to Exceed Minimums

The doors of wisdom are never shut.
— Benjamin Franklin, *Poor Richard's Almanack*

Universal Design

The library is a source of pride to the school, campus, community or place of business. It is considered a "showplace" when it is attractively planned and functionally designed. There are many types of libraries but they generally fall into three broad classifications: educational, public and special. To some degree, all libraries fall within these parameters. "The baby boomer market is the key group universal design is going to affect and improve the lives of," according to John Salmen, president of Universal Designers and Consultants, which provides accessibility consulting services to individuals and new home developers. He continues by saying that "while disabilities have been the catalysts, the real recipients are the people that are aging in the beginning of the twenty-first century." This concept, called "Universal Design," is expanding to design spaces that will serve everyone and will be useful for the future as baby boomers age and begin to experience decreased visual acuity and physical flexibility. Different types of collection layouts and better signage (refer to chapter 10 on wayfinding) are being discussed to meet these needs.

Ronald Mace, the architect who coined the term "universal design," says that one of the more important changes brought on by the use of this term is the elimination of the label "special needs" from a segment of the population who is working to maintain or gain their independence.[1] Four underlying principals for creating universal design are Supportive, Adaptable, Accessible and Safety Oriented.

The first is that the design must be supportive. Consider the lighting used to

On one side of the column a patron uses the computer catalog while an ADA compliant self-check unit awaits its next use on the opposite side of the column.

illuminate a work surface. Lack of lighting can lead to decreased visual acuity. As people grow older they need more light to see well.

Adaptable means that a product or environment should serve a majority of individuals who have a variety of changing needs. The ergonomic chairs and workstation surfaces and monitors are two examples of design that adjust in height, with wraparound work surfaces or detachable keyboards. Products such as these are useful for people with impairments and just as useful for the general public.

Accessible is a term that speaks to removing barriers, both physical and attitudinal, a design that promotes well-being as well as communication and mobility. An example is placing wall sockets at 18 inches off the floor for ease of use from a wheelchair or making doors wider for a clearer pathway. Accessible means "rethinking space and equipment to better enable use by all people."[2]

The fourth principal of universal design is safety-oriented designs to promote health and well-being. Desks and cabinets with soft edges are safer than those with sharp edges. As people age and their abilities change they should not be expected to lower their expectations of what is possible for them to achieve. Universal design says that the environment should be flexible enough to accommodate changing human needs and abilities.

Mimi McCain, supervisor of the Special Needs Center at the Phoenix Public Library, believes that Universal Design is the way to planning spaces in the future and was part of a panel that presented this concept at the ALA Conference 2005. She feels that by using the principles of Universal Design we are planning for the future and saving money by adapting our environment to match our abilities in the future.

ADA: Every Body's Right

The Americans with Disabilities Act was signed into law in July of 1990. The ADA is not just an architectural code, though it has become the subject of major interest and concern among architects and facilities managers as they try to understand what should be done in existing facilities and how new buildings should be built. The ADA is first and foremost a civil rights law. During the five years that followed the ADA being signed into law, there was a timeline in which there was the opportunity given to make these changes and begin building facilities that were useful for all persons. It also was written to help ensure staff was trained and operational policies adjusted to ensure that discrimination was being eliminated. From the occupancy of buildings on January 23, 1993, the ADA stated that newly built facilities must be accessible to all members of the public and that program and communication related accommodations needed to access programs and services were to be provided also.

The term "disabled" applies to anyone with a physical or mental impairment or anyone who has a record of impairment. Disabilities are not always evident. The access rules are designed to ensure that disabled persons have the same access as other customers to a firm's goods or services. The term *disability* as used in ADA legislation applies to the physical or mental impairment that substantially limits at least one of the major life activities (e.g., performing manual tasks, walking, hearing, speaking, learning, and working).[3]

All spaces that serve the public are covered under the ADA with the following exemptions: private clubs, religious institutions, and residential facilities covered by fair housing laws. Also, owner occupied inns with less than six rental rooms are exempt from the requirements of the Americans with Disabilities Act.

RBK Consulting Services, Inc., President Bill Stokes, Jr., who has been a spokesperson for accessibility in the community and throughout the United States, reminds me that the primary rule is to "exceed minimums when possible" and that the guidelines are minimum dimensions. It is always better to be generous with the spaces when possible.

Imagine trying to reach the elevator button from a wheelchair or electric scooter with an ashtray or trash receptacle in the way. Not being able to see the directional signs or hear the warning signals that alert a person to danger are all important issues to consider when planning a building so that every person has the same privileges of use regardless of ability. If a person is not able to gain access and move throughout the building without encountering what are considered "barriers" they will be unable to use it and the building may not be in compliance with the law. A barrier can be anything that limits a person's movement or communications, or an attitude that discourages participation. If you are a wheelchair or scooter user and there are curbs with no ramps or steps, this is an obstruction and therefore a barrier to mobility. If you require someone to help you find something because you are blind and staff are not available to assist, this is a barrier to service.

This entry of the Farmington, New Mexico, Public Library is a great example of barrier free design in the main entry of a library. Note ADA compliant work surfaces and service desk heights.

5. ADA

From the time a person parks their vehicle or uses public transportation to the time they check out or use the material that they need in a library, they are governed by the Americans with Disabilities Act. There must be at least one accessible route from public transportation stops or any accessible parking places, down a sidewalk and to the accessible building entrance that they serve. The accessible route should coincide with the route for the general public as much as possible.

In *Department of Justice* vs. *New Oxford Borough, Pennsylvania*, the department reached an agreement with the council resolving a complaint that the second floor meeting room where the council's public meetings are held is inaccessible to individuals with disabilities and those who are unable to climb stairs. In addition, the complaint alleged that "the Borough's library, located in the basement, is also inaccessible to individuals who use wheelchairs because of the stairs and broken sidewalk leading to the building's entrance. The Council agreed to adopt and publish a procedure for relocating all meeting rooms to an accessible location with reasonable notification and to set aside a room on the first floor for the use of the library so that individuals with disabilities can access library services." The sidewalks were repaired or replaced to open the path to the building entrance as well in this case.[4]

ADA Accessibility Guidelines

ADA Accessibility Guidelines (ADAAG) says that every element inside a building has to be on an accessible path. Aisles between the shelving must be a full 36-inch width. When planning the aisles in the stacks remember that the preferred clearance is 42 inches where possible *after* the end panels are on the shelving, and be aware that the end panels will extend beyond the depth of the steel shelving (usually ¼ to ½ inch per face).

At the end of the aisle 60 inches is needed to turn around if there is no other way to proceed (turning left or right). Maximum reach height is considered 48 inches, irrespective of approach, allowed for reaching up and no lower than 15 inches for reaching down. When a user is approaching the shelf from the side the rules dictate a reach no higher than 54 inches and no lower than nine inches. This means that a three level high periodical shelf unit can be used, since the dimensioning is 53 inches to the top of the third periodical shelf and 35 inches to the top of the second periodical shelf. A height of 48 inches is the preferred reach. Shelf height is unrestricted in stack areas by the code, but I am noticing more libraries that don't use the bottom shelf since the general public has made it clear that they don't like bending over to see and pick up materials from the bottom shelf. Some libraries have chosen to elevate the 42-inch high shelving on platforms to eliminate this problem.

There are rules about placement of wheelchair areas within a meeting place.

If you have an auditorium in your library, be aware that the wheelchair users need to have the same line of sight "comparable to all members of the general public," according to the Federal Register, 1991, Rules and Regulations 4.33, that deals with assembly areas: The wheelchair areas must be level and at least fixed seating space for one companion must be provided with each space that is available for a wheelchair. Some auditorium chairs are designed for the side of the chair to swing open, allowing side-to-side transfer from a wheelchair and upon that transfer the user is indistinguishable from the able-bodied. There are also models of auditorium seating which use hardware that is designed in such a way that the chair can be removed from the floor to make the space available for a wheelchair if the attendee does not choose to transfer to the auditorium seating.

At least 5 percent per "element" of all tables (including carrels, etc.)[5] are to be accessible. If you have 20 tables on a project, that means that at least one of each type of table needs to be ADA compliant. Sometimes, due to the height of the wheelchair or the size of the wheelchair user, the minimum needs to be adjusted specifically to work for the user. The height of the work surface is sometimes a bit higher to a finished height of at least 30 inches (from a standard of 29 inches) to accommodate the wheelchair user. The height from the floor to the lowest point of the underside of the table (knee space) is to be a minimum 27 inches high, 30 inches wide and 19 inches deep before any potential obstruction occurs. The thickness of the tabletop is deducted from the finished height to arrive at a clearance. If a table is 29 inches finished height work surface and 1¼ inches thick, the clearance is 27¾ inches, less than an inch higher than the minimum requirement. The Register says that the tops of accessible tables and counters shall be from 28 inches to 34 inches above the finished floor. This clearance is accomplished by lengthening the legs of the table or by some type of modification of the styling along the apron of the table. Remember there are wheelchairs, scooters and users of all sizes, so meeting the minimum is a guideline only. There may need to be more room given for the employee or patron. Tables that have pneumatic lifts are essential to a special needs area and convenient but still pricey to make available in all areas of the library.

Aisles in the lounge seating area must leave a full 42 inches to accommodate a wheelchair user to pass a person who is using the lounge chair (wheelchair user passing in front of lounge chair) or 30 inches to have an accessible path of travel along the side of a lounge chair.

One of each four of a particular type of check-out lane must be accessible unless the building is less than 5,000 square feet. Examples of check-out lanes of different "designs" include those which are specifically designed to serve different functions such as one to check out books, etc. The counter is not to be higher than 38 inches from the ground and 40 inches high at the highest point in order to accommodate a wheelchair user. Permanent signage shall designate this lane as accessible. Any traffic control or book security gates will not interfere with any person getting into or out of the library. Modification is mandatory to ensure that everyone has the same benefits. It is called "making a reasonable accommodation."

Special Needs Areas of the Library

In the special needs area there are more storage requirements than in any other area of the library, beginning with the service desk, which will use more drawers for items like headsets and magnifiers and other supplies needed by the patrons. Brochures that might be found displayed on the information and service desks are moved to the back of the desk, easily accessible by staff. This keeps the service desk relatively clean of items that can get knocked over by someone who doesn't see them; it is beneficial to organize them in drawers to pass out as needed. It is essential to have an area of this desk at a lower work surface height to provide more welcoming care for patrons that sit at a lower height. It is nice to work with someone eye to eye instead of standing over them or leaning over a counter to see them.

One in every three persons over 65 has a hearing loss. As America's baby boom population matures, these numbers will increase and the audience for closed captioning will grow even larger. Text telephone (TTY) replacing the telecommunications device for the deaf (TDD) phones have been used as an assistive technology by the deaf and are still found at some pay phones (check to be sure that at least one is planned for your library); but individuals are using pagers more frequently with silent vibration for a ringing mechanism and Blackberry or T-Mobile communication devices with text messaging. TTY's are an older piece of technology, while video relay phones are replacing them. All that is required is a small area that has visual privacy and a digital phone line. Two people can use it by having a video camera set up at both ends of the conversation and then the people can see each other and sign.

The American Foundation for the Blind reports that one in six Americans age 65 and older is blind or severely visually impaired; this population is expected to double by 2030.[6] Large print is useful in this situation. It is not usually located in the special needs area since it is thought of as a convenience to those who find it easier to read the large print as well as for those persons who need it to be able to read. In Phoenix, large print text is located across the aisle from fiction in this case and gets much more exposure by the sighted public in the event they decide that they want to use large text. Isolated from the regular size text as a separate type of book and marked over the stacks by a large and unique sign that resembles an eye doctor's chart makes for eye-catching signage.

The Phoenix Public Library in Arizona has won many awards for their Special Needs Center, where they provide all types of disability accommodations. This includes a plethora of information on accessibility issues and a computer lab with many accommodations for people who are blind, deaf or who cannot read or write. If you need information on travel, careers or medical issues surrounding special needs, this is a great resource.

The special needs area serves three target groups: (1) people with disabilities (low vision or blindness, speech and hearing limitations, physical and mental disabilities; (2) their families; and (3) staff from the organizations that serve them. I was fortunate to tour this area with Special Needs supervisor Mimi McCain and learn firsthand what services are provided and how their furniture requirements differ in this area. This area is a microcosm of a full library with dedicated space and is fully funded out of the city's budget. The Special Needs Center is considered a vital component of the services offered, just as children's, reference, and circulation are, and is aptly located on the first floor just beyond the check-in desk.

Origin and Growth of the Special Needs Area

This area originated in the former library in 1982 and started out by being a small area (1,500 square feet) in very visible location on the first floor and separated from the rest of the library by moveable walls with glass panels about 60 inches high. It all began with a few wood shelving units that kept large print books in their own area. Mary Roatch, the original supervisor for the Special Needs Area, said that the center acted as an advocate simply by virtue of its location, and that just seeing the center reminded people of a friend or relative who could use its services. Ms. Roatch supervised the center, whose logo appears on its brochure: a circle within a circle, illustrating Edwin Markham's poem, "He drew me a circle and shut me out ... we drew a circle and took him in."[7] The history of the center is well documented. Thick notebooks crammed with reports, publicity items, publications and photographs tell the complete story.[8]

The library in Phoenix has grown to be the only public library in the state of Arizona which has most of the capabilities that people with disabilities make use of. Documents can be sent in electronic format to Special Needs and, through translation software and an embosser, be produced in Braille. If you are planning to have an embosser, be sure that the embosser has something around it to absorb the sound yet dissipate the heat build-up as it can be quite loud. There is also a Kurzweil machine that translates printed copy to read to the blind. This area began with that one borrowed machine.

This area includes a "Toybrary," which houses therapeutic toys and learning games that can be checked out by parents and educators. These toys are educational and fun for kids so that they have the ability to learn at their own level. These are stored in hanging bags on rods where they can easily be seen. They are sterilized after each use and the plastic bags keep them clean for the next user. Puppets that are stuffed animal arms accept human hands that can teach sign language to children are a part of this library of toys. Mimi McCain shared with me that much of their success is due to two factors: this dedicated staff (both in morale and in funding) works with patrons on a one-on-one basis, and they are an "essential function" of the library, with dedicated funds. They operate, in fact, like a library within a library.

Having all the necessary conveniences like a toilet, drinking fountains and elevators near to an elevator that serves all floors of the library is a goal of a well planned facility. There is not only a fully accessible bathroom in the Burton Barr Library but this area's bathroom exceeds the standards. The room that has been provided could comfortably hold a person who uses a wheelchair, with enough space for assistance of at least two persons if needed. This area was built with the idea of exceeding the minimum guidelines.

Well lit areas are especially important where a person's vision may not be optimal. Electrical outlets placed at belt line height is a convenience for everyone and necessary for those that cannot reach under desks or to the floor to plug in machines.

The experience of the user at Phoenix Special Needs Library's computer workplace for people with disabilities begins by the user filling out a request form at the service desk with pertinent personal information about their special needs. This includes their contact information, their level of ability at a computer and what they need in the way of assistive equipment, whether it is magnifiers or scanners (to increase the print size on documents copied). If patrons are deaf and need adaptive equipment or sign language to communicate this is noted. This form is then kept in their file at the desk outside the Assistive Technology Center so that they don't need to reiterate their needs each time they return. Mimi says that this reinforces the libraries' commitment to get to know their users and provide personalized service. She prides her area on never having to say "no" but rather providing creative, alternative solutions for their customers. This area is fortunate to employ two staff who are deaf and one who is blind. This gives them the ability to relate to users on a different level. The training of the patrons by this staff with specialized skills provides users not only more thorough training but a distinct level of comfort.

The form filled out by all users on their first visit includes an agreement that is signed by the users that they will respect the equipment (by not using food or drink, along with other rules of conduct that show consideration for others), which goes a long way toward making the users feel comfortable, as they know the expectations of using the facility. Ms. McCain feels that this is another key to the libraries' success in having little or no damage to furniture, shelving and equipment.

The desk's location is visible from every area of the library and the lab is visible through high glass half windows for the convenience of the staff and the library users. Inside the lab are completely adjustable computer desks and chairs. There are five fully adjustable workstations. Two of the workstations are outfitted with stations for vision loss, two are for those with learning disabilities and one is specifically configured for patrons who are learning American Sign Language.[9] Each station consists of three adjustable tables. Not only does the keyboard's tray slant and height adjust (21 inches to 27 inches) but the monitor is on a swivel that easily adjusts the screen, both side to side and front to back, with a tilt of nearly 180 degrees for the comfort and ergonomics of all users. The table's pneumatic height adjustment has a range of 27 inches to 44 inches. The tables to either side adjust in height and the scanner is placed on one side and the closed circuit machine is on the other so everything is within arm's reach. This is helpful if not crucial in some cases. One printer per workstation is not required as it is a cost savings for them to share the network and have one printer that is convenient to all the workstations. There is another adjustable table that adjusts to a standing height (estimated at 39 inches high) for those who work standing or require a higher range of operation. In this computer lab there is also a need for lateral drawer storage and covered shelving with locking capability as a place for headphones, microphones and other assistive technology stored for these workstations, as well as for office supplies. Phoenix has used the names of familiar towns in Arizona as workstation names to personalize each station's location rather than using numbers to designate which one a patron is being directed to use.

There is storage available for those who bring their own special paper to use so that they will not have to transport supplies back and forth to the library. The copy machine has the capability to copy to 800 percent and uses oversize paper for its copying. I was informed that good circulatory airflow is something that was missed in the planning of this enclosure for the lab and it had to be retrofitted for the comfort of staff and patron use. Fans are also helpful in creating good air quality.

Reference includes binders for referrals to services and associations that would be helpful. Juvenile, Teen and Children's books are all in the collection on shelving that is vertically adjusted to the sizes required for the oversized books and binders. This library is a clearinghouse of disability associations to get the word out regarding programs and events that will assist patrons in having a higher quality lifestyle. The collection is used to answer questions from any of the target groups or from other divisions or branches of the library and contains statistical data, educational directories, and consumer information and subscription services. Sources of financial aid, advocacy newsletters and governmental regulations and laws dealing with special needs are contained on the shelving. With the introduction of the wealth of data on the computer some of this information is more easily accessed and kept more current, so there has been a departure in keeping a vertical file of resources, whose information becomes outdated. Large print periodicals are included in the shelving for periodical subscriptions that would be of special interest to a person who is blind or deaf as well as to persons with other special needs. This would also be an area to use when a patron wants to learn more about diseases and accidents that has affected their level of ability requiring accessible services.

All areas of the library are finding that the top and bottom shelves aren't as useable. In this area the two bottom shelves are left empty to make the shelving easier to use. Because of this, some of the collection remains in storage since adequate storage is not available in the section. New materials in large print are displayed on the shelving with easel displays to get the attention of prospective readers.

A large collection of American Sign Language videos and VHS tapes that are accompanied by Video Descriptive Service (verbal descriptions of scenes) to help the non-sighted person follow the video are steadily being replaced by DVDs as in the other sections of the library, as videos are becoming a technology of the past. These ASL videos are well used by instructors and students at Phoenix College in their American Sign Language certification program.

A popular area that was designed into this part of the library is a meeting area consisting of a conference size table and chairs available to citizens with special needs who would be more comfortable using this area than other areas of the public library.

The staff offices are located just off the computer workstation area but behind closed doors where staff can retreat to order books, compile statistics, plan programs, write reports and perform other behind the scenes activities.[10] This room is designed for maximum work efficiency, using panel systems to divide areas. The deaf staff member's desk is situated facing the entry so that there aren't needless interruptions to see the patrons' comings and goings and this staff member has an unobstructed pathway to the door. This follows the ancient wisdom of Feng Shui that it is common sense not to have your back to the door and be surprised by what is going on behind you.

Remember, this all started with a commitment to special needs users and a few wooden shelves for large text, telephone reference and information about talking books. If you want to build an area that begins with some of the life changing technology available today, my recommendation is to find an "angel"; that is, a supporter of special needs either because of their own experience or because of the impact they know it can have on someone they are close to. You'll also find that with an advocate in "high places" it can prove helpful to your dream of using the Phoenix model of what is achievable for those with special needs. One way to start is by thinking what is needed to accommodate a specific disability.

This Special Needs Library has created a theme of familiarity as the organizers strive to ensure that staff, the space and the assistive technology is familiar and comfortable for the customers so that they will return and use this area for many years to come. As the needs grow, we trust the size of this library will grow to match them.

The Economics of Universal Design

The future finds that universal design is marketable. As the baby boom generation has changed, so has the money that they are spending. When the boomers were having children, lots of money was spent on products for these babies. As boomers grow into later adulthood more money will be spent on products and an environment that allows them to maintain their independence. If the changes are made initially in the way a building and a person's place within a building are designed, it will be a cost savings since, as the person's abilities change, the environment will still work for them.

Visit this Website to see the most current information (amended September 2002) and under review for approval by ADA Accessibility Guidelines for Buildings and Facilities (ADAAG): http://www.access-board.gov/adaag/html/adaag.htm#lib.

Check This Out: ADA

- Are all entrances accessible?
- If turnstiles are used is there an alternate entrance provided?
- Are there level thresholds to the rooms?
- If the building is on more than one floor does the user have access?
- Are elevator buttons at the proper height for wheelchair use?
- Is there a clearance of 27½ inches under all catalogs, terminals and tables for wheelchair users?
- Are all doors easily opened with lever hardware or do they have a button for automated opening?
- Is there a grab bar and wider stall for restroom (at minimum) and does the door swing outward?

5. ADA

- Is there a sink for the wheelchair user?
- Are there restrooms, elevators and hearing aided phones in close proximity?
- Is there a public telephone that wheelchair users and hearing impaired persons can use?
- Are all areas ADA compliant for use?

6

Seating: Types, Performance Testing and Use

My books are my tools, and the greater their variety and perfection, the greater the help to my literary work.
— Tryon Edwards (1809–1894)

Comfort

Seating is a topic that a person doesn't have a strong opinion about unless they have experienced a really good chair, a chair that supported their body when they felt especially tired or had a problem with their back or legs or the experience of using a poor chair that caused back or leg problems. It isn't something that a librarian thinks about unless they have had a past experience that chairs failed (broke down in use) and they want to be sure that this time when they evaluate a chair for purchase that the seating holds up to the use it will receive. The librarian looks to the "expert," whether it is the furniture consultant or a manufacturer, to know what kinds of use (and abuse) that the seating will need to withstand. This is when performance testing of materials, understanding the joinery methods used to build the product and knowing what types of warranty the manufacturer will offer become important.

The "Sit" Test

First of all, to evaluate a chair you must try it out and think about the fit of the chair for various sizes and shapes of users. At a recent American Library Association conference, specifiers from an architectural firm were visiting furniture booths and they remarked how fortunate they were to be three different heights and sizes who could test the chairs for the comfort of a wide range of users. Be sure that you have a good representation of users who will sit in the chairs.

6. Seating

A distributor will be happy to get a sample to you for a trial period when you are in the market for new seating. The "sit test" will be something of value as a part of the evaluation for seating that will be useful for years to follow. When a person is selecting a chair that is adjustable they should make sure that the chair adjusts so that the person who is in the chair is able to place both feet securely on the ground and that the knees bend at a 45 degree angle from the thigh, allowing the thighs to be parallel to the floor.

Be sure that you understand the adjustments on a chair. Have the chair salesperson spend some time educating you on the chair's features. The back should be supportive and have adjustments that allow the back of the seat to support the user's back and have the capability to be changed (up and down as well as a fixed position) and move with the back (forward and backward) for longer periods of seating. If the back does not have support and the user is leaning forward andrests their arms on their desk, the weight of the shoulders rest on the arms and causes fatigue of the arms in the shoulder region. Each user will have a different ratio of arm, torso and leg length and a good chair will be able to adjust to each person. As the person is seated, the elbow height should be level with the work surface.

Biomechanics, the relationship between our physical environment and the stress it places on the human body, come into play as we educate ourselves more about ergonomic seating. It is not as though we will always sit upright and follow the lines of the ideal seated position. If a chair is doing its job, we should be able to move and readjust our position for comfort. The back should be easily adjusted to follow the back or to "fix" as warranted. The most important factor of the seating is that it provides both comfort and freedom of movement.

In a public use area there shouldn't be many adjustments to a chair since the more moving parts there are the more chance for breakage of levers and knobs. For a chair where more time is spent, staff will want to adjust the chair to fit the user. The more adjustments the better, since chairs may be shared by staff members who can use those adjustments to change the height of the chair to fit their body.

Manufacturers use webbing as seating foundations. Seat belt-type webbing is showing up in furniture as the outer material as it has been shown to have superior wearing abilities. Foam on plywood, sheet webbing, wire mesh with springs, sinusoidal springs commonly known as "no sag" and the "long bow spring seat suspension construction" are a few of the types of supports used in the seat. It is prudent to be able to take the "sit test" as part of the evaluation process and to ask for references for installations both recent and those that were new five to ten years ago.

Performance

Europeans have been involved longer than the United States in their research and test institutes conducting performance testing of furniture and quality assurance programs. Classifying furniture by its intended use is the basis for testing. There are many tests that can be performed. Be sure that the test results that you learn are relevant to the use that the chairs will receive. All of this equipment and testing has a cost and this is passed on to the consumer through the pricing of the furniture. I have always believed that the testing is valuable enough information to be included in any purchasing evaluation as well as an important component in writing specifications for the seating to be used. I have been called upon to visit a work site and determine what needs to be repaired on a chair that I supplied on a project only to find that it is *not* a chair that I supplied that has a problem, but rather one that was substituted by someone who made the decision that they could get a less expensive product and have the same durability. This is where the adage that "you get what you pay for" comes to mind.

Design and Testing

With the different styles the force is imposed on various connections of the chair. This is why it is important that chairs be tested for strength to meet the weight requirements and the forces that are distributed to the connections of a chair that will be exerted in day to day use.

A crucial connection is the one where the back meets the leg at the seat. This must be one of the strongest joints because it is one of the most stressed points in the chair. One of the other points receiving stress is the legs of the chair. That is why you will notice some legs are "splayed" (curved in design) to support the weight that will be imposed on them. The primary function of a chair is to sit, but a user will exert more pressure on the chair when they move the chair while seated in it. In addition to these most common movements, the chair will be moved side to side (with and without weight). If the chair has arms they will be used to support the weight of the user as he lifts and lowers back into the seat but the arms will be designed in such a way that they are not intrusive to his "space" if he is using a computer. It is especially important that the arms provide stability for raising and lowering the body in areas where mature individuals are using the seating or in healthcare libraries where a person may need the extra assistance of the furniture.

Furniture is more inviting when a person has made a quick evaluation that results in knowing that they will be able to rise from it. Performance testing will exert many pounds of pressure on a chair from all angles to assure that strength is sufficient at all connections testing the leg strength, the arm and back strength.

6. Seating

Chairs with stretchers from one leg to another provide additional strength. The chair will also need to withstand the test of standing on the seat as it may be stressed in this way and the drop test will prove helpful in determining the weight that the chair can hold. Usually testing labs test chairs until they fail at one of the connections.

Manufacturers build their chairs differently. Some of the issues that you want to know is how they are connected, one joint to another. Do they use glue in addition to dowels? What about the hardware? Does the mechanical fastener go directly into the wood or does it go into a metal sheath? Is there enough surface area to provide holding power by the glue? Is enough glue used or is it merely a dab that isn't really holding much? More surface space provides more surface area for glue to be used to adhere one piece to another.

Business and Institutional Manufacturers Association (BIFMA) is a trade association standard for office furniture and was established in 1973. In the 1980s there were tests that covered desk and mobile pedestals as well as stability, overturning and drawer function tests. There are standards added every year to address safety issues that arise. BIFMA's performance testing of a lounge chair will test the backrest frame; both horizontal and vertical pressure will be applied to the back. Functional load will produce a cycle of applying weight to the seat simulating a user sitting and rising. A proof load will put the maximum weight that they expect the seat to bear and the last test of a backrest for the BIFMA test will apply smaller loads at greater frequency that would replicate the life span use of the seating. These same tests are produced at various angles. Some of the tests will weight the backrest frame (vertically), backrest foundation and horizontal arm strength (both vertically and horizontally), seat foundation, side thrust leg tests and leg strength tests. There is also a unit drop test that raises one end of the chair or sofa and drops it, noting any particular failures at the joinery. BIFMA's test is equivalent to three 191-pound people sitting on a sofa one at a time (a total of 573 pounds) every 52 minutes, 24 hours a day, 365 days a year for 10 years. This is called a ten year useful life span model. Government Services Administration (GSA) has their own standards of performance to meet for governmental purchases and most often heavy duty is met. Performance testing by GSA divides its results into three categories: light, medium and heavy duty. Light duty is equivalent to three 225-pound people sitting on the sofa simultaneously (a total of 675 pounds) every 45 minutes, 24 hours a day, 365 days a year for 10 years. Medium duty is equivalent to three 263-pound people sitting on a sofa simultaneously (a total of 789 pounds) every 30 minutes, 24 hours a day, 365 days a year for 10 years. Heavy duty is equivalent to three 281-pound people sitting on the sofa simultaneously (a total of 843 pounds) every 25 minutes, 24 hours a day, 365 days a year for 10 years.[1]

Unlike the GSA performance test BIFMA is a pass or fail, with no intent to provide a graded scale or to compare it with other tests. BIFMA is a less stringent test and doesn't satisfy performance test specifications which give specific results. There are administrative costs to the manufacturer in maintaining a GSA agreement with the federal government, but the manufacturer hopes to be included in purchases that he might not qualify for without it. The benefit to buying from the GSA is that the bid process can be avoided by the purchasing department if they are part of a federal agency.

Warranties from the manufacturer run from five to twenty years, with ten years being the most common, excluding the upholstery which varies with the fabric chosen and carries its own separate warranty. If you are purchasing a higher priced chair, ask if the manufacturer will extend the time given on the warranty.

Types of Seating

Most guest chairs supplied as office furniture will not supply the pitch that is optimal for a reading chair. How does the back of the chair feel? Is it high enough? Does it occur at a comfortable place? Is it supportive? What about the height of the arm? Does the elbow rest easily on the arm or does it feel too low or too high?

Work situations vary and the practical work solution approach is to customize the use of the chair to the needs of the user. As we will learn in the chapter on accessibility issues, not all "rules" fit. Wheelchair users have different size chairs and they are of different sizes and have different abilities, so the solution for one situation may not fit the needs of another user. Each set of needs should be evaluated to choose a product that will work for the user since this chair will be in use for a period of years.

Task seating usually means the ergonomic (adjustable to the body) seating that is on casters and used at service desks. In some cases this may be the seating that is chosen for the computer areas where people will sit longer. The backrest must provide support for your lumbar area. The seat pan area must be large enough to physically accommodate the size of the sitter, and the front of the seat pan (toward the knees) should be cushioned and not apply pressure on the back of the legs but rather have a shorter seat pan and fall away, hence the name of a "waterfall" front.

Some of the things to look for when you are evaluating a lounge chair are to notice the pitch of the chair, which is the relationship of the slant in the back of the chair to the seat, and to take note of the depth of the seat. Will most users be able to easily rest their feet on the floor as they sit in the chair?

Take the time to learn the materials that are used in lounge seating, sometimes referred to as "soft seating." There is foam, and within foam there are various densities (pounds per square inch) and compressions (how fast the foam returns to its original shape). This is important to the length of time that the materials will function for you. Aside from durability, denser foam makes for a more supportive piece of furniture. In general, the greater the densities the more a cushion conforms to you and cushions your movements in a lounge chair. You don't want a lounge chair to be too soft, as it envelopes your body and isn't good for circulation. A chair that is "too soft" may feel good in short term sitting but is not as comfortable as having support when a person sits for a longer time period. The body needs support to keep its proper alignment.

The task seating in a library is the one used for the reading chair at a table. These chairs are the ones that need to be the most durable, as they accept the most use and abuse of any seating in the library. There are basically two types of base, four legged and sled based chairs. There are also variations in styling that allow the chair to be lighter in design, as well as the actual weight of the reading chair. Materials include types of metals, woods, plastics and fabrics as well as combinations of these materials. In schools where budget is an issue, fabric backs and wood seats are used. As one looks across the landscape of the room, it will appear that they are all fabric, as you will not notice the seats. There is another philosophy that speaks to fabric seats being more comfortable with padding while the backs remain all wood. All wood seating is also used and the seat may be hollowed out for comfort rather than completely flat. Plastic seating has become more comfortable over the years. The plastic shell used to be the only style of seating. Now there are plastic seats that give with the body and are built with comfort and style in mind. They are not purchased for the purpose of buying the least expensive chair any longer. Always look into the hardware connections used and the structure of the chair.

The four-legged chairs will be used by people who sit four-square as well as by those who try to use the back two legs to rock on as they naturally change positions while studying. There are chairs built with this in mind. Two-position chairs are especially popular at the university level. They are not rockers but rather have the two positions engineered and level the "sled" at two places. Be sure to see their testing for safety and to determine that they do not overturn easily. The task chair should fit the users when the user's feet can comfortably rest on the floor. Unless a body has short legs and a longer torso, there should be a chair that fits them. Two-position and sled-based chairs of the same style can be intermixed as they will look the same unless you examine the bases closely. Study furniture should be planned for comfort, because time spent in the library is likely to increase in the years ahead. Particularly on residential campuses students may use the library to escape from the activity of the dorms.

It is becoming common for the seating used in libraries to be classified as office/commercial seating and to be put into use in the library. This is due to the fact that the library manufacturers are not producing as many of the contemporary offerings as those coming from the commercial furniture designers. My experience has been that many of the planners for libraries are looking outside of the library manufacturers for more modern designs. Just be aware that office seating is not always made for the heavy use that libraries get. Ask for testing and referrals for similar use.

Designs coming from Italy, Denmark, Germany and other European countries are popular, with their fluid lines and unique materials for upholstery. There is always the potential challenge of getting the imports into the United States in a timely manner. Some manufacturers use parts and pieces of the chair that are imported or "sourced out" from another manufacturer. Whenever parts and pieces of seating are brought together by one manufacturer to assemble and sell, it is always a factor to be considered. It is difficult for a manufacturer to be totally responsible when there are various suppliers involved. It is still another issue to be factored into the lead time (the time from placement to the factory until the product leaves the factory) and is on its way to the project. The use of product coming from another country is not something to be avoided but rather to be aware of the additional pitfalls.

Furniture for restaurant and healthcare industries are another source of well engineered seating designed to withstand the heavy-duty use of the public. A variety of styles and materials are found in those chairs that may not be available from a library manufacturer.

In the discussion of chairs as they relate to sizes of users we want to include a relatively new concept being marketed and what one manufacturer has named "Plus Size Seating." Since 60 percent of the American population are overweight and one third of those are clinically obese, planners are beginning to install 10 to 20 percent of the seating to accommodate those users. The larger users do not want to be discriminated against or singled out as needing to use special chairs, but would rather the chairs look like the standard ones. These larger chairs can be worked into a project without being obvious in the overall look. There is a need for this type of seating on every public project, including libraries. Chairs are available in sizes from the traditional 18–21 inch width (without arms) and can be made additional sizes in increments of two inches, and sometimes as large as 40 inches wide. Independent test results show that "Plus Size" chairs will pass a 1200 pound static load test[2] and a 600 pound drop test. A 600 pound test drops a 600 pound weight from six inches above the seat to simulate use and the way a body falls into a chair.

Wood, metal or upholstered benches are options. They are designed with backs and for shorter periods of seating they do not need to have backs. When the seat level is higher they create a perch for leaning. Metal has the advantage, in a public area, of the fabric not getting stained with dirt, nor does metal hold germs like fabric does.

Fabric Choices and Testing

The furniture industry demands stricter performance for furniture used in public spaces. In 1991 there were two California versions of the California Bureau of Home Furnishings' Technical Bulletin 133 concerning flammability codes. Many states followed by requiring that the furniture used in an installation pass CAL133. States and municipalities have their codes as well as borrowing and making their own other codes that they find would work for them.

Public buildings codes address the issues of preventing disastrous fires. The furniture in public buildings is more easily regulated than in residential housing, since fire marshals don't routinely monitor residences looking for code violations like they do public occupancies. Underwriters Laboratory issues other standards for safety that apply to flammability and electrical capabilities. All of the standards and tests are designed with the safety of the persons in mind who will be in the area impacted by the furnishings and the safety issues in using the furniture located in the area that would be impacted should the equipment fail, as well as the consequences if the furniture would burn. There is a smoke tunnel test in which an item is burned and rated as to how the flame spread and what type of smoke developed. There are independent testing laboratories that provide these types of services. Fire retardant fabrics are those treated with special chemical agents or finishes to make them retardant or resistant to burning. Today many fabrics achieve this property by using fibers that have it built into the polymer. This treatment makes the fabric highly durable and some predict that all fabrics will have this property in the near future if major governmental watchdogs and consumer advocates get their way.

The Association for Contract Textiles addresses issues such as resistance to fire, colorfastness of the fabric (the rubbing off of color under wet or dry conditions), colorfastness of the fabric when exposed to light and the physical properties of the fabric to tearing or to withstand wear and rubbing over time. Fabric grade options should be evaluated by the look and feel of the fabric as well as the testing of what is termed "double rubs," and the ability to clean the fabric as needed. American Society for Testing and Materials abrasion testing for general contract upholstery is 15,000 double rubs while 30,000 to 40,000 double rubs is considered heavy duty upholstery. Light use is 3,000 double rubs, according to the ASTM standards.[3]

The durability ratings of the grading systems, numbers (i.e., 1 to 8) or letter grades (A to G, for example), are not necessarily the lowest to the highest in durability. Designer fabrics are sometimes more costly but not necessarily more durable. Areas of high use should be carefully considered when it comes to fabric choices. Areas of high use (service desks, etc.) should dictate using more durable fabrics.

Manufacturers also offer the price grade called "COM" which designates "customer's own material." In this case the fabric is sent to the factory for use but it should be noted that the planner will be asked to notify the manufacturer of their intention to use a particular fabric so that the factory can relay two pieces of information back to the planner. The factory will let the planner know how much of this fabric is required per chair (based on patterns of the fabric so that they will be sure to have enough to upholster) as well as whether the factory has had any prior experience with the fabric that allows them to know if it will perform well over time. Fabric is usually used the way it comes off the bolt. The easiest way to explain this is by taking the example of a striped pattern where the stripes are long coming off the bolt instead of across the width of the bolt. The stripes would usually run top to bottom on the back or front to back on the seat of the chair. If the fabric was used the other way, perpendicular to the way the stripes run, the stripes would now occur across the seat on back. This method of laying out the pattern on the fabric is known as "railroading" the fabric.

Wood or laminate caps the arms of the chairs for the sake of durability and cleanliness. If the arms are fabric be aware that the natural oils from the skin will discolor the fabric over time and the fabric will need to be cleaned or replaced. This is one of the areas that the choice of upholstery fabric based on its performance testing is especially important. Leathers and the new faux leathers test well for long lasting use. The only drawback to leather is the ability to remove stains if they aren't noticed and cleaned right away. Check out the care and cleaning recommendations when evaluating materials for seating. Color choices are common sense when it comes to choosing neither the darkest (it shows dust) or the lightest (shows ink or other forms of stains). Staying somewhere in between is beneficial for hiding most of what will happen over time. There are puncture-proof fabrics that spring back when a sharp object goes through.

There are fabrics that can take stringent cleaning from the like of bleach products. Fabrics can be sprayed or otherwise integrated by some type of *protectorant* for longer wear and cleanability factors. There is a "Scotchgard Fabric Protector," a brand name owned by the 3M company that provides protection from a wide range of stains and soiling, while silicone based products are claiming to do a good job as well. Both repel water and water based stains. Evaluating their properties is difficult, since I have noticed that some chemicals actually appear to cause fabric to soil faster than untreated fabric. Scotchgard sells their product to mills and finishers under a license agreement which establishes standards of performance. Evaluate the options for cleaning fabrics once a protector is applied and weigh the advantages.

In both public and academic libraries the use that seating must withstand places the burden on decision makers to choose those types of materials that have superior test results or to minimize the use of fabrics. In the University of Nevada, Las Vegas, evaluation of their campus library nearly four years after opening, they said that "Our experience with fabric-covered chairs has been mixed. Chairs/stools for our service desks are worn. We should have purchased a higher quality fabric that would have withstood heavier use. We have had to have many of the fabric-covered public seats cleaned as they have become dirty in a variety of ways.... We have not experienced problems with the upholstered lounge chairs located throughout Lied Library. Early in the planning a decision was made that no sofas would be installed. Their absence has not been a problem. One of the most valuable types of furniture we acquired was stackable sled-based chairs. Stacked on wheeled carts these can be easily moved from one location to another in Lied Library in response to the changing needs. They have been quite useful at mid-terms and finals when students want to study in groups. Stacks of chairs are located strategically on first and second floors and students take them as needed to where their group has assembled. That is the only instance in which library customers are permitted to move furniture."[4]

It is not necessarily a bad thing when furniture is heavy. Sometimes it is an advantage, as it is less likely to be moved. If the intent of the furniture is to be moved often and the design is to stack the chairs, the chairs are likely to be lighter materials and thus easier to move. If rearranging seating is a concern many manufacturers have ways of addressing that problem by accessorizing their chairs with various types of ganging mechanisms. These ganging mechanisms are supplied as an accessory by the manufacturer and bolt the chairs together in a way that they can be moved only as one larger piece or not at all, dependent on the type of mechanism. If the idea is to stay the way they were originally placed you might ask if any type of attachment is available (one chair to another or bolting seating to the floor). Depending on the type of chair the connector may be joined underneath and not visible or it may become a part of the design when added to the seating.

In high traffic areas you may want to look for seating that will be easily reupholstered on-site. Some manufacturers have additional covers available for purchase at the time of original purchase. Others will quote reupholstering at the factory or in the field when the time comes for new fabric. It is prudent to ask how that is accomplished should the time come that you need new fabric. It may be a smart thing to purchase in the original purchase enough fabric to recover additional chairs since the availability of fabric over a period of time may change. If the seating is designed to be reupholstered in the field, additional covers could be priced when you make the original purchase. If the chair uses fabric, understanding the methods available for replacing the fabric is important. Some are attached using Velcro, while others require tools to remove and replace. Some chairs are easier to reupholster in the field, eliminating the cost of returning them to the factory or a local upholstery shop. There is always the option of using a professional upholsterer as well. If you have learned the complexity of the task, it may well save some time (and money) in the future. Especially in public libraries, there is a lot of discussion on whether to use fabric in heavily used libraries or areas frequented by the homeless, which is likely to be a challenge in inner city libraries. Wood, metal or plastic seating has an advantage that fabrics don't in that they won't absorb some of the things like food, body oils or other undesirable substances that are left behind. There are architects who use materials so easily cleanable that the area can practically be hosed down if needed. There are also fabrics that will accept being washed down with a bleach mixture, recognizing that fabric can become a breeding ground if not dealt with. Metals and plastics are some of the best materials that will not harbor dirt and germs. If the choice is made to use fabric and there are concerns, the fabric can be treated with an antimicrobial or a shield can be added between the foam and the fabric to keep any liquid from destroying the structure of the chair.

What Seating Can Provide

There is more time being spent in the library than 50 years ago when there was not as much leisure time for the common folk. It had also become better known that libraries hold the means to look up information in a card catalog and periodical index tables and to speak with the librarian concerning the use of these tools. Currently most of the research is done on the computer, and that can be done on the library's computer or in carrels or study areas with the individual's own computer. The library of today is built more with a stay and browse attitude. The librarian's concern remains one of assistance; now it is more navigating the computer programs for obtaining information and there are still those people who don't own computers and come to the library to use them. It is one of the best kept secrets to use local libraries when traveling to obtain information on local events or to check your e-mail from the road until you choose to catch up with technology that allows e-mail and Web access from your own phone.

With libraries being built in areas that have commanding views of the city, parks or riparian areas, the seating expands to enjoy those popular areas for browsing a book or an area of quiet contemplation. Lounge seating was originally found only in the periodical area, but with the use of computers it expanded lounge seating to practically any area of the library. Lounge seating is sometimes used for creating a divider between areas. Curved modular seating can create traffic patterns or enclose areas for specific purposes like a reading area. The periodical area of the library is a browsing area and most likely will hold most of the soft (lounge/upholstered) furniture that is used in a library.

The need for lounge seating has expanded but some of the requirements remain the same. With the addition of computer usage, the chairs will accommodate this need by widening the chair to accommodate the user and a comfortable width for use of a laptop. Some chairs have built in tablet arms that swivel in front or to the side when not in use. Ports for electrical and data are sometimes integrated into the seating for convenience or on a table that is attached to one side of the seating. Electrical outlets and data planning are crucial in these areas, as these two items are brought to the area through the walls or in the floor. This electrical planning is important to the discussion in early stages of planning the building, as this is when the decisions are made as to how and where outlets will be placed. Be sure to plan a quiet seating space so that the customer pursuing serious study or those who prefer a traditionally quiet library setting are not in close proximity to students working on a group project. An ottoman with fabric that has properties that make it cleaner-friendly or is easily recovered is being used in easy reading areas to support the feet or to sit down for a short time.

These types of rooms on reserve for meetings are commonplace in today's libraries. As the cultural center of the community, the library has public meeting room areas of various sizes and accommodations. There are large screens and sound and video systems included in the newer facilities. In addition to having an area for art work display, a community room is a place where authors speak and topics of general interest are held. These rooms are set up with moveable seating in classroom style, one row behind another, or if the area is large enough it could be planned as permanent auditorium seating, with seating attached to the floor. In the Carnegie-financed libraries more areas were devoted to public service (children's rooms, reference rooms and lecture halls) than in the modern library.

If the area is used as a multipurpose room for the public an option is to choose moveable stackable seating which can be wheeled away on trucks designed for stack seating and to store them in a back room or closet. These types of chairs need to be most durable as they are moved often and are usually lighter in weight. Hand holds (a small area designed along the upper back of the chair to pick the chair up) are helpful as it provides an easy way to move them.

Seating Over the Years

From 1890 to 1896 reading and desk chairs were all derived from the bentwood chairs popular in Victorian offices. The earliest recognition of recent artistic trends came in 1897, with the introduction of the Windsor chair. The company followed the trend of the Arts and Crafts style of furniture in 1899 and discontinued the Bentwood chairs, offering only antique oak finish depicting the whole Arts and Crafts movement. They began to address aesthetic issues instead of insisting on the company's "particular attention ... to mechanical points of construction" (as had the 1897 catalog) and adopted the rhetoric of the Arts and Crafts movement with statements speaking to the "purity of design, structural excellence and perfect finish ... free from any form of fantastic ornament." The choice of the Arts and Crafts aesthetic is telling in the context that it allowed the Bureau (the supplier of the times) to bridge the gap between librarianship's emphasis on functional design and architecture's growing interest in classicism. The Bureau blended the classical and Arts and Crafts movement as the bases of the card catalogs and file cabinets were shown with "massive square legs with three wide flutes, and could easily fit into a classically detailed library without offending an Arts and Crafts sensibility."[5]

In the early days of the library there was more all wood seating and less upholstery. Carnegie Libraries were being built in mining and industrial towns populated predominantly by men who worked in the day and frequented the libraries in the evening in their leisure time to read. The libraries were furnished with materials that were locally available and built or fabricated at the site with the types of materials that were plentiful in the area. The areas that had limestone used it for pillars and it made a grand entrance. Carnegie Libraries have distinctive styles; more than half were designed as Classical Revival, often called Carnegie Classical, identified by columns and a large pediment over the main entrance. At some point the pillars were considered to be too formal and structures were built that looked more like houses of the time but larger. While not all bear the Carnegie name in their title, their appearance generally indicates their genesis. Carnegie Libraries were impressive in size and many had massive staircases to their buildings. Even though there were no known specifications for the furniture, the library was given a requirement that they must spend 10 percent of the cost of the building for annual maintenance. This included the salaries for those who worked in them, so the pay was low according to other types of work. Most of the librarians were women and the planning was usually done by men.

The Carnegie-funded library was less likely to have a room to reserve for its trustees than the libraries funded in other ways. There was no agreement about the use of separate rooms for reference reading, for cataloguing and for trustees meetings: Only 58 percent of the libraries surveyed included these rooms.[6]

6. Seating

All of the 2,806 libraries donated throughout the English-speaking world by Andrew Carnegie were required to receive an annual subsidy from their home municipality. In most cases, this annual maintenance pledge, which became known as "The Carnegie Formula," was calculated as 10 percent of the cost of the library building. All of the early libraries funded by Andrew Carnegie were required to have the words "Free Library" or "Free to the People" inscribed on the front of the building. He wanted these words to be literally engraved in stone, to ensure that no library he funded ever charged an admission fee! [7]

Check This Out: Seating

- Are finishes maintainable, with durable fabrics and finishes that can be replaced or cleaned? Is the fabric porous enough to breathe and able to absorb and evaporate moisture?
- Is there a variety of comfortable seating (for various purpose/age level of users) and is there enough seating?
- Can people get into and out of chairs easily?
- Is furniture designed for ease of repair or replacement of parts?
- Is furniture designed and constructed for user safety, with rounded edges and free of projections that could snag clothing?
- Can chairs be pushed close to the tables and carrels?
- Is staff seating easily adjusted and adjustable for many sizes of persons?
- Do chairs with castors move easily on the floor surface?

See OSHA Ergonomic Solutions; Computer Workplace and Seating e Tool excerpt in Appendix B: Evaluation of Work Station Seating or visit http://www.osha.gov.

7

Children's Areas: (Quietly?) Entertain While Encouraging Learning

"Reading is the Building Block of Life."
—Charlie Gibson, Anchorperson for the *Today Show*

Larger Spaces for Small People

A larger percentage of the library is being designed for the younger patrons, since three in five of library users are youth. The areas for children and youth are growing, as many baby boomers have now become grandparents. There are baby time programs geared to the newborn to twelve month and programs for one and two year olds so that parents can positively interact with their children and help lay the groundwork for future learning. "Early literacy" is the buzzword driving the creative surroundings of furniture and programs to serve the toddler to six-year-old. How do you raise a child to be a reader? The answer is as simple as just "read to them, early and often," says Elaine Meyers, manager for teen and children services at Burton Barr Central Library in Phoenix. Don't wait for kindergarten or preschool to ensure literacy skills, Meyers tells parents. "The best teacher for a child," she says, "is their parent."[1]

Tests show that colors and shapes stimulate interest and learning. There are many studies that prove that the child who is read to at a young age learns to read easier and faster. A children's area must accomplish a few things to be successful in its goal to encourage children to spend time there and to return often. A good library is stimulating and engages as many senses as possible. The editor from *Parenting* magazine says that "reading must be fun." To work toward this end furniture manufacturers supply chairs using the process of laser cutouts in the backs of

7. Children's Areas

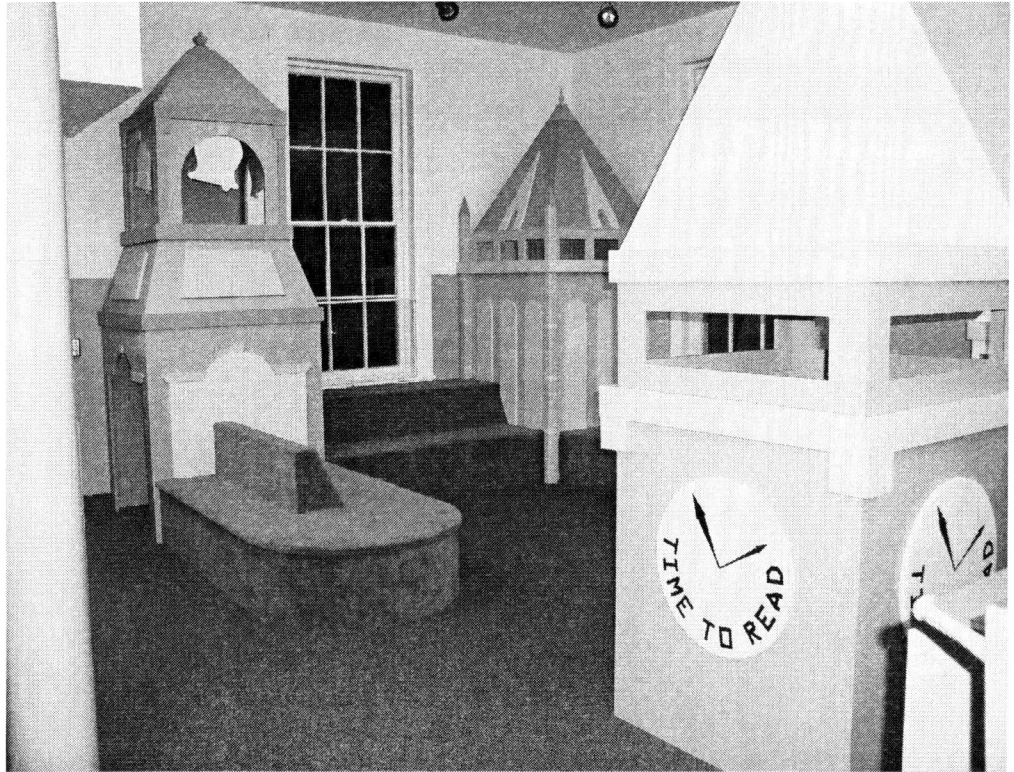

This children's library exemplifies an area that stimulates learning by using bright colors and shapes. It also functions as a reading area complete with built in bench seating.

the chairs. The laser cutouts are in the end panels of shelving as well as the end panels of tables or carrels. Shaping the backs of chairs or end panels in desired patterns is another way of defining this area. This would be determined by the ideas of the designer or planner working on the new area with the librarians at the facility.

Tables, chairs and computer carrels should be scaled down to the appropriate size rather than using full scale furniture and merely shortening the legs. There will most likely be two different sizes of tables and seating (see Recommended Furniture Sizes Based on Average Student Heights) for your children's area, one for toddlers and another for older children who don't qualify for the Teen Area yet. Fun shaped tables that are able to work as a group for projects or stand alone are advantageous. It is good to build flexibility into all sections of the library to meet future needs.

Provided is a chart that shows heights of tables and seating for various stages of growth for youth. If possible, shelving or some type of display should separate

Children's plywood formed seating uses laser cutouts painted in a myriad of colors.

7. Children's Areas

these two groups within the children's area. If the preteens are able to get to their area without walking through the younger children's area that is of benefit since it gives them their own identity.

Recommended Furniture Sizes Based on Average Student Heights, 6 months to 12 years

Age	Chair Height*	Table Height**
6–18 months	5" H	12" H
1–2 years	6½" H	14" H
2–3 years	8" H	16" H
3–5 years	10" H	18" H
4–7 years	12" H	20" H
6–8 years	14" H	22" H
1st Grade (4–7 years)	11½"–12" H	22" H
2nd Grade (6–8 years)	13½"–14" H	22"–24" H
3rd Grade	15½"–16" H	27" H
4th Grade	15½"–16" H	27" H

*Refers to height of seat   **Refers to finished height of table

"Board books" in baskets are shown to work well. Toddlers love to pull out all of them and "reshelve" or place them back in the baskets just like they do at home with their toys. That way *they* get to choose which books they want read to them. These bins can be made in shapes or in rectangular or square boxes with designs applied to the sides of the "boxes" to make them more kid friendly. Cutout panels in the shape of animals make a bold and fun statement. That way monkeys, crocodiles or poodles can hold the book bins, dependent on the style desired.

Upon entering the children's area I always am eager to see if there are bright colors and objects or an obvious theme that has taken shape. Sometimes a castle or a fairytale comes to life, zoo animals flourish on columns or bare walls

Book bins adorned with colorful jungle-themed vinyl covering create a fun storage system.

Additional children's book bins use the large animal shaped cutouts, keeping the jungle theme intact. Both of these jungle book bins are at a child friendly height, where children can browse for their favorite book.

become a mural of underwater life. End panels and doors are easily used for representations of larger than life books. The youth services librarian is often excited about the area and anxious to share what she and the children have been able to create. In many libraries a theme evolves that is relevant to the area. (Some examples are Southwestern and Western regions that use Native American items to educate users; Hispanic communities might highlight their history or culture). The theme and décor of the area could be based in traditional stories from childhood complete with castles, moats and forests, using end panels that are scribed or shaped like animals in that forest. Local artists or creative craftsmen (patrons of the library or professional artists) in the area might get involved by working on a focal point. A focal point in the Telluride, Colorado, Wilkinson Public Library is the larger than life storyteller. The librarian has told me that this carving, measuring eight feet seated, was created by a local craftsman and provides the showpiece of the children's area. This is one of those times that the library benefits from the support of the community.

7. Children's Areas

At the Wilkinson Public Library, in Telluride, Colorado, is a large carved storyteller seated on a throne. Colorful fabric and rugs festoon this area and add a lot of color and textures.

Similar to other commitments in life, once a desire is known the universe brings together those people with the talents or resources to make it happen.

Common ways of bringing themes to the area without the donation or purchase of artist's work are using cutouts to resemble objects from nature, maple or oak leaves, plants, flowers or animals on the backs of chairs or end panels. When a child is excited about recognizing the shape of a leaf, education becomes fun. Shaped tables with feet of colors or shapes and anodized paint colors on metal or wood are all available from manufacturers (see Appendix F: Sources of Information). In Delores, Colorado, a caterpillar became the "mascot" of the library and now marches in town parades (with a little help from volunteers who serve as the many legs). The children who use the library wanted to see a caterpillar theme follow into the new library when the building was complete.

Lenora Nicoli, youth services librarian of Telluride, says that they moved the picture book browsing bins toward the entry, finding that this maze created an area where the small children tended to slow down and get ready to use the "quiet voice" that she encourages. She also says that flexibility of these bins is helpful and the castors make it easier to move them into the desired pattern. Some librarians may alphabetize the picture books; others don't even try, as with the picture books on the children's level they are likely to be heavily used. The most important thing is that the children look at them and the more that a "box" system can be created to search through the books, the more successful the result.

When selecting seating, there are a few things to keep in mind. The fact that adults accompany children is one of them. Some libraries provide areas where both a child and an adult can sit together comfortably and look at a book. Chairs used at small tables should be able to support an adult who may help a child. Kids sometimes like to snuggle into a window seat or a niche that is built-in with a cushion for comfort. Furniture should be safe, having rounded edges without metal welds

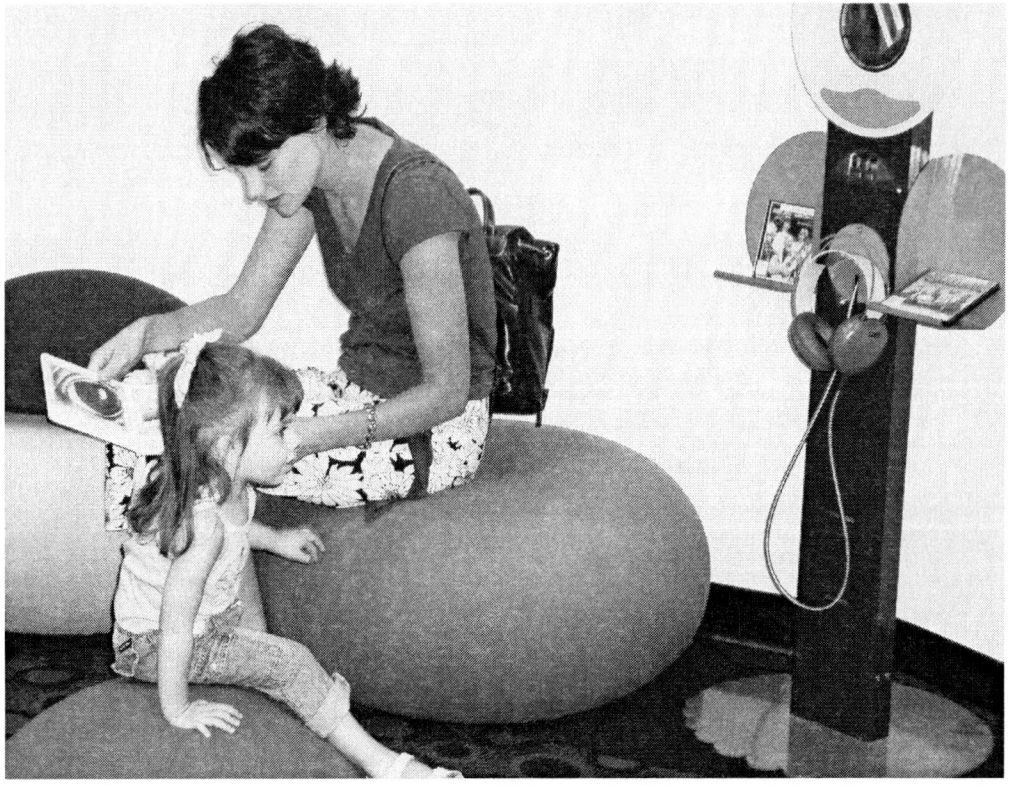

In the Farmington, New Mexico, Public Library an adult reads to a child on brightly colored cushions. Note the listening station in the background that invites children to enjoy audio books and music.

7. Children's Areas

and the wood edges finished (more about this in the chapter on writing specifications). Upholstered benches work well, as the sizing holds two or three persons in one seat. This is also a good use of what is called "Plus Size Seating," wider than standard seating to support the use of the chair for parents and children.

Fully upholstered lounge seating is not used often but when it is used it is quite effective, especially if the covering can be replaced easily. Since upholstery can harbor germs, the choice of fabric is important in this area. Fabrics developed for the health care industry are worth consideration. Fabrics that have good wearability and good cleaning options are essential. There are collections of fabric within the major textile companies that are specifically designed patterns with children in mind. Crypton[2] fabrics were developed for health care and public facilities, a process to sanitize fabric encapsulated within the threads of the fabric. It is promoted as a safe, easy and effective upholstery cleaning system that eliminates tough stains while also preventing the growth of germs and odor-causing bacteria. The cost of using this patented system within the fabric is an upgrade, but in the long run it pays for itself.

The goal of keeping the levels of sound low has always been a challenge for the librarian. It is most effective when there is supervision by both the librarian and the persons who accompany the exuberant children. It is the librarian's hope that the person who brought the child will be staying in that area with them. If they aren't, the librarian is left to supervise them.

The hands-on computer areas are well-spaced in children's areas rather than grouped, which appears to make sense when planning electrical outlets. Grouping of users (children in this case) tends to promote conversation, and if a child does get enthralled in the game or interactive program that they are enjoying they are not disturbing their "neighbor" in the library when the stations have space between them. Part of the listener's enjoyment is to sing along with the CD, unaware of the impact their small voices have on the library's sense of tranquility.

Baffling in the ceilings or some type of acoustical treatment or banners of artwork are helpful in these areas if the ceiling is high. In the interest of deterring the transferring of germs, headsets have been taken away and external speakers are used in these areas where noise is not considered a problem. In this case those carrels might be grouped. Placement depends on the personality that the library is creating. Soft seating and decorative displays may be a factor in lowering the undesired noise in an area. The public library in Camas, Washington, used whimsical custom seating in the shape of a flower for their children's area and as the children are enjoying sitting in the flower it is also providing acoustical benefit. Music piped through the system at low volume may enhance the calm atmosphere desired in an area of the library.

In the Telluride Public Library a child plays a hands-on computer game while seated on a stool at a children's size computer workstation. Note that the adult size lounge chair is in the same area.

In a public library, the program areas must be large enough to accommodate story time and special events. Sometimes the spaces are similar to a wraparound amphitheatre, with areas for puppet shows, interactive theatre and more. The library has something for everyone. A story time for even younger patrons has been added to the offering and mothers bring their children two and under for special time together. Provisions for slide or video presentation on retractable screens are useful. Be sure there is wall space provided to display ongoing information for events or new books or themes being featured. The newer building plans make much more use of monitors that can play educational series or run topics of interest to the public.

A parenting corner is a new concept in the library. The periodicals concerning child rearing as well as some other periodicals that may be of interest to parents are displayed in the children's area and are duplicated in the main periodicals area. This is conveniently planned to encourage the parents to stay in the area with

7. Children's Areas

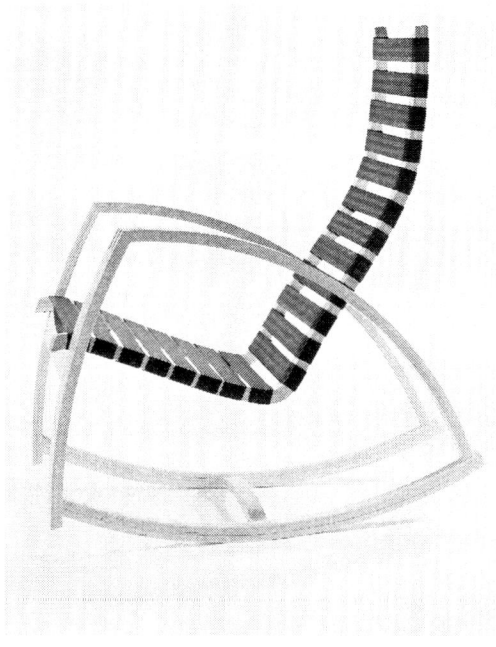

Top: The Farmington Public Library's story time room is a mini-amphitheatre area with multimedia presentation board ready for children to fill the tiered and carpeted seating for programs. *Right:* The Gotham wood ply-bent rocking chair offers a choice of colors of seat belt material from the automotive industry as the support. Rocking chairs are a great addition for toddlers in this area.

the children. Placing some furniture and activities for the comfort of parents in this area will work toward achieving this goal. A rocking chair is a popular item for nursing the newborn in a sense of privacy and creates a relaxing place, with the familiar rocking movement to soothe the restless toddler.

It is important to have some adult seating as parents will sometimes want to stay in the area as their children enjoy story time. Children get more out of programs conducted in the same area where related books and other materials are located. Media bag racks on steel shelving are good for grouping these materials for check-out. A knapsack filled with related materials is also a popular solution.

The Carnegie Corporation Forms

In 1911 Andrew Carnegie presided over the first meeting of the Carnegie Corporation in Carnegie's music room in the presence of his daughter and wife. The Carnegie Corporation was chartered to administer the library program. This was one of the first modern foundations and Carnegie "did not have a term to distinguish a corporate body whose purpose was to make money from one whose purpose was to give it away,"[3] so it was and remains the Carnegie Corporation. Carnegie's reforms and his insistence on public support for his gifts meant that the libraries' funds drawn from public monies had to convey fiscal responsibility; so as a result the buildings to follow were to be built smaller and less elaborately, limiting the building to library functions and a small lecture hall.

Some of the best and earliest public library services for children, with spacious buildings, customized equipment and furniture and well-qualified staff, were found in the USA. Specialist training was instituted there in 1898. However, in the 1920s advances in library work with teenagers were being developed in the UK. A pioneer intermediate library opened at Walthamstown in 1924 with over 4,000 volumes, and the Carnegie United Kingdom Trust provided book grants to youth clubs in 1926. As the quality and quantity of children's literature increased in the 1930s and 1940s, bookstacks were enhanced by new authors, although there were still concerns about the range of titles being provided. In 1936 the first modern reviewing journal, *Junior Bookshelf*, modeled on the U.S. *Horn Book Magazine*, was published, and surveys of children's reading began to be considered important. A more professional approach to service delivery was also evident in the Library Association's greater interest in children's work; the Association of Children's Librarians (ACL) was established as their Youth Libraries Section (later group) in 1945. In commitment to young adult services, however, they lagged behind the USA somewhat; there, as early as 1929, the Young People's Reading Round Table had been founded as part of the ACL.[4]

At the turn of the century the public library was quite different than the library of today. As one entered the library a patron's direction was gender determined. The men's reading area was separate and distinct from the women's area. There was a division between the children's areas; again male and females were separated and then the children's areas were isolated from the adults.

7. Children's Areas

There was actually a separate entrance to the library for children to enter and exit rather than using the main entrance to the library.[5] This gives credence to the adage that not only should children not be heard but that they should not be seen. There was a glass screen that would allow the boys and girls to see each other. The boys were accompanied by an attendant to monitor their behavior and there was a detailed Rules of Daily Conduct posted. The layout was L-shaped and the adults were in the opposite side of the library from the children. At some point the librarian ceased monitoring both areas from the one charge desk and the children truly were out of sight. "The idea was not as much to protect children as to ensure that the 'genteel' library user enjoyed the illusion of 'ordered and serene opulence' that the architect, librarian and library commissioners had worked to create in the stage set they thought of as the real library."[6]

Service to children was the first feature of the "modern library idea" to receive serious consideration in the period that Carnegie libraries were being built. As early as 1876 librarian William I. Fletcher pointed out the inconsistencies between the library's claim to educational function and the usual practice of barring children under twelve from library use.[7] The ten years that followed would be the transitioning period, until children would be trusted with books. By 1897 a survey in *Public Libraries* showed that a children's corner was specifically fitted with low tables and chairs[8] in Pawtucket, Rhode Island. The survey revealed that many city libraries had all provided separate reading rooms for their young readers and by the turn of the century most librarians regarded the children's room as a necessary component of the public library.[9]

Check This Out: Children's Area

- If you were a child would you like to be in this environment?
- Are the shelves, furniture and the convenience facilities scaled for children?
- Is there comfortable seating for adults to sit with children to read and is the arrangement such that adults are not intimidated while in the area?
- Does staff have visual control over the area?
- Is there sufficient room for staff to prepare programs?
- Has space been provided for display and materials geared to children?
- Is play area designed to avoid interfering with other library functions and are the areas arranged to minimize noise and disruption to adjacent adult/teen areas?
- Are washroom facilities near the children's area? (preferable *in* the area)
- Is access available to preteens without going through the young children's area?

8

Teen Spaces: Created from *Their* Input

If we wish to attract our young people, our children, our new audiences, then we must encourage fun.
— E. Ethelbert Miller, poet, writer, commentator and educator

Getting Teens Involved

If the library doesn't provide programs for the youth between school age and adulthood, the youth coordinator at the City of Scottsdale, Arizona, Medina Zick, says that they may lose that person as one who does not think of the library as part of their life. If the teen center is successful in keeping that person active in using library facilities, she says that success will most likely make them a library user for life.

In Farmington Public Main Library the youth have designed seating for viewing the large high tech displays and listening areas complete with earphones. Computer games, CD player listening stations and DVD monitors are abundant since this is what the teens are interested in. All of these types of media require some type of electrical requirements in the building that will need to be available in the furniture, shelving or displays that will house them. Knapsacks hanging from the bag racks are a convenient way to organize, protect and easily carry these types of educational media for check-out.

It is useful to determine the electrical and data requirements early in the project, as you want these areas to be designed with comfortable seating, listening booths or stools for perching. "In Phoenix more than 30 students met to brainstorm ideas for the center which modeled the new "Teen'Scape" in the central branch of the Los Angeles Public Library."[1] Even with requests for beanbag chairs, metallic décor and strobe lights, architect Will Bruder said, "all the ideas are possible." Athia Hardt, president of the Friends of Phoenix Library said, "Once you get kids in the library, they find out what a resource it can be."

The planner's goal is to design an area with freedom for the users while defining the use (in this case a library, not a recreation center). Teens can be part of a youth panel that is interactive and creative in designing their area. In Farmington, New Mexico, the youth panel brought the idea of multimedia stations. These are screens that can be viewed from angles (like a sports bar) while a film or other favorite music video can be playing simultaneously. Computer screen placement is important in that staff will want to be able to view the screen if it can be controlled by the user.

Five years after the design of Teen Central at Phoenix Main Branch, little remains of the mostly Italian designs that were appropriated for the grand opening. Even though the original furniture cost the same as furniture that was "durable," constant use up to 200 teens a day, some of them staying for hours, meant the furniture could not withstand the use and abuse that it received. The lighting that was originally planned is also not intact as it was installed. The lighting that was chosen invited tampering, as it consisted of pieces of paper on which poetry could be written and displayed. Graffiti is a constant problem as this library is located in an area of downtown where it is common to see many of the young people who use the library leave their mark. As many of the users of this Teen Center spend a few hours at a time in the area the fabric on the beanbag seating quickly wore out. It was replaced by automobile upholstery and has been wearing well.

Some of the design concepts originally used in the Phoenix teen zone didn't work. The sheer curtains that softened and enclosed areas couldn't stand the constant abuse as they were pulled into the restaurant-like booth seating and used to wrap around the teens. Some design ideas are creative and visually refreshing, but not practical. Ideas for this area have shown that they need to be low maintenance and durable because of the heavy use that the furniture will need to endure. The tables they chose worked out since it was learned by trial and error that the tops could be scrubbed and sanded down if necessary. Acrylic bookcases seemed like a good idea — opaque colors integrated into the plastic — but they had no adjustments as would be standard in traditional library shelving and that has become a problem in that there is material that cannot be shelved due to this restriction in the size of the openings. If the shelving takes a hard and direct impact and it is damaged, it is also impossible to repair. Damage could be as simple as the result of vandalism or taking the brunt of a cleaning machine. The types of lightbulbs were expensive and not easily changed as they burned out. The cost of the furnishings over the life cycle must be taken into account in addition to the purchase price. It is interesting to note that even though they do not fit the design scheme for Teen Central, the library chairs that were brought from the former library and had been in service for at least 20 years are now showing up in the area newly reupholstered, so that they have seating they know will hold up.

Teens frequent libraries if the facilities appeal to them. Inflatable or soft seating and lava lights can be a part of a teens "wish list" for including in their space. The idea of the centers being designed by the users is not new, but it is being done more often. Involving teens in the design stage should help foster a greater sense of ownership for them. Shera Farnham, assistant city librarian, says, "It's a way for them to learn and mature, while knowing they're trusted and respected."[2]

Scottsdale Arizona's Civic Center Library, "Knowasis," opened this year and was named by the teens who were a big part of the design. The multi-zone 4,000 square foot area has come to fruition after three or four years of making choices that were inspired by the teen committee and orchestrated by the architect and the city. It is Thunderbird's Charities Teen Learning Center, a privately funded project that arose out of a need for a place to do homework (the "homework zone") and watch a movie on the plasma television located in a central point of the space and with lounging chairs where teens can be welcomed to "hang out" with their peers in a positive and safe environment.

When the homes of the students don't have the technology and the school system is not equipped or does not have hours that are convenient to study or do research, libraries are finding that it is a real benefit to provide these services. The computer chairs that were chosen have castors as the teens requested and are comfortable fabric covered foam, while the remainder of the seating is plastic covered or hard plastic as they feel that this will work better than upholstery fabrics. The floor has a fabric feel with the carpet alternate chosen to not only wear well but, also to be comfortable to sit on if the floor is chosen as a resting spot while listening to an iPod or talking on a cell phone, which is permitted unless the conversation is disruptive to the other library users.

The café zone has tables and chairs that can be used when teens are snacking from vending machines. The cyber zone has twelve computers with seating on castors and this teen area has a special zone in that there will be an outside area which should prove popular by bringing a feeling of nature to the space. This was one feature that was unanimously voted upon. Teens will be able to lounge on brightly colored solid geometric foam chairs and benches for watching a 52-inch screen flat panel television and for movie night or visiting with friends. Their listening station areas will be cutting edge technology. The music will be ordered at the service desk and the listener will return to a chair that is beneath a dome shaped amplifier filled with music directed down and surrounding the listener. The foam chairs have been a popular addition and it really helps that they can be wiped off with Clorox since they are a solid color and show marks from shoes. It is important to note that when solid colors are used stains, lint and other marks from daily use will be more obvious and you need to know that there is an effective way to clean the material.

If patterns are used, whether this is for the fabric, work surfaces or flooring materials, this is more forgiving of showing wear.

With the concept of the zones in the Scottsdale library, both quiet and active areas are available. If one area doesn't work for study, the group or individuals have choices that match the way they work best. There are choices as unique as each of us. Some people are best working or studying without any noise or distraction while others can only study while listening to music or with activity going on around them. This concept of zones allows them to choose. Wi-Fi (wireless fidelity) incorporated into the library will allow teens to bring laptops from home to continue progress on homework or to surf the Internet. Some teens will bring their music and headphones so that they can block out surrounding noise. Architect Wendell Burnette shared that "They were very interested in a kind of balance between entertainment and the traditional quiet library atmosphere."[3] "The entertainment separates you from the stereotype everyone thinks of as a typical library," says Jake Morgan, who participated in the design and concept process.[4]

Another way that a feeling of nature will be brought into the space is through the use of fabric that will catch the multicolored light provided through a system of ceiling lights. There will be lights that simulate sunset (orange, pink and red) and sky blue colors. One of the most desirable features of the teen area was to make patrons feel as if they were outdoors. Some libraries have designed an outdoor area in a courtyard or a patio surrounded by the wall of the building or a wall of plant life or shrubbery. Some areas were an unused service courtyard in their former life. In these areas some type of commercial outdoor furniture would be used rather than residential quality, which wouldn't last long in a public space.

The key in supervising the teen area is to be able to accomplish that goal without the monitoring being obvious to the users of the library. Glass enclosures sometime provide this ability but the tradeoff is the lack of absorptive qualities to handle the noise due to the hard surface of glass. Areas for teens are much less of a "quiet area" than other parts of the library, as they have become areas of activity. Lines of sight for the librarians are more important in the area serving children and youth (through the teen years) than any other age group. The service desk is ideally placed in the center of the area so that this can be accomplished.

The use of other teens in a volunteer or part-time paid position as a librarian's aide has worked well, as teens are more likely to ask another teen for help instead of a staff person. The advisory group of teens will continue to have input into their area concerning any additions or programming.

Flexibility with placement of tables is valuable as well as fun and creative projects allow teens to gather around them for assignments. One of the newer libraries in Farmington, has used stainless steel tables, chairs and counters complete with

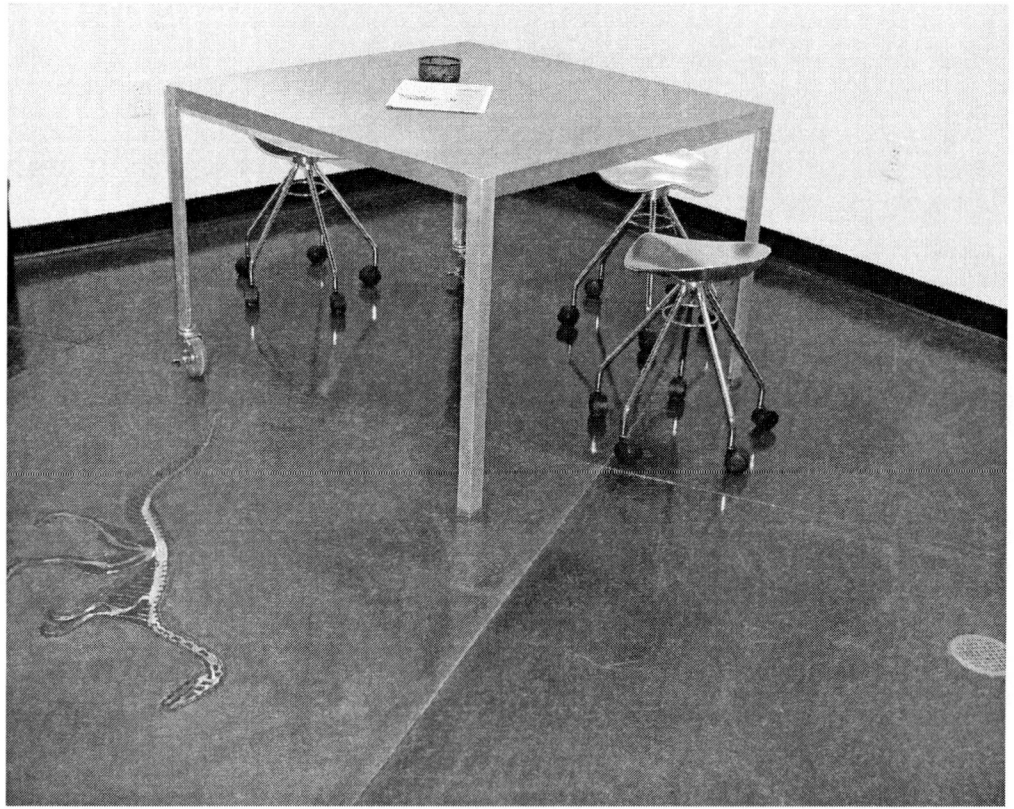

Stainless steel tables and tractor seat stools on castors allow easy clean up in this all purpose craft room for the teen area of the Farmington Public Library.

sink area available for heavy duty crafting projects and for easy cleanup on completion of projects. When crafts are part of the program, sinks are a helpful addition for staff and participant cleanup. A public library is less similar to a school library in this case, where group interaction is not as strongly encouraged. It is generally agreed that in a school library needs in the educational program require areas for reading, reference work, group work, audiovisual listening and viewing, library instruction and (sometimes an area of its own) teacher preparation material. The school library houses all the books, magazines and audiovisual materials as well as the academic collection to support the specific school's curriculum that would not be found at a public library. The library instruction or computer lab has many computers on tables and chairs placed in classroom style. This is an area that computer/classroom tables and chairs are more often used than library furniture, as it is more apt to carry the wire management in the more contemporary styles that are desired.

In all of the teen inspired areas two themes are consistent: using color and looking at seating arrangements for groups of teens. Very different from the libraries that were once part of the "Modern Library Idea," interaction is encouraged by the type of lounge and casual seating — different from the days where separation, formality (seated at tables) and quiet were the way of life in the library. "Whether aimed at young or old, reading rooms offered readers an orderly space with tables regimented in neat rows. Period photographs depict readers in approved postures, seated with both feet on the floor, chair pulled up close to the table, and with their attention focused on the books immediately in front of them."[5]

Some of the areas today will use bistro-like counter height (24"–30" seating height) stools around a smallish (30"–36" diameter) table for gathering and conversing. Others will use chairs around larger tables to be able to spread out studies or hobby interests.

The modern library and its planners have a genuine interest in providing a safe and inspiring area for its younger patrons, realizing that these users are our future. If they are not inspired to continue learning and growing, then educated decisions will not be possible. My experience has been that as much attention is paid to this area as any other adult area of the library. In the past five years I would say that the interest has grown in getting the teenage users involved in planning their own areas of use. Ten years ago the teen section at your public library was probably an afterthought. At best, it boasted a few posters and languished at the edge of the children's section, all but consumed by munchkin-size tables and chairs. But libraries are changing, and the Phoenix, Arizona, metropolitan area is leading a national trend to create the kinds of interactive, noise-friendly spaces that Generation Y wants.

Recommended Sizes Based on Average Student Heights, 12 years to Adult

Age	Chair Height*	Table Height**
5th Grade	17½"–18" H	30" H
6th Grade	17½"–18" H	30" H
7th Grade	17½"–18" H	30" H
8th Grade	17½"–18" H	30" H
Middle School	17½"–18" H	30" H
High School	17½"–18" H	30" H
College/University	17½"–18" H	30" H

*Refers to height of seat   **Refers to finished height of table

Check This Out: Teen Areas

- Is the physical and psychological climate pleasant for teenagers?
- Does the staff have visual control of the area?

- Is the area clearly distinguished from the adjacent areas?
- Is there comfortable seating?
- Is there a display area?
- Is there an area so that they can socialize without disturbing other teenagers who may want a quieter area to read?
- Are there listening stations for music?

9

Lessons Learned from the Past to Embrace Technologies of the Future

Books are the treasured wealth of the World and the fit inheritance of generations and nations.
— Henry David Thoreau

Gone are the pre-computer days when obtaining information took literally hours in the research library. With all the search engines available on computers sitting on tables or study carrels, the same information can be accessed in minutes. In June 1992, in an article titled "Librarian Jobs opening up through the 1990s," Jenny Upchurch says that "the librarian has become more of a manager, rather than a caretaker of the information resources." She says, "Gone are the days of the gorgons who guarded the bookshelves and card catalogs from inquiring minds — if they had dirty fingers."[1]

I believe it is safe to assume that the future will bring even more ideas to the way a library accomplishes its mission with the community it serves. Currently the newest technology brings LCD and high definition televisions. New electronics have changed the look of wall units and artwork because televisions are now being hung over fireplaces and counters or on walls. It is surprising all of the creative ways a library can provide different types of information to its users. It is interesting to remember that some of the younger patrons have never been without interactive media.

Classes, lectures, and movies dealing with topics important to daily living as well as specialized interest and educational topics are all available in today's libraries. The libraries need to present these opportunities in a few ways to catch all three groups of searchers: the group that has never known the library without computers, the users that are in transition of using both types of media, and the group, though it may seem small, that will never use or have only limited knowledge of what the computer can bring to them. The type of class or lecture will determine what area of the library is used and the furniture requirement for that area.

Keeping chairs light and stackable and tables sized to be easily flexible for reconfiguration would be of benefit. Some of the discussion groups will want to break out into smaller groups, while some are set up as more of a lecture. If the program is a hands-on class, tables may be needed and if clean-up is required a counter with sink and water may be useful.

The traditional library furniture — beefy and very dark or very light stained wood and all wood chairs — are still part of the library design world, but there are many more choices now. More design elements are used in libraries, including paint, fabrics and ideas taken from residential and other commercial buildings.

The Study of Books and Places to Read Them

A book called *The Book on the Bookshelf*, by Henry Petroski, explains books, bookshelves and study spaces, so eloquently tracing the history of the book and its storage from the beginning as a scroll through all the materials that were used prior to the printed word and finally bound into the books that are so common to us today. He states that "The furniture changed to meet the need of the reader to support the book."[2]

The fourth century BC scribe Ezra is shown here working before an open armarium (courtesy of Henry Petroski, used in *The Book on the Bookshelf*).

The background of reading areas is an interesting study in itself. They came about through the evolution of the bookshelf.

9. Lessons Learned from the Past to Embrace Technologies of the Future

Yes, the shelving that held the books didn't always look the way it does today. I find the progression of this library furniture fascinating! In Medieval times, books were stored in trunks. When a trunk was open, the front edge was conveniently positioned where the reader could use it as a book holder and at a height that it was easier to pick up to move due to the weight of a trunk full of books. Later the trunks were turned on end in a vertical positioning and segmented with boards so that the books were separated and didn't fall down to the bottom. This design was most likely the genesis of shelving. One armoire-like closet, called armariums in the fourth century BC, is pictured with a scribe named Ezra working in front of the armarium.

This piece of furniture evolved to another type of storage for books, which was a podium-like stand next to a chair. That was followed by sloped display for

Lecterns in the library of this twelfth-century church have books chained to rods above the lecterns (courtesy of Henry Petroski, used in *The Book on the Bookshelf*).

viewing books. That storage and display evolved to church pew styled seating, using the sloped display on the back of the pew to hold books. The reader would be using the seat behind this display, which was also the seat in front of them. This appears to be the beginnings of a bookshelf/study space (the carrel?) by meeting the humble needs of the monastery, as the library was part of the monks' daily studies. At this time books were still chained to the shelves that held them.

Books were precious because they were not plentiful. Chains were taken off the books in the library of Peterhouse, Cambridge, in the late sixteenth century and the shelving were still called "presses" into the mid-seventeenth century. "Note the projecting wings at their base which once formed the ends of benches that extended the length of the press and along the wall between adjacent presses. These seats were also known as podiums, having served as places to stand on to reach the books on the upper shelves."[3]

Presses from the mid-seventeenth century, including the seating that they called podiums that doubled as stepping platforms to reach the higher shelves (courtesy of Henry Petroski, used in *The Book on the Bookshelf*).

Because there were alcoves in monasteries (where the first libraries were found) it made perfect sense to make use of the partial enclosures of the alcoves as this helped keep down the noise and distractions of the "outside world" and made a natural study carrel. The natural light from the outside streamed into the carrel, so carrels were most useful during daylight hours, as candles (and later kerosene lamps) were used until electricity was supplied.

Revisiting Our Beginnings: Library of Congress

I was reminded at a recent visit to the Library of Congress that libraries are all about direction and instruction. Seeing remnants of what

9. Lessons Learned from the Past to Embrace Technologies of the Future

the library of the turn of the twentieth century looked like, I realized how much *and* how little has changed in libraries in the past 100 years. Although this library arguably is the mother of all libraries, the largest library in existence and sometimes known as the depository storage of knowledge, so much of what has followed in libraries has been the influence by what is provided in the Library of Congress.

Thomas Jefferson said he believed that learning is a lifetime experience and the decisions that are made today in libraries are made for the same reason. He felt that there is no subject that Congress should not have an interest in because by increasing their education they are able to make better decisions. Although the laptop I was carrying seemed out of place in the palatial grandeur of the sixteen story high and one hundred foot wide circular grand area of the reading room, computer use was designated to the south side of the rotunda. Linton Weeks says that "The elegant expansive reading room, with its 160-foot high dome and its concentric arrangement

The Thomas Jefferson Library Main Reading Room at the Library of Congress in Washington, D.C. All the curved reading tables and seating radiate outward and face the circular reference desk; note the highest level is where the librarian sat to have a 360 degree view of the entire reading area.

of oak reading tables is one of modern civilization's grand temples of learning."[4] All the wood reading chairs are carved in the back and the massive dark wood curved desks mirror those on the other side of the one hundred foot diameter circle. Book-lined alcoves are well suited to the quiet studious atmosphere. Plato, Shakespeare, Homer, Moses and other scholarly and wise men's statues stand beneath each window opening, facing into the circle and gazing at each other and into the rotunda with light pouring through stained glass into the area designed for 236 researchers.

The architectural materials in this room are magnificent. They are the most expensive examples of their time and still impressive today as the rarest type of marble was used. The softness of the curves and the arches are embedded with shadowbox effects and with rows of framed gold rosettes that are exquisite 23K gold. The "silver" is aluminum, the most costly material of the day. The materials are functional in that they take very little maintenance. Silver would need shining, the tour guide explained and aluminum was more expensive and the idea was to make the boldest statement that this was the most opulent building built to date.

The Jefferson Building was the first building in the Federal Maze with electricity, so that in itself was something visitors traveled from afar to see. Artisans from a previous World's Fair were asked to come to Washington in 1889 to be a part of a project that would be heralded throughout the world. The building budget was 6.5 million dollars and it came in nearly $200,000 below budget. The interior finishes cost about $200,000, which was an exorbitant cost in those days, just as the cost in today's dollars would be. That $200,000 reflects $4,081,632[5] that would be spent today for the same interior finishes *if* the materials were available.

The Jefferson Building opened in 1897 and it was an important way in the United States to show the rest of the world our prosperity as a nation. The Library of Congress was established in 1800 when Congress set aside $5,000 for the purchase of "such books necessary to Congress." When the British invaded Washington in 1814 and destroyed the Capitol Building and its library, Jefferson, who by then was living in Monticello, sold his collection to the Library of Congress, a collection devoted to art, science, literature, psychology, religion and mythology. Jefferson began the collection, which now numbers over 130 million items, with a Congressional appropriation of $23,970 for his 6,487 book collection.[6]

The original artwork and décor were designed to teach Christian stories to people who couldn't read. The globes throughout the library represent universal access — open to everyone — while many of the drawings and sculptures reinforce that this knowledge is available to every class of society and honors all vocations of the time, whether electrician, mechanic, doctor or architect. Jefferson's library was broken down into three categories: Imagination, Reason and Memory, as he encouraged people to choose knowledge over ignorance.

The sculpture in the Library is worth noting. The winged *Father of Time* is a large bronze sculpted by John Flanagan as a classic example of how clocks are used architecturally to make a statement about time. *Human Understanding* is a beautiful feminine figure draped in cloth and flanked by two cherubs. "One cherub seems to be dancing and the other is holding a rectangular object in his hands. For a minute it appears to be an ancient tablet. But the longer you stare the more it looks like a laptop,"[7] according to Weeks.

Artwork is becoming more common in and around library buildings today as some cities have been given the mandate that when they build a certain percentage of that cost is to be spent on art to enhance the building.

Architecture and Library Science Professions

The professional fields of architecture and library science were forming at the same time in the late 1800s and were sharing a desire to become part of the culture of professionalism. Both were building their fields by getting professional education and developing standards of professional achievement through efficiency. "In the turn of the century architects found that they had more in common with librarians than had their predecessors and that librarians were more persuasive in their means to convey their ideas on library design. No longer content simply to describe their ideas on library design, they began to translate their ideas into material form. Starting with small pieces of library equipment, librarians steadily increased the size of the library fittings in which they shaped their work environments,"[8] wrote Abigail Van Slyck.

The Library Bureau was founded by Melvil Dewey, whose interest in introducing efficiency into library work prompted him to serve in American Library Association's (ALA) Co-operation Committee formed in 1877. Dewey had such a great interest in efficiency that he went so far as to develop a shorthand of sorts in which he shortened words, which first appear to be misspellings. In fact, his intention was to be efficient and it is interesting to note that he convinced Carnegie to support and use this simplified spelling scheme.

In addition to evaluating available library supplies, the committee Dewey was a member of was a clearinghouse, buying in bulk and passing on the savings to small libraries. Dewey continued with the supply house idea and in 1888 he established Library Bureau, whose motto was that they supplied a library "everything except the books."

After trying for the next ten years to seek involvement with the architect to offer their services for planning libraries, the Bureau introduced the Furniture Department, whose task it was "to take the library building from the general contractor, its exterior walls completed, its interior walls and floors and partitions done, and equip it with all other fixed and moveable furniture" from stock items. The same catalog offered Library Bureau's willingness to fabricate custom interior pieces from the architect's drawings or their own drafting department.[8] This appears to be the beginning of architects and people who call themselves library consultants working together. Librarians and architects each brought their own expertise to the library project and when libraries are planned that way today, keeping this philosophy from history, they tend to be the most successful projects. Library Bureau's sales meetings and lectures suggest long-standing tensions between architects and librarians had not completely dissipated and may have prevented architects from seeking out the company's (Library Bureau) expertise.[9]

Library Bureau's annual catalogs began to mention donors and trustees as clients for their consultation and custom woodwork, a change which suggests that the Bureau was trying to get their most powerful players in the library process to force architects to consult with them. During the same time period Library Bureau added illustrations to their catalogs. These became a tool for librarians to communicate their preferences to the architects. When the Bureau first used illustrations they identified the library without giving credit to the architect who worked with the library.

By 1909 the architect was given credit in the catalog, not only receiving recognition but free advertising in a nationwide market. This was quite an advantage for firms marketing themselves as library specialists and may have been the Bureau's attempt to reward the architects who used their products and services. As Library Bureau began to take into consideration the more contemporary trends in architectural design, architects began to use the company. The thought that aesthetics placed a role in library design was new to the "library world," since an earlier generation had felt that "aesthetic concerns had led architects to ignore the needs of library function."[10] It was said that Dewey's departure from Library Bureau freed the company officials to forge new ties with those in the architectural profession.

Libraries of the Past

According to Abigail Van Slyck, "Even in public areas, central libraries did not welcome all readers with equal enthusiasm. Most library boards (and the head librarian whom they employed) expressed their sense that the library was divided into two groups: serious readers or 'scholars' and casual visitors. Their written descriptions further reveal that the difference between these two groups was not the frequency that they visited the library, but the sort of reading that they did there."[11] They believed that serious users consulted reference materials and read nonfiction books, whether technology to further their business or the study of humanities and arts to use their leisure time in pursuit of "highbrow interests." In contrast to "working class habits" (like reading the daily newspaper in the library) or a preference in fiction, the library boards reinforced this class-based hierarchy by isolating these two groups. The isolation was reinforced by the fact that the social sciences, music and drama areas all flanked the magnificent entrances and were articulated on the exterior by projecting pavilions and classical urns, while the newspaper and periodical rooms were located to minimize their connection from the grand entry. The ground level and back areas held the working-class users closer to the staff areas, which were also hidden from view.

At first the Carnegie Corporation did not require that a library be designed by an architect, and no stylistic criteria were attached to the building's appearance, other than that it should signify the importance of the building to the community. The issues of exterior and interior origins were not identical. There was more the issue of exterior image so planning and the users' experience set up independent variables that created the interior that filled the needs of the community.[12] Some architectural firms built their business working on Carnegie libraries because once the architects completed a project they were considered "experienced" and were called upon to design buildings in other parts of the country. Much like today, there are not a lot of architects and designers that specialize in this field of endeavor. Cass Gilbert built his library design career working on Carnegie libraries and created a narrow band of circulation space and staff rooms to insulate the quiet rooms (for reading) from the bustle of the delivery area,[13] where library patrons retrieved their requested book. The shelving at that point in history was in the rear of the library and closed off to the public and only staff could access the books for their patrons.

"Almost every community which received a donation from Mr. Carnegie in years gone by to erect a library building came back with a plea that they had used the money in the building and no money was left to purchase book stacks and furniture,"[14] writes Van Slyck.

Middle-class women organized into fundraising groups to build libraries conflicted with Carnegie's insistence to deal with elected officials in planning libraries. The club women of Nevada, Missouri, made this connection, explicitly emphasizing the role libraries would play was in supplying "home influence" to the young unattached men of the town.[15] These women felt it their moral obligation to offer wholesome alternatives to the saloons for these men and agreed that the library location be distanced from the saloon's location. This sense of obligation was used to lobby for funding for the library and its continued growth, while the men who wrote to Carnegie took the stand that it would be good for business and act as a "magnet for development, citing the need for the library in economic rather than moral terms."[16]

Influence of Computer Usage

Furniture must be designed for much different uses than in the past. Spaces once used for reference collections, journal runs and microfilms have been traded for areas containing the maximum number of computer spaces. Services at public libraries, like downloading DVDs to personal MP3 listeners, encourage use of the library by new users who otherwise might not be patrons. Professors and students download materials for their studies now as well as spending hours in the private study quiet rooms of the library and using the reserved rooms for group study as in the past. Retirees check their stock portfolios daily at the library on the computer as they used to check the newspapers but now information is faster and more up to date. They are now also able to perform research on the stocks, allowing them to make their own decisions. Public computers are used to search genealogical research. Books can no longer stay as current as computers can, especially on topics like medicine, legal advice and business. When a health issue arises the computer allows more information to the user than they can absorb, and all because computers are available at our libraries as a free service to their patrons.

From Central to Neighborhood Branches

There is a resurgence toward community libraries as it costs more in time and money for the patrons as well as in the operation of a central library building. Branch libraries may be smaller but the convenience sometimes makes up for their size. It takes more time to travel to a central library which is located in the middle of the city. The rising square footage cost of building, leasing and maintaining space is another vote for libraries of the future. There is a movement toward building vertically, rather than spreading out, to save land. The percentage of circulation of materials is down except where it is offset by areas that are increasing in population. Computer age techniques allow so much to be gained by the patrons from using the technology. Computer classes are flourishing as part of the libraries' free classes. These classrooms are part of planning in every new or refurbished library and in attracting new users to the library.

Lighting and Utilities in the Future

Light, heat and other climatic influences are sometimes a challenge to work with. Lighting continues to be an essential design problem and glare, contrast and shadow control should be analyzed. Lighting design will continue to become more efficient and affordable as lighting options that are more natural and kinder to the eyes are available. Architects are orienting the buildings on the land and taking advantage of the terrain, learning what is helpful and what could become a detriment to building on the site. For example, opening a building to the north for natural daylight and insulating the west and east sides from the sun and heat while the south remains open to a view outside is something that our primitive ancestors did instinctively, and architects are making more use of these types of reasoning. The south face of the Phoenix Public Library's central branch is protected from the sun by motorized adjustable louvers on the exterior of the building called "shade sails," whose continual movement is regulated by a programmed computer.

Lighting is also available where computer sensors analyze lighting conditions and are programmed for dimming lights to save energy. I think we are moving toward the use of sensors that absorb the occupant's routines. When a person enters an area, lighting will be adjusted for use in that area and sensors will make an adjustment for heat or air conditioning to be turned on just before they arrive.

Comparison of the Past to the Present

Typically the entries of libraries reflect the great buildings of the past in that they are rotunda-like and spacious in their feel. The styling of libraries on the East Coast of the United States typically use pillars and the heavier wood look of libraries of the past and have a sense of stability, while the libraries in the warmer climates frequently use lighter colors and airier styles.

Until the second decade of the 1900s books in most libraries were not available to browse as they are today. You would request what you needed and it would be delivered to an area called the "delivery area/desk," which was always central to the library, like the circulation desk in today's library. It was called a charging area and was a straight desk which provided a barricade to keep the public outside and to separate the staff from the public. The public brought a request slip to the librarian and the librarian returned with a book and a charging slip for the borrower to sign. The request was named a "call slip" and books thereafter had "call numbers" to identify them in cataloging. Due to a rash of thefts and mutilations of books, the Library of Congress had to reinstate their closed stack policy in 1992 to protect their collection.

Behind the desk were the tools of the librarian, which consisted of rubber date stamps and the supplies for completing this transaction. The charging desk was arranged so that a person could reach all the necessary materials without changing position, most often seated. There was a charging tray divided into rows for the charging cards. "Patent adjustable blocks maintained the proper angle of the cards in any position. At either side of the center a large drawer arranged with extension slides for borrowers pockets. Other drawers are devoted to cash and general utility, while two contained the alphabetic register of borrowers." Even the smallest desks included a pull-out desk surface, a card catalogue on a swivel base (for the use of library staff and patrons), a storage tray (for the storage of book cards), a card sorting drawer (divided into compartments) and a drawer for a list of borrowers. Date stamp, rubber bands, paper clips and every piece of equipment had its place at the charging desk. Serving to ward off dust and to hide the clutter of cards, roller covers left the desk with an unencumbered surface that, at the turn of the century, was associated with efficiency.[17]

New York's Science, Industry and Business Library (SIBL) has returned to this method of retrieval by which visitors requesting research materials hand in requests at the "Delivery Desk" to be sent to the stacks via pneumatic tubes. Kristin McDonough, the director of SIBL, whose database is split between paper products (1.2 million volumes) and information technology supplied by computers with outlets located at each station, says that a research library thus far must supply both. "I do not see a totally digitalized environment for our purposes," says Ms. McDonough. New Yorkers are not intimidated by the new technology, as 12,000 people had signed up for the courses on how to make the most of their time at SIBL. A visitor can step up to the computerized kiosk, press a button and after an introduction by the New York Public Library's president, receive instruction on the use of the library.[18]

The Case for the Book

A project called "Library 2040: the Future in Progress" is "based on the premise that books will live on and that books enrich society and will remain forever a part of our culture. For that reason there will always be room in our civilization where we can keep books, places of collective inspiration, attractive places that are pleasant to spend time in and where we can meet books."[19] Rodeane Widom, Glendale, Arizona, Library director, agrees when she says, "I don't think libraries will be out of work for a long time because people need help with research.... A lot of students don't have the patience we do. It's helpful to have someone walk you through it instead of working on your own. Libraries will stay, but they will change."[20]

10

Using Wayfinding: Signs for Identification and Information

A library is the mesmerizing crossroads of creativity and fact.
— Johnathon Scott Fuqua

More Is Not Better

Signs are an essential part of libraries. Function and design are the most important elements when choosing signs. They are at their best when they are not noticed as signs but perform the function of guiding and are an integral part of the design. Tina Lockwood, the owner of All Sign Systems in Phoenix, Arizona, for the past 20 years, says that "More is *not* better" when it comes to good signage. Some libraries have many signs with large lettering; their intent is that the larger the sign the better it will be seen. Tina says that this is not the case, as the signs "compete for attention" with all the busy-ness of people, information and book display and often make things more confusing to the user. Too much signage in the same area can cause the user to ignore it because they are constantly bombarded with stimuli. Good signage begins with guiding the patron to the entry of the library by signs on the exterior of the building and continues to inform and direct them with directory cabinets that have information, and site maps that help to get them where they are going. "Generally," Tina says, "there will never be enough signs to satisfy everyone," so an information desk near the entry of the library is the first line of defense, as some patrons choose not to look for direction but rather to get assistance from a person.

In an article concerning the factors that contribute to the success or failure of the reference interview — the way a patron relates to the reference staff members — the data gathered confirmed that a client can be influenced positively or negatively by the interior environment. In this study, the students who were acting as the persons using the library were asked to comment on the physical setting: signs, lighting, position of the reference desk within the room, the height and appearance of the reference desk. Eighty-nine percent of the students commented on signage. More than half of them found "Information" or "Reference" signs in libraries they visited. Maps of the layout or directories of the departments and signs seemed to enhance a student's comfort level in the library. As one of the students commented, "The signs really help make this a user friendly place." When there is a lack of signs, especially for the reference and information areas, it creates a feeling of confusion. At least one student wrote:

> There was no signage for either the circulation desk or the reference desk. I did not see any signage at all in the library and at first; I thought the reference desk was part of the computer section as they are located in the same area.

Although some of the signs were seen upon entering the library, another student found that:

The signage at the information desk at Desert Broom Branch Library in Phoenix, Arizona, is a very simple question mark design applied on a vinyl material.

There were signs for checkout and the children's area, but not for the reference desk, computers, catalogs, adult fiction and nonfiction or other specific parts of the library.... The overall tone of the library was pleasant, but if I were a new client, the lack of signs or obvious direction in floor plan would leave me wondering where to start. There were no clues to help a client without asking for help the first time.[1]

Keeping it simple seems to be the best advice when it comes to providing legible and effective signage. Try to see your library for the first time with new eyes that don't understand how a library works.

Classifying and Scheduling Signs

Effective wayfinding, a term that I consider as finding the best path, uses a combination of signage, signs hung from ceilings, attached to walls, beams and facades to provide direction and give instruction. Most signs fall within three classifications: Department or Area, Room Identification and Information.

The budget for signs begins with a schedule listing of what signs you think will be needed. This will be helpful when you meet with a sign consultant. They will help you determine what is needed (by regulatory code) and in looking at the plan of your building they will be able to help you with placement of the signs. At this point you can create a sign schedule that will calculate how many signs will be needed.

The amount that you have to spend on signs will determine the options that you have in the way of materials. Although a high percentage of the signs are constructed with a variety of plastics, material choices are as varied as construction materials, including metals of all types that you might use in your home or work environment.

As with all the other areas of planning for a facility there are many decisions to be made. Will you use solid surfaces or laminates for your signage? Will it be framed, unframed or have a border to cut the cost of a frame but simulate a frame? Another clever idea is to use a transparent material that will not detract but rather blend with the surface where it is hung. Encapsulating a logo or something in keeping with the overall design concept (a leaf or a photo as examples) will complement other materials but still blend with the design and architectural feel of the area.

Large signs are also used for the major classifications that will be found in the library: fiction, nonfiction, biographies, reference, magazines and newspapers and any special collections. Large signs are used to denote major service areas, and in a school library they may designate the place to pick up student or staff handouts. In a school it is also helpful to place signs at the circulation desk with names of staff who are on duty to assist students at various times.

Signs most commonly seen in multipurpose areas are changeable "occupied/unoccupied" sliders on the front of a conference, meeting or reading room to show if it is currently in use. This type of sign can also reflect whether a person is available as a part of their name plate on the outside of their office door or hung on the fabric of a systems furniture partition. There are signs that use magnets to change the sign or to advertise events as they change. Another idea is to have a photograph of a person on their nameplate. Bronze is appropriate for signs that memorialize a person, dedicate the space or acknowledge someone for their contributions to the library.

A brass plaque is a way to honor contributors to the library. This plaque is found at the Allegany County Library in Cumberland, Maryland.

Consistency in style, design, font and color make the signage work in a library. Effective signage reduces the number of directional questions and contributes to a welcoming library and helps a person feel comfortable in the space. Signs can be constructed as individual letters, etched on the sign's surface, or applied letters to the front of the sign. Signs can be reverse engraved, which etches the back and then color fills the etched areas with a contrasting paint. The design of a sign should be simple and when the sign package is complete, the signs should complement each other.

ADA Signs

Signs today must comply with the ADA (Americans with Disabilities Act). There are three grades of ADA signage; however, only Grade 2 is approved to meet ADA regulations. Grade 1 spells out the words exactly as a sighted person reads them. Grade 2 Braille, which is a type of shorthand for the blind, and Grade 3 Braille signage use symbols that can be read by those who are trained to know by touch what the symbols mean.

Room identification sign placement is dictated by ADA to be installed between 48 inches to 60 inches from the floor on the wall in the latch side of the door. With the Grade 2 Braille the test is required to be tactile and is raised $\frac{1}{32}$" from the sign face. With this standard in place a blind or visually impaired person can easily identify and locate the room.

ADA Federal Requirements[2]

Building Signage

A) Signs which designate permanent rooms and spaces shall comply with 4.30.1, 4.30.4, 4.30.5 and 4.30.6.

B) Other signs which provide direction to or information about functional spaces of the building shall comply with 4.30.1, 4.30.2, 4.30.3 and 4.30.5.
Exception: Building Directories, Menus and all other temporary signs are not required to comply.

4.30.1 **GENERAL.** Signage required to be accessible by 4.1 shall comply with the applicable provisions of 4.30.

4.30.2 **CHARACTER PROPORTION.** Letters and numbers on signs shall have a width-to-height ratio from 3:5 to 1:1 and a stroke width-to-height ration from 1:5 to 1:10.

4.30.3 **CHARACTER HEIGHT.** Characters and numbers on signs shall be sized according to the viewing distance from which they are to be read. The minimum height is measured using an upper case X. Lower case characters are permitted.
MINIMUM CHARACTER HEIGHT: 3 inches (75 mm)

4.30.4 **RAISED AND BRAILLE CHARACTERS AND PICTOGRAMS.** Letters and numbers shall be raised 1/32" upper case, sans serif or simple serif and shall be accompanied with Grade 2 Braille. Raised characters shall be at least 5/8 inch (16 mm) high, but not higher than 2 inches (50 mm). Pictograms shall be accompanied by the equivalent verbal description placed directly below the pictogram. The border dimension of the pictogram shall be 6 inches (152 mm) minimum in height.

4.30.5 **FINISH AND CONTRACT.** The characters and backgrounds of signs shall be eggshell, matte or other non-glare finish. Characters and symbols shall contrast with their background — either light characters on a dark background or dark characters on a light background.

4.30.6 **MOUNTING LOCATION AND HEIGHT.** Where permanent information is provided for rooms and spaces, signs shall be installed on the wall adjacent to the latch side of the door. Where there is no wall space on the latch side of the door, including double-leaf doors, signs shall be placed on the nearest adjacent wall. Mounting height shall be 60 inches (1525 mm) above the finish floor to the centerline of the sign. Mounting location for such signage shall be so that a person may approach within 3 inches (76 mm) of the signage without encountering protruding objects or standing within the swing of a door.

4.30.7 **FINISH AND CONTRAST.** An eggshell finish (11 to 19 degree gloss on a 60 degree gloss meter) is recommended. Research indicates that signs are more legible for persons with low vision when characters contrast with their background by at least 70 percent.

4.30.8 **IDENTIFICATION.** Each area of rescue assistance shall be identified by a sign which states "AREA OF RESCUE ASSISTANCE" and displays the international symbol of accessibility. The sign shall be illuminated when exit sign illumination is required. Signage shall also be installed at all inaccessible exits and where otherwise necessary to clearly indicate the direction to areas of rescue assistance. In each area of rescue assistance, instructions on the use of the area under emergency conditions shall be posted adjoining the two-way communication system.

—January 1992

Planning Your Signage

After the walls are constructed, measurements should be verified to assure that all the signs needed are included on the schedule and will fit in the space allowed. Planning room identification signage includes signing any permanent rooms such as janitors' closets, electrical rooms and other utilities as well as restrooms. Also, identifying open areas by name and informational signs like emergency exit maps, stairwell identification and area of rescue assistance can be done by a walk-through and noted on the plan.

An "Area of Rescue Assistance" is an area that is predetermined by the architect when the building is laid out. It is an area that a person who could not leave the building on the best planned escape route would travel to in an emergency to wait for assistance to arrive. That area would be checked by the emergency responders to determine if there is any person in this area that needs assistance getting out of the building and at that time that person would be rescued from the emergency.

A clever solution to signing an area is illustrated here by using cut-out letters on a hanging chain link fence curtain.

End Panel Signage

To identify the placement of all the books that reside in the library, the stack ends are numbered consecutively as well as carrying the individual book's number given to it by the Dewey Decimal or the Library of Congress numbering system. This way the librarian can direct a user to the appropriate stack in which they will find a particular call number that they are looking for. Signage, Jeffrey Hoover says, must explain the subject area in a way that makes sense, and the arrangement of the collection should be as intuitive as possible. Rem Koolhaus's design for the Seattle Public Library's central library presented a solution that consisted of the collection gently sloping along a spiral through four floors. In Dewey Decimal order the books are displayed for browsing and easy access.[3] The spiral on Levels 6 through 9 allow all patrons the freedom to move throughout the entire collection without depending on stairs, escalators and elevators. Escalator and elevator stops are labeled with Dewey Decimal System numbers corresponding to materials on each floor. In addition, floor mats throughout the Books Spiral highlight Dewey Decimal numbers that correspond to nearby stacks. The Books spiral houses the majority of nonfiction collection in a continuous run and the collection can easily be expanded on the spiral, avoiding the problems of having to move books and materials to other locations and floors when various subject areas grow.

10. Using Wayfinding

The Desert Broom Public Library in Phoenix, Arizona, uses hanging chain link fence material to define areas and to hold lighting and signage for designating the areas.

End panel signs vary by shapes and sizes in the material used. ADA guidelines dictate minimum sizes and level of contrast from the background to the letters and numbers and deal with the glare issue. (See ADA Requirements for Signs.)

There are signs that are permanent as well as the type made on the computer that require a few strokes to change and mount. The signage software packages were proprietary in the past and could be used with only one manufacturer. The last few years this has changed. They are no longer proprietary so the software that you purchase can be used with any manufacturer that is chosen. The paper can be purchased from your sign supplier but you have more options of both paper color and textures if you visit a paper supplier. The paper that you get from the sign company may have perforations for tearing but that is not usually an issue since the programs predetermine sizing using an 8" × 11" sheet and then half sheet sizing. The paper inserts for changeable signs are based on using standard paper sizes as well.

There are other ways of signing a stack. The manufacturer of the steel shelving

Beaverton City Library in Oregon shows stack ends with removable signage that can be easily changed with a permanent sign identifying the area as Nonfiction.

10. Using Wayfinding

most likely will provide a basic metal with paper insert available for mounting on the end of the stack or along the front edge of a shelf. If the end panel is flat, there are more options than if it is curved. Signage can become a part of the design of the end panel, complementing the theme that has been chosen. Do not use stick-on labels on metal or wood as they will permanently mark and destroy finish or the paint.

Miscellaneous Signage

There are instructional and information signs throughout the library. Some of them are needed to instruct users on the use of the computer, the conduct that is expected in the area or where to pick up print jobs. Sizing of signs that are not determined by ADA requirements are determined by how far away it needs to be seen and how visible you want it to be and if it is something that may change (pricing of copies or hours of operation). Displays for brochures, single pages, and books as well as employee badges and name tags are available from the sign company.

Specialty framing or a kiosk can be built to coordinate a directory to the design and finish of the furniture or the interior. Neon signs can reflect the mood of the CD collection as it designates the music and movies from the rest of the CDs.

Using signage to denote quiet areas in university libraries is not always necessary because some of the areas are not designed to be quiet, as a university library might determine the need for "quiet study" floor by floor. The students develop an evolving culture in which they "self regulate," designating quiet areas by

This signage has been designed to change the event notification and hours of operation. Signs can be designed to be changeable where it is needed for maximum flexibility (courtesy of Tina Lockwood at All Sign Systems, Phoenix, Arizona).

consensus. According to Susan DiMattia, "Putting up signs or having policies for quiet study is like a speed limit on a highway. People read them as suggestions, not requirements!"[4]

To see many examples of signage and get ideas for your projects see http://www.signsearch.com. Not only will it provide ideas of materials but you can also search for local sign companies and national manufacturers in the industry.

Check This Out: Wayfinding/Signs

- Are signs on the wall, by the doors, on the stacks and hanging from the ceiling complementary in style and color?
- Are the signs simple, easy to read and logical in placement to get you from one area to another?
- Are all permanent rooms identified for the low vision and blind person?
- Are Braille markings and signage adjacent to elevator buttons?
- Is Sans Serif font used for ADA compliant signs?
- Do signs have non-glare illumination when they are backlit?
- Do wall signs at 60 inches above the floor have characters and symbols on signs raised at least $\frac{1}{32}$"?
- Are characters and background in eggshell gloss, matte, or other non-glare finish?
- Is character size in compliance with the ADA guidelines concerning optimal legibility? Is character width-to-height ratio between 3:5 and 1:1? Stroke width-to-height between 1:5 and 1:10?

ll

Green Libraries That Work

Where is the wisdom we have lost in knowledge?
Where is the knowledge we have lost in information?
Choruses from *The Rock*
— T. S. ELIOT

"Specifying wood with a clear conscious is attainable now with the right information," says Jennifer Thiele Busch in *Are You a Good Wood or a Bad Wood?* She suggests this as a basis for evaluation when specifying and procuring wood products. The key is to know what you are specifying and where it comes from, along with learning how responsible the source is to sustainable forest management. She explains that 45 percent of the cause of tropical deforestation is slash and burn agriculture and not the industrial logging (accounting for only 15 percent) that we sometimes blame for the problem.[1] The Tropical Forest Foundation in Alexandria, Virginia, a not-for-profit organization that promotes tropical forest conservation, estimates that "only a small percentage of harvested tropical hardwoods actually end up as aesthetic elements of our nation's architecture, interior design and furniture projects,"[2] but a lot of attention is paid to this subject since the design industry's use is highly visible.

Rapidly renewable materials like cork flooring are encouraged as are wood products from well managed forests. Cork, recycled resins and repurposed biodegradable pressed woods are some of the renewable sources of materials found in libraries built with the thought of preserving our environment. Furniture of the future will most likely include materials similar to the pressed wood called "Maplex" from FK Importation, a Barcelona based business focused on importing ecological and sustainable products. Bamboo is becoming more popular. The hard part is finding it in Europe and the United States. FK Importation was importing the beech from a forester who follows sustainable practice and uses recycled resins. "Ipewood" is a renewable material being researched that comes from the Rain Forest.[3] Writes

Matthew Power in "From a Bamboo Crisis — Innovation," "Lightweight, durable, and more easily renewable than wood, bamboo can be woven, mashed into pulp, and pressed into fiberboard. Bamboo's utility, and its ubiquity in some of the world's poorest regions, has led some, including India's former prime minister, Atal Bihari Vajpayee, to refer to the plant as 'green gold.'"[4] There is also a product called "plyboo," which is like plywood but made with bamboo.

Fewer Books in the Landfill?

A little closer to home, Peter Danko Designs in Pennsylvania began buying thousands of yards of overruns and mismatched dye lots of seat belting material from suppliers in the 1990s and had joined recycling efforts to use the discards from the automobile industry. As colors went out of vogue for use in new cars, crash-tested, post-industrial automotive seatbelts are given new life in eco-aware furniture by Peter Danko Design. This company was one of the pioneers in promoting green furniture. Danko educated us by explaining that "ply bending (of wood) yields 8–10 times more useable wood from a log than solid lumber."[5]

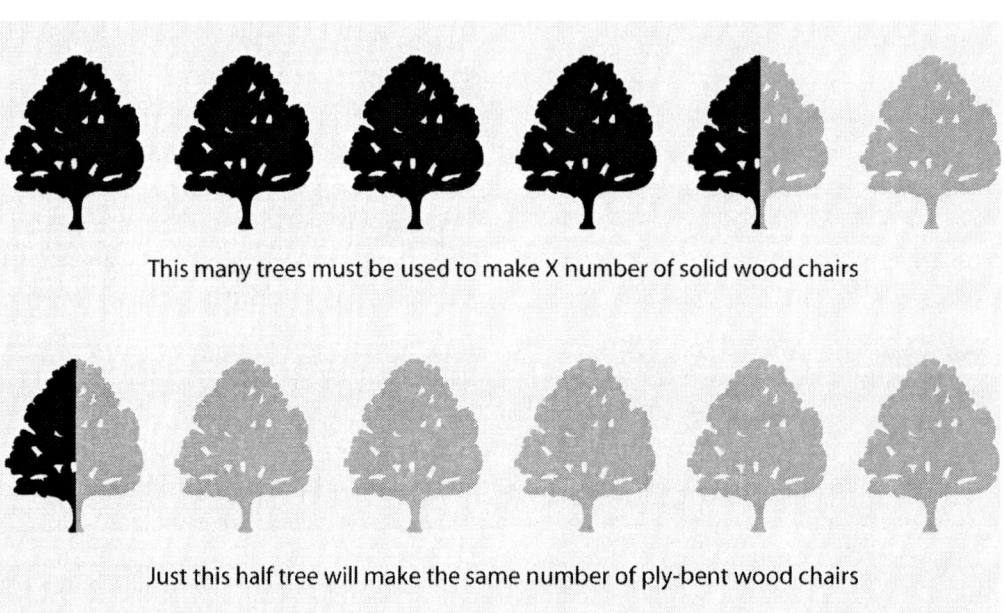

This many trees must be used to make X number of solid wood chairs

Just this half tree will make the same number of ply-bent wood chairs

Even though trees are a renewable source, this illustration shows the amount of trees affected by the decision to use solid wood for the construction of chairs as compared to using plywood (courtesy of Peter Danko Design).

11. Green Libraries That Work

Wood, Ply-bent

Ply-bent (or molded ply) furniture techniques have been around for a little over 100 years and have been explored by a handful of designers including Aalto, Eames and Danko. It is extremely efficient as the previous chart demonstrates.[6]

PLY-BENDING FACTS:

1. Ply-bending yields 8 to 10 times more usable wood from a log than solid lumber.

2. Ply-bent furniture has greater potential to outlast solid wood furniture.

3. The energy utilized in converting wood from a raw material to a finished product is minuscule when compared to any other industrial material.

"Making solid wood furniture can be an extremely wasteful process. Just think about the fact that a log is round while a wood board is rectangular. When a rectangular board is cut from a round log, all that wood in the circumference is wasted. Sure, some of it is recycled into chip-board, but chip-board is mixed with an almost equal volume of urea formaldehyde resin, an extremely toxic substance. Not cool and not healthy," says Peter Danko.[7]

Peter Danko has been building furniture this way since the 1970s and Dan Binford, a Cincinnati, Ohio, based furniture distributor who sells Danko chairs says,

These are the wood ply-bent chairs that efficiently use the lumber depicted in the illustration on page 166 (courtesy of Peter Danko Design).

"Seat belt chairs are attractive to environmentally conscious companies because the furniture helps keep belt webbing out of landfills."[8]

Some universities are talking to Google about scanning library books, called Rocket E-Books, and creating an online reading room of hard to find books on its widely used Internet search engine. This will change the landscape of the library. Rocket E-Books have become an option for reading and as they become less expensive this might replace texts for schools so that instead of carrying five or six textbooks only one could be carried. This reduction in textbooks would also be beneficial in that it would reduce the number of books that end up in landfills.

Supply and Demand

Building material pricing and availability are based according to their popularity. This is called supply and demand because as the demand

An interwoven material using surplus industrial seat belts stretched over a ply-bent chair frame that uses industrial waste and very little new lumber to create this seating (courtesy of Peter Danko Design).

increases and supply diminishes the goods' perceived value goes up. The trends follow these cost issues. As oil prices increase there are many materials that increase proportionately. Steel prices have skyrocketed due to the use of oil in processing steel. All types of laminate pricing continue to increase due to oil prices. When the Library of Congress used aluminum in the Thomas Jefferson Library (Library of Congress) it was one of the most expensive materials available. These days it is not thought of as an expensive material and is cost effective to use as a decorative trim.

As consumers who believe that our resources are being depleted and that our decisions do make a difference, we can have an impact on supply and demand. Learning about ways to save our environment and putting what we feel comfortable in supporting into action will gradually swing the pendulum of green materials cost, and the cost will begin to come down as more people get involved.

Sometimes it is just a matter of making different choices in fabricating methods (for a company) or knowing that good design exists and as a by-product it is built in a way that is good for the environment.

Businesses Good for the Environment

Josh Dorfman, cofounder and CEO of Vivavi[9] eco-friendly designed furniture and host of a radio show called *The Lazy Environmentalist*, has a mission. He feels that "consumption is damaging and will continue to deteriorate our way of life." He adds that it is possible to align our lifestyles with cleaning the planet without making sacrifices. His philosophy is that "if we care [and he says 80 to 90 percent of us do] and we don't take action then we must be 'lazy' and there is probably some of that [laziness] in just about all of us." He promotes the idea that it doesn't have to be a burden, that one can fit environmental consciousness into a lifestyle they are accustomed to and if we are provided better options to align our lifestyles for a cleaner planet[10] then we will do it.

Ira Flatow, a host on NPR who was interviewing Josh Dorfman, says that we will "'ipodicize' the environment; make products more desirable in their quality and desirability so that it has a certain 'buzz' that relates to the environment," and Josh agrees our goal would be met, "If we could create furniture that is so iconic that it stands on its own and it stands for environmentalism."[11]

LEED Certification

To encourage doing business with companies that have good environmental practices in place in their manufacturing, LEED (Leadership in Energy and Environmental Design) buildings become more prevalent. The U.S. Green Building Council, the nation's foremost coalition of leaders from across the building industry working to promote buildings that are environmentally responsible, profitable and healthy places to work and live, helped develop the LEED Green Building Rating System. The Green Building Program encourages a whole-system approach through design and building techniques to minimize environmental impact and reduce energy consumption of buildings while contributing to the health of its occupants. While controlling volatile organic compounds and reusing materials, it is a win for everyone. Materials that are reusable, recyclable or biodegradable all accumulate credit in the way of points.

There is a point system that is followed to determine LEED certification. More points elevate the level which a facility can achieve. Of 69 possible points, projects must get 26 points to be certified, 33 to give it a silver rating. Gold level is reached at 39 points and Platinum is the highest level of the LEED with a total of 52 points. One of the criteria for credit is that 25 percent of materials purchased for the building must be purchased locally or within a 500 mile radius to the project. Fayetteville Public Library in Arkansas got points for using a walnut tree harvested on the library building's site to fabricate a meeting room podium and table. The library's fireplace and retaining walls will be built with rock from the site. Using recycled, remanufactured or salvaged materials is part of obtaining LEED certification. The south-facing views allowed natural daylight to eliminate the use of some of the artificial lighting. The construction weight that they recycled or reused throughout the project would fill the University of Arkansas football stadium up to the sixth row.[12]

This is an oversimplification of the LEED process. It adds cost in the short term but may give back over time in money spent and a satisfaction that we have done something to better our conditions in the world, one building at a time. The materials don't cost more, but it is all the monitoring and documentation of the data that is costly. LEED is a voluntary consensus-based national standard for developing high performance, sustainable buildings. The library building itself can become a learning tool by setting an example of what can be done by using green building materials. It might be an inspiration to patrons to try some of the materials in buildings where they are involved.

One of the Phoenix branch libraries built in 2005 is the Desert Broom Library. This library building is the second City of Phoenix (Arizona) building considered "green." It is a LEED-certified building making extensive use of highly sustainable products. Ninety percent of the trash from the construction was recycled. Beams in the roof are recycled wood and over half of the wood used was harvested from certified sustainable forests. Countertops are recycled plastic and the backing on the flooring is made from recycled materials. All the millwork is made of wheat board, a fiber particleboard that relies on the residual straw farmers once burned after harvest. Insulation is free of formaldehyde and the columns in the building are rusted and covered with clear coat paint, eliminating the need for paint and lowering the level of volatile organic compounds. The outside lighting was designed to reduce light pollution. I found it to be comfortable and to blend into its desert setting in the park. As you walk across a bridge (also naturally rusted steel) over a wash to the entry one of the first things you notice is that there is outdoor seating around tables so that you can actually take your materials outside on patios. These areas, as well as all of the indoor areas, are defined by steel rebar on the vertical, while the inside area has few walls to divide one area from another. The architect has used flexible chain link hung off of a serpentine track to enclose the copy area, the children's area and the Teen Zone. There are also small and well-directed light

11. Green Libraries That Work

This award-winning "green library" exterior reflects the use of surplus industrial materials that are used throughout the Desert Broom Branch of the Phoenix Public Library System and creates unique new uses for them.

fixtures hanging off of the track. There are skylights to let in natural light and glass curtain walls on three sides of the building, reducing the use of electric light. Projectors are set to add lighting that reflects off the walls when the amount of natural light is deemed insufficient in the library.

Even if getting green certification is not part of your plan, you should have an interest in using vendors that manufacture using good environmental practices. Working with an architect who is interested in using environmentally friendly materials, natural ventilation and natural lighting and is concerned with proper utilization of natural energy will be an educational process by planning for the future by using sustainable design.

From all indications the libraries of the future bring more client service, as the librarians' roles are changing day by day to more of a retail assistant who is available to patrons and one who sells their services by creating an environment like that of shopping. Libraries may even end up in malls as square footage becomes more costly and the library's services are thought of as one stop on the shopping trip. A convenient and innovative option for patrons in Elmhurst, Illinois, was a drive-through window for returns. Baltimore's Enoch Pratt Free Library has its first "anchor branch" in the Highlandtown community featuring a drive-up window, a meeting room for 175 and a large enclosed atrium. The patrons are even able to sort their own returned media by using separate slots for each type of media, which frees up some of the duties of staff in the process.

Desert Broom now has one of the first drive-through windows in Arizona. Books that are on hold can be picked up, fines can be paid and any transaction except the service of staff going to the bookstacks and searching for a book can be completed at the window.

Art, discussion about books and movies and social aspects of the library are on the rise. How the library relates to the community is becoming more important in that it becomes a thriving entity and fulfills its community's wishes by providing needed services and the community responds by using its services.

The open spaces will be built, while still creating the intimate spaces to be with a book, providing flexibility that only open spaces can achieve. If the spaces are adaptable to the future and flexible today they have set the mark for buildings of the future.

To Our Health

According to the Environmental Protection Agency, "At present, not much is known about what health effects occur from the levels of organics usually found in homes. Many organic compounds are known to cause cancer in animals; some are suspected of causing, or are known to cause, cancer in humans."[13] Nontoxic finishes remove uncertainty and ensure healthier homes and a healthier environment.

Finishes like adhesives are an essential part of the furniture making process because they help preserve and protect furniture from water, household spills and general everyday use. Nontoxic finishes like Danish Oil Wax help eliminate volatile organic compounds (VOCs) from entering our homes and are safer for the environment. VOCs can be highly toxic and dangerous to human health. The Forest Stewardship Council (FSC) is an international not-for-profit organization founded in 1993 by environmental groups like Greenpeace, the Sierra Club and World Wildlife Fund. Its mandate is to protect the world's forests through globally recognized principles of responsible forest stewardship. FSC-certified sustainable wood is the only wood that is accepted under the U.S. Green Building Council's stringent LEED program. Part of what makes the FSC unique is the way in which it protects the rights of aboriginal peoples to utilize the forest for their culture, livelihood and spirituality.[14]

The following is from Vivavi's Website:

> John Wiggers is a studio furniture maker who specializes in contemporary and Art Deco inspired designs. His holistic approach to furniture making often combines exotic veneers with unusual inlays such as metal, glass, stone and mother-of-pearl. The spirit of John's work reflects his deep philosophical commitment to environmental responsibility and sustainability, largely by way of his involvement with the Forest Stewardship Council (FSC) and his use of FSC-certified woods. On Earth Day 1998 John became one of the first furniture makers in the world to become certified by Smartwood to the rigorous chain-of-custody standards of the FSC. Between 2000 and 2004 John also served on the board of FSC Canada in a variety of roles, including treasurer and chair. In his travels and through his work with the FSC John has met a variety of aboriginal peoples, from the Kogi of the remote mountains of Columbia in South America to the Haida of the Pacific Northwest in Canada. These experiences have given John considerable insight into the profound ancient wisdom held by many aboriginal cultures, including some of the traditional holistic and medicinal uses of various plants and trees from the forest. This has translated into a holistic perspective that manifests in John's design aesthetic by way of subtle manipulations of natural forms and materials.[15]

I have selected some of the sustainable wood resources from the Vivavi furniture Website to share some of my research on how we could improve our health by our choices in materials.

Excerpt taken from "Eco-Glossary" on Vivavi.com

Wood, Acacia

This superior wood comes from pod-bearing trees and is known for its beautiful grain and rich contrasting colors. In addition to being environmentally friendly, acacia has another unique distinction — it appears to change color and luster in different lighting conditions (a property called "chatoyancy"). The wood can morph from a light tan to dark brown. Acacia is also naturally resinous which makes it waterproof and impervious to stains and odors. A quick wash with soapy water is all the maintenance your acacia items require.

Wood, Amboyna

Amboyna is a lustrous reddish/gold colored hardwood that is sometimes referred to as Narra. The particular Amboyna used in the John Wiggers Collection carries a special provenance in the world of sustainable forest management, because it comes from the last remaining board known to exist of the very first wood to be sustainably harvested on the Solomon Islands in the early to mid–1990s.

Wood, Black Walnut

In his furniture pieces, designer John Wiggers will often inlay a rare sampling of Black Walnut wood into areas that are frequently touched. Native American medicine women discovered through many generations of trial, error and observation that this sampling of Black Walnut wood has medicinal properties that are useful in the prevention and treatment of disease. It is believed that simply touching this wood will allow the active molecules (known scientifically as ellagitannins) of the tree to contact the surface of one's skin, where these molecules can be absorbed into the pores. In recent years a scientific basis for this ancient wisdom has been discovered, and these ellagitannin molecules are now at the leading edge of ongoing cancer research.

Wood, Hawthorn

Hawthorn is an extremely rare hardwood that was well known to ancient Greek herbalists, and has been used in Ayurvedic medicine dating back over 5,000 years. In North America the bark, root bark, leaves, fresh and dried fruit, together with the nutlet seeds were used as a source of medicine. Hawthorn gives off natural aroma therapeutic properties that are found to be hypotensive (they help relieve stress). Hawthorn extracts are used in modern medicine as cardio tonics and also as effective coronary vasodilators.

Wood, Sassafras

Sassafras wood is native to North America, although variations of this tree species can be found in different parts of the world. The word Sassafras comes from an aboriginal people known as the Narragansett, whose home was Long Island Sound. These people used the Sassafras as a source of medicine, as have many eastern tribes since time immemorial. Sassafras wood produces an aromatic fragrance that is easily absorbed by the body, and produces an overall sense of well being. This fragrance is very closely related to Myrrh, one of the legendary spices of the ancient world. Sassafras is also used for purification in the Native American tradition of the sweat lodge ceremony. John Wiggers will often use Sassafras to make pencil trays or drawer components. This allows the aroma therapeutic qualities of the Sassafras to accumulate naturally inside the drawer while it is closed, so that it can be released each time the drawer is pulled open.

Wood, Kiri

Kiri wood comes from the fast-growing paulownia tree and is praised not only for its striking natural grain, but also for being lightweight, strong and durable. Unlike most woods Kiri also avoids warping.

12

Forward Thinking

A camel is a horse designed by committee.
— Sir Alec Issigonis

Whose Vision Is It?

Since it takes a team to create a successful building, a choice will need to be made. Is the architect hired to help manifest *your* visualization of your library or will they be given the authority to create the vision? Neither is the right way and neither is the wrong way. Just be aware that there are two different ways of working and it is your choice. If the architect is chosen to help make decisions based on their expertise in the area of making buildings work and the librarian contributes by sharing what they know about how a library works, this is the best scenario. One issue that will impact your choice is the time that staff desires to spend or has available to invest in the project. If the staff is already stretched thin with the responsibilities of keeping the library operating, then the decision may be to give the architect more leeway in learning the needs and concerns of the library and to design the building reflecting what is important to the library. By going through the process of finding the right architect at the right price with the right attitude (and I use the word "right" not to mean correct when compared to incorrect) but rather one that will appear to have the qualities that match the requirements and personality of the project.

The team will need to have a plan of their own before bringing the architect into the picture. It would be helpful, thus saving time and money, if inventory is made of any existing furniture, noting size, condition (if it needs refinishing or reupholster of seating) and some idea of what type of furniture the library will use in the future. Looking at catalogs and other recently completed libraries and exchanging information with those on the staff who have been through a building project or renovation and who may have ideas is a start. Keep photos on the computer or in a paper file of the things that you like while doing your research.

If the committee changes their mentality along the way, without consideration to accomplishing the desired end result, the building will lose a part of what it was to be. Not that a project does not evolve. It is always changing according to new information brought to the decision makers. For example, if the library director has decided that they want a library that will use furniture they imagine will last 20 more years they will be vested in choosing something that is found to be low maintenance, with the ability to withstand use but they may be aware (maybe from past experience) that they have to pay more for this type of furniture. If they do not know this, as they become aware of this fact the choice may change.

And this is where it gets tricky. They may have in their mind that they want all these things, but feel that they "can't afford it." They should get their equipment list together and have a budget compiled for their project. That is the *only* way they will be able to determine initial cost. If only they can see that by buying the better furniture they will be further ahead, happier along the way (not having problems that poorly made furniture causes) and know that they are not contributing to a throwaway society. If they buy goods that are *not* made to last, they contribute to goods being made by low cost (under unfair trade agreements) labor and sold cheaply, and *that* is what we get more of. We as consumers create the offering by what we will pay for. If people continue to have the idea that it doesn't matter what they contribute to, they will under cut the manufacturers that are still making goods to last, and at some point these higher priced goods will no longer be in the offering.

It is helpful to work with a manufacturer through their representative to compile specifications for the desired product. If you are going to go this direction it is important to inform the rep up front that they are going to bid against other manufacturers. The rep can then help you compare apples to apples and will realize from the start that they might not get the job. That way, even if they do not get the job and you need to work with them in the future, you are building a fair and honest relationship.

If the decision is made to purchase from a particular manufacturer based on value for the dollar and the decision makers allow another manufacturer to bid product that is of a different (lesser) quality and a decision is made to go with the less expensive product only because it is cheaper, the end user is making it harder for the manufacturer who worked with them through the process to the end and then didn't receive the job. If all parties are honest from the beginning in the budget that they have to work with and what they are truly interested in, everyone can work toward making sure that they get what they really want.

12. Forward Thinking

Thoughts on Books and People

Historical library buildings were most likely to have thick walls and few windows. The purpose of the library structure in those times focused on warehousing books and protecting materials rather than circulating them. Today the library is competing with book stores and other retail venues, especially when located in neighborhoods, where branch libraries tend to be built. Making the spaces spacious and inviting is the challenge of working on the remodeling of historic buildings. Instead of filling them up with more shelving, mobile units are used as display opportunities. As I've spoken with librarians about what they would like to see from the manufacturers in the future, they have mentioned shelving that moves. The problem with the existing shelving is that, although the shelving can be adjusted up or down at one inch increments within the shelving, when a librarian is back shifting as is necessary as the circulation grows, the deeper shelves that once were appropriate for deeper books are now being used for regular books, while standard depth shelves end up with the deeper sized books. "It isn't good for the book to not be supported by a full shelf. The deeper book when sitting on a deeper shelf is more likely to fall off the shelf," says Kelly Hudson, page supervisor for the City of Scottsdale Civic Center Library.

Archival storage teaches us that books like to be cool and stored in dark places. A refrigerator was suggested as being perfect except one is never sure that it is dark in there without checking (and then it isn't). I've learned that books can literally be frozen for long term storage protection. It is all "basic chemistry," says Michael McColgin, conservation officer for the State of Arizona Archives and Records. If you want to speed up a chemical reaction (in this case the reaction of the book materials to aging) you warm it up. On the other hand if you want to slow down the chemical reaction, you cool down the elements. When the new building is built for Archives in Arizona, the collection will experience a cool 55 degrees. Wouldn't you love to have a job there in the middle of an Arizona summer?

Through the ages, it has been said that the book likes a temperature cooler than people and darker than is comfortable for a person to spend their time in, let alone read. Bernard Green directed the construction of the Library of Congress as well as the erection of the shelving that he engineered and created for that building. The shelving was designed with metal shelves that were slotted to improve air flow.[1] Green felt that daylight was "the most unequal and unsteady of all human dependencies, under the ever-changing position of the sun and condition of the weather." Furthermore bright sunlight is the enemy of the book — "books in fact are much better off in the dark" — and so he noted that when we make anxious provision to let it in, we must make similar expensive provision for keeping it out."[2]

Independently wealthy collectors of books, like Paul Getty of Oxfordshire, England, didn't want to risk the books being exposed to sunlight. The director at Getty's castle pointed out that central heating is no friend of books, and the cooler they are the better for them. Getty said that "books, like wine, need to be kept at a regular, unfluctuating temperature."[3] And we all know how cool the typical castle's temperature was.

Places for People, Places for Books

In 1991 the main Library of California State University opened a new robotic book retrieval system in the Oviatt Library located in Northridge, a suburb of Los Angeles, California. The goal was to save students time and to save the school money. Students use the computer to request a book and the robotics get the book from a bin in an 8,000 square foot area designed to hold more than one million volumes. Doug Davis, the acting dean of the university libraries, said that they would "need an area 100,000 square foot of space just for the books," if they used traditional open shelving. He added that "it would cost $100,000 per year to maintain the robotic system compared to $400,000 to care for the volumes in traditional library stacks. Our motivation in getting the system was the reduction of long term costs."[4] Digital libraries are definitely a viable option. In 1998, it cost about 20 cents to store one megabyte of information, or $2.00 a book; a book's total cost is closer to $40.00.[5]

To retrieve a book from the system at California State University, a student types a code into the computer library computer, which directs the robotic crane to the appropriate storage bin. The last two digits of the bar code are used. The bin is placed on the electronic track vehicle and carried through the ceiling to a librarian at the circulation desk who removes the book and forwards it to the main circulation desk. In this library this system is used only for older periodicals and books that are used infrequently, while the frequently used books are found in open stacks. "Time from the initial request to availability to the circulation desk is under ten minutes,"[6] estimates the library.

Theories of what a future library may look like include an idea of silo-like storage in which books could be placed on their sides in a pigeon hole which would be the size to comfortably house a book on its side with spine out, its ID chip placed so that the robotic spider on a web that consists of a moveable apex of the horizontal and vertical cables is controlled by the book's address. The robot moves between two horizontal bars. These bars move up and down the column so that the spider can fully access the matrix of addresses. There might be two notches on the shelf, which would allow the book to be properly supported by two mini-fork lift "hands" grabbing the book securely toward the midline, protecting the top and bottom of the spine. Traveling on that matrix a retrieved book could scan to retrieve, return and make note of any repairs or cleaning that it might sense needing upon return. Periodically and when time permits the books that need to be viewed by staff would be gathered and mended or weeded out to make room for a more heavily circulated book.

The chip embedded within the book would keep records of the ongoing maintenance and its replacement with a new book. Giving the average book a 2" H × 12" L × 10" D home, 1,260 books could be housed in a space approximately 10' L × 10' H × 20" D. In a traditional bookshelf, using the same footprint would give you storage of less than 500 books on a double-sided unit 90 inches tall.

Since robots are just as happy "climbing" 100 feet as they are 10 feet, this new type of storage could hold 12,000 books in the same footprint. The benefit to this theoretical storage arrangement would be threefold; the book could stay in an environment optimal for its life cycle to counteract the wear, tear and discomfort it might be subjected to on the "outside" of its new home (while in circulation). Stored in its ideal temperature, darkness, and humidity while dustfree are great advantages. Its spine is not subjected to the downward weight causing pages to splay. Continuous dusting will no longer be a problem. Energy costs could be reduced because the silo could remain dark except for any needed maintenance of the area. Large openings could be used for the larger books while smaller books could be housed on smaller shelves, as they would each have permanent addresses.

People would be able to expand into the areas that are currently warehousing books and there would be a distinct plan of creating places for people and places for books. Not only is some of the layout reclaimed for people but there are no restraints on the temperature or light that streams into the reading rooms that surround this core of book storage, or any changes that make the places for people the most comfortable place that they could enjoy being.

Similar to the way that teens are creating their spaces, community input could assist planners in designing their ideal concept of a comfortable space. While the teens' area needs to be a stimulating area and a place for hanging out with friends and the children's area needs to be playful while educational, I'm confident that adults have their ideas for an area they'd enjoy. People who imagine the ideal reading area as cozy, complete with relaxing lounge seating and floor lamps, could spend time there. People who are comfortable in an outdoor area with benches could read in a park-like atmosphere where the indirect lighting poured throughout the area like a sunny day. Those who want to bring even more nature inside could spend time in an area next to fountains or a waterfall element with a sky that changes overhead. There could also be the possibility of allowing people to choose the theme or surroundings which match their mood for that day. Many of the technologies for creating these types of environments currently exist. You need to look no further than Las Vegas's casinos' public areas to see ideas like these put into their entertainment venue.

Current periodicals and popular books would be traditionally shelved on display, while the books requested by patrons and brought by robots would be at the retrieval station in a matter of minutes. Staff might take a different role, continuing to advance in cross-training for a variety of job descriptions and providing even greater technical support for the patrons.

Embracing Technology

Dr. James H. Billington, Librarian of Congress, says that "At the heart of the National Digital Library effort is something important to all libraries: the belief that old institutions, in order to survive, must embrace new technologies while maintaining old values."[7] If the library patron had an objection to this new concept of a virtual library it might be that they would no longer be able to physically hold a book and peruse the book to see if they indeed would have an interest in reading it. What if they still could do this — in a *virtual* way? That is, to be able to view the book's spine as shown on a traditional book stack. Imagine this: each published book comes from the publisher equipped with its own record, a unique file showing the image of the book, spine and cover, information about the author and publisher with pertinent details, the table of contents, index and the physical address of the book (where it resides by the number given it). The reader could open that book on the screen and view the table of contents, etc., to determine their interest in the book and to see if it is a book they want to take a closer look at or maybe check out. They select the virtual book, which automatically launches the robot to bring the book to the retrieval desk closest to their location. At the retrieval desk where they physically pick up the book, they check out the book. If you decide against taking it out of the library, or when you are ready to return it, you scan the book at a reader and it is returned to its address by the robotic spider until it is called again by another reader.

The library could become first and foremost a place for people, while it remains not only a safe but ideal place for the book. The success for the library of the future rests with the library planners now and in the future. If there is a new concept that combines the familiarity of today's library (the way it looks and works) and the automation available today for tomorrow's libraries, the new models of the library could attract more users and provide the comfort to keep them for a longer time. Libraries are changing. Let's become a participant in that change.

12. Forward Thinking

Do you think that a virtual library makes sense? Log on to http://www.libraryfurnishings.com and send us your comments.

In Conclusion

We have come a long way from the libraries' beginnings, where user's spaces were dictated by their gender, age and social standing. Now our goal is to plan spaces that no one, regardless of age, ability or any known classification, is treated any differently than anyone else; rather it will be a place where everyone has the same opportunities to learn and advance their knowledge. As we learn more about our environment and how to preserve it for future generations, and more about a person's comfort and what needs to be done to take good care of our books so that everyone can enjoy them, our libraries can only get better.

Appendix A:
Defining Tasks and Responsibilities of the Development Team*

> *"Planning is an Art, not a Direct Science."*
> — Keyes Metcalf

Librarian/Library "IT" Professionals Tasks

    1. Involve other areas of the library such as AV (audiovisual) technicians, IT (information technology) person, teachers (in the academic library) and children's librarians (in a public library).

    2. Develop the electronic equipment schedule, listing size of equipment, amperage or wattage requirements along with special requirements like shielding, surge protection or proper ventilation.

    3. Determine the equipment to be placed at each carrel work station, table and desk.

    4. Anticipate future requirements such as online catalog, computer lab. Locate these data/electrical requirements within the furniture and shelving.

    5. Determine how many receptacles (electrical and data) are required for patron appliances and anticipated power requirements, determining access location of data and power above or below work surface.

    6. Determine the data medium based upon current standards.

    7. Determine the work flow of the circulation desk and the way your patrons approach the service desks to receive assistance.

    8. Learn what the architect expects you to provide and what the architect/interior design person will provide you along the way as a "reality check" that the interior is moving in the desired direction (i.e., periodic meetings at the start-up becoming more frequent as the project nears completion).

Interior Architect/Designer Tasks

    1. Select the type of electrical for the building.

2. Develop the electrical plan for the building to include electrical requirements of furniture and equipment.

3. Designate a contact person at both the architect and the library that all the correspondence will go through along with a process to get questions answered.

4. Create a set of documents that translate and satisfy the needs of your project both functionally and visually.

Designer/Planner/Library Consultant Tasks (often the Architect)

1. Identify the needs for each station or service desk. Determine the appropriate electrical system for the furniture and the total number of wires to be pulled to each range of furniture.

2. Evaluate existing furniture for reuse in the new building. Could it fit in the overall concept? Does reupholstering or refinishing make good cost sense? Are there any pieces that have historical significance to the library?

Furniture Manufacturer Tasks

1. Develop electrical plan for the furniture being chosen.
2. Provide proper installation instructions.
3. Be technologically informed.
4. Stay in compliance with standards and codes.

Government or School Administration Authority Tasks

1. Coordinate issues with purchasing department.
2. Interact with architect concerning community issues.

Owner Agent Tasks (on large projects)

1. Protect the owner's interest, acting as a liaison between the contractor, owner and architect.
2. Check blueprints for accuracy to actual build-out
3. Keep a paper trial of answers to concerns and question of owner
4. Provide for a smooth installation from the planning stages to construction phase, making sure that the construction is completed in a good workmanlike manner.

Conclusion

The development team consists of many constituents who must be represented. Some of this team might wear a few hats. Failure to include any of the above broad categories may result in a facility that either has duplicated or omitted requirements. To avoid changes in the plan of building it is imperative that the furniture be planned and be electrically specified before the architect and the electrical engineer plan the circuitry and power locations for the building. It is always necessary to appoint one person who monitors the building to assure that it matches the blueprint for dimensions and location of power.

*This appendix was adapted and expanded from *Current Solutions* (copyright 1987) by The Warden Company.

Appendix B: Evaluation of Work Station Seating

- **WORK POSTURES**— The workstation is designed or arranged for doing computer tasks so that it allows your: YES   NO
  1. Head and neck to be upright or inline with the torso (not bent down/back). If this is false, see Monitors, Chairs and Worksurfaces. ____ ____
  2. Head, neck and truck to be face forward (not twisted). Refer to Monitors or Chairs if false. ____ ____
  3. Trunk to be perpendicular to the floor (may lean back into backrest but not forward). If false refer to Chairs and Monitors. ____ ____
  4. Shoulders and arms to be lined up with the torso, generally about perpendicular to the floor and relaxed (not elevated or stretched). If not, refer to Chairs. ____ ____
  5. Upper arms and elbows to be next to the body (not extended outward). If false, refer to Chairs, Worksurfaces, Keyboards and Pointers. ____ ____
  6. Forearms, wrists and hands to be straight and inline (forearm at about 90 degrees to the upper arm). If false see Chairs, Keyboards and Pointers. ____ ____
  7. Wrists and Hands to be straight (not bent up/down or sideways toward the little finger). If false, refer to Keyboards and Pointers. ____ ____
  8. Thighs to be parallel to the floor and the lower legs to be perpendicular to the floor (thighs may be slightly elevated above the knee). If false refer to Chairs or Worksurfaces. ____ ____
  9. Feet rest flat on the floor or are supported by a stable footrest. If false refer to Chairs and Worksurfaces. ____ ____

- **SEATING**— Consider these points when evaluating the chair:
  10. Backrest provides support for your lower back (lumbar area). ____ ____
  11. Seat depth and width accommodate the specific user (seat pan not too big/small). ____ ____
  12. Seat front does not press against the back of your knees and lower legs (seat pan not too long). ____ ____

Appendix B

	YES	NO
13. Seat has cushioning and is rounded with a "waterfall" front (no sharp edge).	___	___
14. Armrests, if used, support both forearms while you perform computer tasks and they do not interfere with movement.	___	___
"No" answers to any of these questions should prompt a review of Chairs.	___	___

- **KEYBOARD/INPUT DEVICE**-Consider these points when evaluating the keyboard or pointing device:

15. The keyboard/input device platform(s) is stable and large enough to hold a keyboard and an input device.	___	___
16. Input device (mouse or trackball) is located right next to your keyboard so it can be operated without reaching.	___	___
17. Input device is easy to activate and the shape/size fits your hand (not too big or too small).	___	___
18. Wrists and hands do not rest on sharp or hard edges.	___	___
"No" answers to any of these questions should prompt a review of Keyboards, Pointers or Wrist Rests.	___	___

- **MONITOR**— Consider these points when evaluating the monitor. The monitor is designed or arranged for the computer tasks so the:

19. Top of the screen is at or below eye level so you can read it without bending your head/neck down/back.	___	___
20. User with bifocals or trifocals can read the screen without bending the head or neck backward.	___	___
21. Monitor distance allows you to read the screen without leaning your head, neck or trunk forward/backward	___	___
22. Monitor position is directly in front of you so that you do not have to twist your head or neck.	___	___
23. Glare (for example, from windows or lights) is not reflected on your screen, which can cause you to assume an awkward posture to clearly see information on your screen.	___	___
"No" answers to any of these questions should prompt a review of Monitors or Workstation Environment.		

- **WORK AREA**— Consider these points when evaluating the desk and workstation. The work area is designed or arranged for doing computer tasks so the:

24. Thighs have sufficient clearance space between the top of the thighs and your computer table/keyboard platform (thighs are not trapped).	___	___
25. Legs and feet have sufficient clearance space under the work surface so you are able to get close enough for the keyboard/input device.	___	___

- **ACCESSORIES**— Check to see if the

26. Document holder, if provided, is stable and large enough to hold documents.	___	___

Evaluation of Work Station Seating

	YES	NO

27. Document holder, if provided, is placed at the same height and distance as the monitor screen so there is little head movement or need to refocus, when you look from, the document to the screen. _____ _____
28. Wrist/Palm rest, if provided, is free of sharp or square edges that push on your wrists. _____ _____
29. Wrist/ Palm rest, if provided keeps your forearms, wrists and hands straight and inline when using the keyboard/input device. _____ _____
30. Telephone can be used with your head upright (not bent) and your shoulders relaxed (not elevated) if you do computer tasks at the same time. _____ _____

"No" answers to any of these questions should prompt a review of Worksurfaces, Document Holders, Wrist, Rest or Telephones.

- **GENERAL**

31. Workstation and equipment have sufficient adjustability so that you are in a safe working posture and can make occasional changes in posture while performing computer tasks. _____ _____
32. Computer work station, components and accessories are maintained in serviceable condition and function properly. _____ _____
33. Computer tasks are organized in a way that allows you to vary tasks with other work activities, or to take micro-breaks or recovery pauses while at the workstation. _____ _____

"No" answers to any of these questions should prompt a review of Chairs, Worksurfaces, or Work Processes.

Reproduced from: OSHA Ergonomic Solutions: Computer Workstations e Tool-Evaluation Checklist August 2003 available at: http://www.osha.gov/SLTC/etools/computerworkstations/checklist.html (see also Purchasing Guide Checklist at www.OSHA.gov)

Appendix C: Survey 26 ADA with Diagrams

Use with the Minimum Requirements Summary Sheets and ADAAG. Use Survey Forms 1 to 22 as applicable, as well as this form.

Facility Name:

In addition to the requirements of ADAAG 4.1 through 4.35, libraries must comply with ADAAG 8.

Library Location:

Section	Item	Technical Requirements	Comments	Yes	No
8.2	Reading and Study Areas:	Do at least 5% (but not less than one) of fixed seating, tables, or study carrels comply with 4.2 and 4.32 (See below)?			
4.2.4 4.32.2	Seating Clear Floor Space:	Do spaces provided for wheelchair users have a 30 by 48 inch clear space which overlaps an accessible route?			
		Is no more than 19 inches of the 30 by 48 inch clear space measured under the table? (See Figure 45)			
4.32.3	Knee Space:	Is the knee space under the table at least 27 inches high, 30 inches wide, and 19 inches deep? (See Figure 45)			
4.32.4	Height:	Is the top of the table between 28 and 34 inches from the floor?			
4.3.3	Aisles:	Are the aisles leading up to and between the tables or study carrels at least 36 inches wide?			

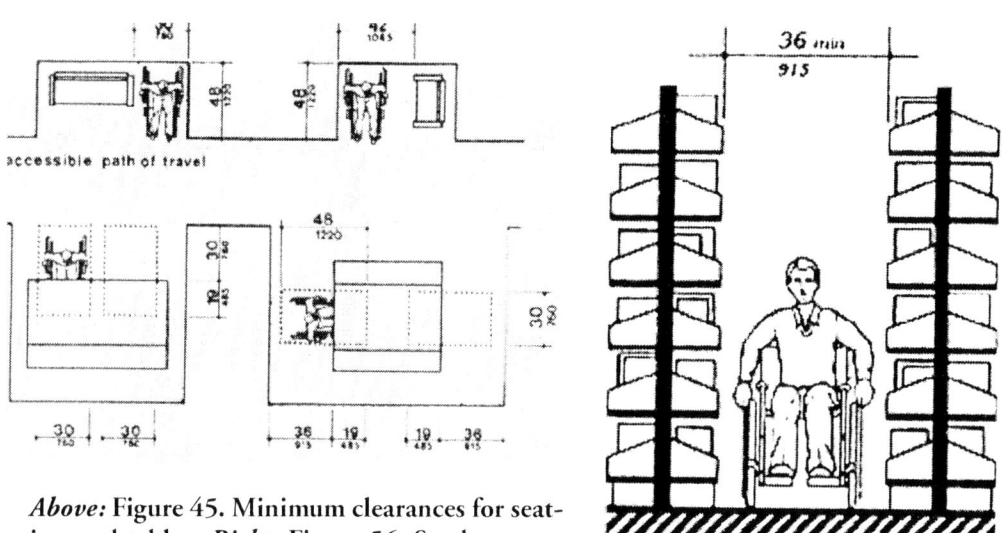

Above: Figure 45. Minimum clearances for seating and tables. *Right:* Figure 56. Stacks.

Section	Item	Technical Requirements	Comments	Yes	No
8.3 7.2(1)	Check-Out Areas:	Is there at least one lane at each check-out area where a portion of the counter is at least 36 inches long and no more than 36 inches high?			
8.3 4.13	Security Gates:	Do security gates or turnstiles comply with 4.13? (Use Form 10: Doors and Gates) OR Is there an accessible gate or door next to a turnstile or security device?			
8.4	Card Catalogs and Magazine Displays:	Is the aisle between card catalogs and magazine displays at least 36 inches wide?			
	Reach:	Are the card catalogs between 18 and 54 inches from the floor? (A height of 48 inches is preferred.)			
8.5 4.3	Stacks:	Is the minimum clear aisle width between the stacks at least 36 inches? (See Figure 56) (A minimum clear aisle width of 42 inches is preferred where possible. Shelf height in stack areas is unrestricted.)			

Appendix D:
Electronic Planning Table

Electronic Planning Table

ELETRONIC PLANNING TABLE

EQUIPMENT	QTN	SIZE			LOCATION ON PLAN	Data?	Telephone?	AMPS	Ventilation Required?
		Width	Depth	Height					
ANY ADDITIONAL INFORMATION									
Make a copy of this sheet for your project to document requirements for electrical and data									
Tish Murphy http://www.libraryfurnishings.com									

Appendix E: "Watt" Amperage Is Required?

It is important we do not overload the circuits. National Electrical Code (NEC) advises to plan loads only to 80 percent of the 20 amp rating (16 amps per circuit).

The following are examples of the amperage draw of some common equipment used in a library. (Exact amperage draw must be determined by reading the electrical placard on the equipment.)

Equipment	Amps	Equipment	Amps
Calculator	00.050 amps	Printer, Laserjet	06.400 amps
Clock/Radio	00.100 amps	Reader Printer:	
Coffee Warmer	01.500 amps	Fiche	6.0–10.00 amps
Copier	15.000 amps	Film	10.0–13.0 amps
CPU	2.0–4.0 amps	Reader:	
Fax Machine	01.000 amps	Fiche	1.0 amp
Folding Machine	04.200 amps	Film	1.0 amp
Letter Opener	02.100 amps	Scanner	00.450 amps
Monitor, 15"	01.800 amps	Slide Projector	01.500 amps
Monitor, 20"	02.500 amps	Space Heater	10.500 amps
Paper Shredder	04.500 amps	Task Light, 17 watt	00.750 amps
Pencil Sharpener	00.560 amps	Task Light, 25 watt	01.000 amps
Postage Machine	03.400 amps	Typewriter	01.500 amps
Printer	01.500 amps	Visual Display Unit	01.000 amps
Printer, Deskjet	04.000 amps		

Appendix F: Sources of Information

General

www.augustinc.com	Children's furniture with replaceable upholstery on-site
www.afb.org/info	American Foundation for the Blind, Facts About Aging & Vision
www.allsignsystems.com	Interior and exterior signage
www.bigcozybooks.net	Upholstered book furniture
www.buckstaff.com	Furniture
www.cryptonfabric.com	Fabric with "permanent protection"
www.gressco.com	Children's furniture
www.librisdesign.org/docs/furniture finaltext_newdoc?bbatt=y	
www.libraryfurnishings	
www.librarydisplayshelving.com	Acrylic shelving for display
www.litecontrol.com	
www.loc.com	Library of Congress
www.theledlightcom/lumens.html	
www.otherpower.com/otherpower_lighting.html	Efficient lighting
www.lib.az.us/archives/g-preservation.cfm	Preservation of materials
www.lib.az.us/archives/conservation.cfm	Conservation
www.mockett.com	Doug Mockett—grommets, electrical management
www.mjshelving.com	Cantilevered library steel shelving company
www.nessenlighting.com	Lighting company
www.nedcc.org/plam3/tleaf24.html	Protection from light damage
www.proloconline.com	

www.peterdanko.com/greendesign.html	Green design of furniture
www.sustainabledesignguide.unm.edu/MSDG/materials_pi.html	
www.signsearch	Examples of signs
http://www.3m.com/us/home_leisure/scotchgard/furniture.jhtml	3 M Scotchgard fabric protection
www.totalibra.com	Furniture and shelving
www.tmcfurniture.com	The Midlands Company-cutout designs on furniture
www.treehugger.com	Green materials archive
www.usgbc.com	United States Green Building Council-LEEDS certification
www.universaldesignonline.com	
www.universaldesign.com	
www.ul.com/consumers	Underwriters Laboratory
www.westinnielsen.com	Plus Size seating

ADA Links

www.janweb.icki.wvu.edu/kinder/linkframe.htm	ADA Document Center-index of federal disability-related documents
www.access-by-design.com	Guide to ADA including hints and product resources and bulletin board
www.adaptenv.org/schools/default.asp	The National Information Center for Children & Youth with Disabilities(includes state by state resource list)
http://indie.ca	Integrated Network of Disability Information & Education-Canadian Resources
http://members.aol.com/jylbear/	Jillene's Disability Resources-site for parents & educators of children with disabilities
www.human.com/mkt/access/	Access Media Information offers compliance information and "how-to" aids for businesses, schools and government agencies
www.know-the-ada.com	Arizona Office for Americans with Disabilities specific to Arizona laws and implementation
www.usdoj.gov/crt/ada/adahom1.htm	U.S. Department of Justice-extensive list of resources and information relating to ADA

Other Helpful Contact Numbers

Office on the Americans with Disability Act
(202) 514-0301

Architectural and Transportation Barriers Compliance Board
(800) USA-ABLE

Chapter Notes

Introduction

1. Abigail A. Van Slyck, *Free to All: Carnegie Libraries and American Culture 1890–1920* (Chicago: University of Chicago Press, 1995), 33.
2. Richard J. Bazillion and Connie L. Braun, *Academic Libraries as High-Tech Gateways: A Guide to Design and Space Decisions*, 2nd Edition (American Library Association 2001), 66, from *Planning Academic and Research Buildings*, 3rd edition, ed. Philip D. Leighton and David C. Weber (Chicago: American Library Association, 1999).
3. *Single Building: Phoenix Central Library; Process of an Architectural Work*, ed. Oscar Riere Ojeda, with an introduction by Nader Tehrani (Rockport Publishers, 1999), 22.
4. Vicky Hallett, "Teaching with Tech, " *U.S. News and World Report*, 17 October 2005, 55–58.

Chapter 1

1. Brian Kenney, "The Library Reloaded," *Library Journal* (December 2003): 8–10.
2. Allan Konya, ed., *Libraries: A Briefing and Design Guide*, 2nd edition (New York: Architectural Press Series, London: Vos Nostrand Reinhold, 1986).
3. http://www.homepage.ntlworld.com/g.blaike/interiors.htm, "Inside the Libraries, 1907"; photographs of Langside Library contributed by Wilma Moore.
4. Lynda M. Baker and Judith J. Field, "Reference Success; What Has Changed Over the Past Ten Years?" *Public Libraries* 39, no.1 (Jan/Feb 2000): 23–30.
5. John Cotton Dana, *The Public and Its Library* (1897) (Freeport, NY: Books for Libraries, 1969), 249–250.
6. Richard J. Bazillion and Connie L. Braun, *Academic Libraries as High-Tech Gateways: A Guide to Design and Space Decisions*, 2nd Edition (American Library Association 2001), 37, from *Planning Academic and Research Buildings*, 3rd edition, ed. Philip D. Leighton and David C. Weber (Chicago: American Library Association, 1999).
7. "Latte-da! New Library Has a Café," AZ Republic, *Washington Post*, August 30, 2000.
8. Diane Boulerice Lyons, "No Food, No Drink—No More? A Study of Food and Drink Policies and Practices in Public Libraries," *Public Libraries* 39, no. 6 (November/December 2000): 338–339.
9. Ibid., 340
10. http://www.osha.gov/SLTC/etools/computerworkstations/wkstation_enviro.html#lighting.
11. http://www.otherpower.com/otherpower_lighting.html.
12. http://www.osha.gov/SLTC/etools/computerworkstations/wkstation_enviro.html#lighting. (The U.S. Department of Labor Website includes a checklist guide and purchasing evaluation.)
13. Lightscape program @ Lightscape software (Discreet, a division of Autodesk, Inc.) http://www.autodesk.com.
14. Richard J. Bazillion, "The Wisdom of Hindsight: A New Library One Year Later," *American Libraries* (April 2001), 72.
15. Martyn Shaw, "Top Valley: A Joint Use Success Story," *School Libraries* 38, no. 2 (May 1990): 51–2.
16. Shared Use Facility presentation Debo-

rah Tasnadi, Deborahtasnadi@mail.maricopa.gov.

17. E. McC., "Scottsdale PL branch boom built on school partnership," *American Libraries* 26 (1 October 1995): 871.

18. Ty Young, "Centers (don't say senior) look to get hip to draw baby boomers" *The Arizona Republic,* December 12, 2005, A14.

Chapter 2

1. Richard J. Bazillion and Connie L. Braun, *Academic Libraries as High-Tech Gateways: A Guide to Design and Space Decisions*, 2nd edition (American Library Association, 2001), 36, available at http://www.intertek-etlsemko.com.

2. http://www.intertek-etlsemko.com.

3. Wikipedia contributors, "Underwriters Laboratory," in *Wikipedia: The Free Encyclopedia*, available at http://en.wikipedia.org/w/index.php?title=Underwriters_Laboratory&direction=next&oldid=35201366 (accessed March 13, 2006).

4. Winn L. Rosch Lab Notes, *PC Magazine* (August 1991): 397–406.

5. National Electrical Code, Article 605: Office Furnishings, 70–576.

Chapter 3

1. Richard J. Bazillion and Connie L. Braun, *Academic Libraries as High-Tech Gateways: A Guide to Design and Space Decisions*, 2nd edition (American Library Association, 2001), 116–117.

2. Ibid., 116

3. Tish Murphy, Some Considerations in Choosing Library Furniture, *Public Libraries* 38, no. 4 (July/August 1999): 245.

4. Industrial Standards for Particleboard, ANSI A208.1-1999; Industrial Standards for MDF ANSI A208.2-2002, available at http://www.pbmdf.com.

5. Judith Davidsen, "Particleboard: A Look beneath the surface shows there is nothing to hide," *Interior Design* (1990), 176.

6. Jeffery Swiggett, "Peel Me a Log," *Contract Design* (April 1999), 98.

7. Ibid.

8. Marilyn Farrow, "How Do They Do That? The Process of Selection," *Fine Furnishings International*, no. 3: 23–24.

9. Nancy Lohrer, "How to Select Furniture for a Library," *Media and Methods* 42, no. 1 (Sept/Oct 1997): 44.

Chapter 4

1. *Library Technology Reports* (November/December 1998): 848–852

2. Ibid., 852.

3. Creating Library Spaces: libraries 2040, Rob Bruijnzeels, available at: http://www.ifla.org/IV/ifla68/papers/037-094e.pdf, Wilson 16.2M 6/86.

4. http://www.wes.army.mil/REMR/bulls/v0113/n03/text/voc.html.

5. MJ Industries Color Selector Card, 2005.

6. *Library Technology Reports* (November/December 1998): 692.

7. "Test Reports on 15 Models of Bracket-type Steel Library Bookstacks," *Library Technology Reports* 34, no. 6 (November/December 1998).

8. Federal Register/V01.56, No. 144/Friday, July 26, 1991/Rules and Regulations 4.2.1 Space Allowance and Reach Ranges; Wheelchair Passage Widths.

Chapter 5

1. Roberta L. Null, PhD, with Kenneth Cherry, *Universal Design: Creative Solutions for ADA Compliance* (Belmont, CA: Professional Publications, 1996), 25.

2. Ibid.

3. Christopher Lewis, "The Americans with Disabilities Act and Its Effect on Public Libraries," *Public Libraries* (January/February 1992): 23

4. http://www/usdoj.gov/crt/ada/janmar99.htm.

5. Federal Register/V01.56, No 144/Friday, July 26, 1991/ Rules and Regulations 8.0 Libraries, p 35668.

6. American Foundation for the Blind, "Facts about Aging and Vision," June 2002, available at http://www.afb.org/info_documents.asp?CollectionID=2.

7. Eunice G. Lovejoy, *Portraits of Library Service to People with Disabilities,* chapter 3 (Boston, MA: G.K. Hall, 1990).

8. Ibid.

9. Mimi McCain, "What's So Special About Special Needs?" *Public Libraries* 42, no. 1 (Jan/Feb 2003): 52.
10. Lovejoy.

Chapter 6

1. ANSI/BIFMA X5.4–1983 and GSA specification FNAE-80-214.
2. "Static Load Tests on Westin-Nielsen Chairs," Twin City Testing Corporation Project No. 30160-04-61699 (September 1, 2004).
3. American Standards for Testing and Materials.
4. Ken Marks and Tom Findley, "Lied Library at the University of Nevada, Las Vegas: Post Construction Thoughts" *Library Hi Tech* 23, no. 1 (2005): 16–21, available at http://www.emerald insight.com/0737-8031.htm.
5. Library Bureau, *Classified Illustrated Catalog* (1902): 23, 43.
6. Abigail A. Van Slyck, *Free to All: Carnegie Libraries and American Culture, 1890–1920*, (Chicago: University of Chicago Press,1995), 100.
7. Vivian F. Thomas, "The First Carnegie Library," *Wilson Library Bulletin* 9 (1995): 52–54.

Chapter 7

1. "Garden of Literacy," *The Arizona Republic,* October 20, 2004.
2. http://www.Cryptonfabric.com/test_specifiications.aspx.
3. Abigail A. Van Slyck, *Free to All: Carnegie Libraries and American Culture, 1890–1920*, (Chicago: University of Chicago Press) 1995), 100.
4. Ibid., 26.
5. http://www.homepage.ntlworld.com/g.blaike/interiors.htm, "*Inside the Libraries, 1907*"; photographs of Langside Library contributed by Wilma Moore.
6. Van Slyck, 25.
7. Ibid.
8. Harriet Long, *Library Service to Children: Foundation and Development* (Metuchen, NJ: Scarecrow Press, 1969), 80–94.
9. Van Slyck , 26.

Chapter 8

1. Jacqueline Simone Gayle, "Library Space with a Teen Twist Youth Panel, Architect Design 4th Floor Center," *The Arizona Republic,* June 30, 2000, p. 1.
2. Marcia Gaysue, "Not Your Padre's Library," *The Arizona Republic,* January 6, 2006, p. 1.
3. Elias C. Arnold, "Library turns teens' ideas into a cool learning space," *The Arizona Republic,* Valley and State, March 1, 2006, sec. B4.
4. Ibid.
5. Abigail A. Van Slyck, *Free to All: Carnegie Libraries and American Culture, 1890–1920* (Chicago: University of Chicago Press, 1995), 109.

Chapter 9

1. Jenny Upchurch, "Librarian Jobs Opening Up through 1990s," *San Jose Mercury News,* June 14, 1992, classified sec.
2. Petroski, Henry, *The Book on the Bookshelf* (New York: Alfred A. Knopf, 1999).
3. Ibid.
4. Linton Weeks, "The Library of Congress and the Future of the Book," *The Washington Post Magazine*, Sunday, May 26, 1991, p. 13.
5. Consumer Price Index Conversion Factors, 1800–2015, to convert dollars to 2005 dollars http://www.oregonstate.edu/Dept/pol_sci/fac/sahr/cv2005.pdf.
6. http://www.loc.gov/about/history/.
7. Weeks, 31.
8. Abigail A. Van Slyck, *Free to All: Carnegie Libraries and American Culture, 1890–1920* (Chicago: University of Chicago Press, 1995), 47.
9. Library Bureau, *Classified Illustrated Catalog* (1897), 5.138.
10. "L.B. Training School; Enthusiastic opening of eight weeks summer course for prospective salesmen," *Salesmen's Bulletin* 40 (22 July 1903).
11. Van Slyck, 52.
12. Ibid., 98–99.
13. Ibid., 92–93.
14. Ibid., 95.
15. Ibid., 34.
16. Ibid., 135.
17. Ibid., 137.
18. Ibid., 169.

19. "Store of Knowledge" *Contract Design* (June 1997): 6.

20. Rob Bruijnzeels, "Creating Library Spaces: Libraries 2040," 68th IFLA Council and General Conference, August 18–24, 2002, available at http://www.ifla.org/IV/ifla68/papers/037-094e.pdf.

21. Betty Beard, "Libraries Start to Join the High-tech Revolution," *The Arizona Republic*, July 17, 2000, sec. B5.

Chapter 10

1. Lynda M. Baker and Judith J. Field, "Reference Success; What Has Changed over the Past Ten Years?" *Public Libraries* 39, no. 1 (Jan/Feb 2000): 23–30.

2. Excerpts relating to signs from *The Federal Register*/V01.56, N0.144/Friday, July 26, 1991, Rules and Regulations

3. Brian Kenney, "The Library Reloaded," *Library Journal Buyer's Guide* (December 2003), 9

4. Susan DiMattia, "Silence Is Golden," *American Libraries* (January 2005): 49

Chapter 11

1. Jennifer Thiele Busch, "Are You a Good Wood or a Bad Wood?" *Contract Design* (April 1996): 78

2. Ibid.

3. Treehugger Archives, available at http://www.treehugger.com/files/materials/index.php.

4. Matthew Power, "From a Bamboo Crisis — Innovation," September 9, 2004, available at http://www.csmonitor.com/2004/0909/p14s01-sten.html.

5. http://www.peterdanko.com/greendesign.html.

6. http://www.peterdanko.com.

7. Reprinted from http://www.peterdanko.com with permission.

8. Jayne O'Donnell, "Designers buckle up whole line of seat belt fashions, furniture" *USA Today*, December 2, 2004, sec. 4B.

9. http://www.Vivavi.com (environmentally friendly furniture).

10. Ira Flatow, NPR interview with Josh Dorfman on *Talk of the Nation: Science Friday*, March 10, 2006 (new design-centric environmental movement).

11. Ibid.

12. Louise Levy Schaper, "Public Input Yields Greener Library Design," *Library Journal* 128, no. 20 (December 2003): 63

13. Available at http://www.epa.gov/iaq/voc.html.

14. "Eco-Glossary," available at http://www.vivavi.com/materials.php.

15. http://www.Vivavi.com (environmentally friendly furniture).

Chapter 12

1. Henry Petroski, *The Book on the Bookshelf* (New York: Alfred A. Knopf, 1999), 183.

2. Ibid., 181.

3. Ibid., 217.

4. "Quiet, please! Robot librarian hard at work: Book-retrieval gear cuts costs, time," *The Arizona Republic*, November 4, 1991, p. A3.

5. Richard P. Hulser, "Prepare Today for the Digital Library of Tomorrow," in *The Future Compatible Campus: Planning Designing, and Implementing Information Technology in the Academy*, ed. Diana G. Oblinger and Sean C. Rush (Bolton, MA: Anker, 1998), 225.

6. http://library.csun.edu/About_the_Library/asrs.html, Northridge Oviatt Library Website, "Automated Storage & Retrieval System" (ASRS).

7. http://www.questia.com/pm.qst?a=o&d=5000447490.

Bibliography

Books

Bazillion, Richard J., and Connie L. Braun. *Academic Libraries as High-Tech Gateways: A Guide to Design and Space Decisions*, 2d edition. American Library Association, 2001.

Bisbort, Alan, and Linda Barrett Osborne. *The Nation's Library: The Library of Congress, Washington, D.C.* London: Scala, 2000.

Breisch, Kenneth A. *Henry Hobson Richardson and the Small Library in America*. Cambridge: Massachusetts Institute of Technology Press, 1997.

Dana, John Cotton. *The Public and Its Library* (1897). Freeport, NY: Books for Libraries Press, 1969.

Highsmith, Carole M., and Ted Landphair. *The Library of Congress, America's Memory*. Golden, CO: Fulcrum, 1994.

Hulser, Richard P. "Prepare Today for the Digital Library of Tomorrow," in *The Future Compatible Campus: Planning Designing, and Implementing Information Technology in the Academy*, ed. Diana G. Oblinger and Sean C. Rush. Bolton, MA: Anker, 1998, 225.

Konya, Allan, ed. *Libraries: A Briefing and Design Guide*, 2nd edition. New York: Architectural Press Series; London: Van Nostrand Reinhold, 1986.

The Library of Congress: An Architectural Alphabet 2000. Library of Congress Publishing Office, Pomegranate 2733.U6.L542000.

Long, Harriet G. *Library Service to Children: Foundation and Development*. Metuchen, NJ: Scarecrow, 1969, 80–94.

Lovejoy, Eunice G. *Portraits of Library Service to People with Disabilities*. Boston: G.K. Hall, 1990.

McCarthy, Richard C. *Designing Better Libraries: Selecting and Working with Building Professionals*, 2nd edition. Highsmith Press Handbook Series, 1999.

Null, Roberta L., with Kenneth Cherry. *Universal Design: Creative Solutions for ADA Compliance*. Belmont, CA: Professional Publications, 1996, 25.

Oehlerts, Donald E. *Books and Blueprints: Building America's Public Libraries*. New York: Greenwood, 1991.

Petroski, Henry. *The Book on the Book Shelf*. New York: Alfred A. Knopf, 1999.

Single Building: Phoenix Central Library; Process of an Architectural Work, edited by Oscar Riera Ojeda, with an introduction by Nader Tehrani. Rockport Publishers, 1999.

Van Slyck, Abigail A. *Free to All: Carnegie Libraries and American Culture, 1890–1920*. Chicago: University of Chicago Press, 1995.

Journal Articles

Baker, Lynda M., and Judith J. Field. "Reference Success: What Has Changed over the Past Ten Years?" *Public Libraries* 39 (Jan/Feb 2000): 23–30.

Busch, Jennifer Thiele. "Are You a Good Wood or a Bad Wood?" *Contract Design* (April 1996): 78–80.

Chelton, Mary K. "Three in Five Library Users are Youth: Implications of Survey Results from the National Center for Education Statistics." *Public Libraries* 36, no. 2 (March/April 1997): 104–108.

Davidsen, Judith. "Particleboard: A Look Beneath the Surface Shows There Is Nothing to Hide." *Interior Design* (1990): 176.

DiMattia, Susan. "Silence Is Golden." *American Libraries* (January 2005): 49.

Goldberg, Beverly. "Scottsdale PL Branch Boom Built on School Partnership." *American Libraries* 26 (October 1995): 871.

Hellett, Vicky. "Teaching with Tech." *U.S. News and World Report,* 7 October 2005, pp. 55–58.

Kenney, Brian. "The Library Reloaded." *Library Journal* (December 2003): 8–10.

Levy Schaper, Louise. "Public Input Yields Greener Library Design." *Library Journal* 128, no. 20 (December 2003: 63.

Lewis, Christopher. "The Americans with Disabilities Act and Its Effect on Public Libraries." *Public Libraries* (January/February 1992): 23.

Lohrer, Nancy. "How to Select Furniture for a Library." *Media and Methods* 34, no. 1 (Sept/Oct 1997): 44.

Lyons, Diane Boulerice. "No Food, No Drink — No More? A Study of Food and Drink Policies and Practices in Public Libraries." *Public Libraries* 39, no. 6 (November/December 2000): 338–344.

Marks, Ken, and Tom Findley. "Lied Library at the University of Nevada, Las Vegas: Post Construction Thoughts." *Library Hi Tech* 23, no. 1 (2005): 16–21, available at http://www.emeraldinsight.com/0737-8031.htm.

McCain, Mimi. "What's So Special about Special Needs?" *Public Libraries* 42, no. 1 (Jan/Feb 2003): 52.

Murphy, Tish. "Some Considerations in Choosing Library Furnishings." *Public Libraries* 38, no. 4 (1999): 244–246.

Shaw, Martyn. "Top Valley: A Joint Use Success Story." *School Libraries* 38, no. 2 (May 1990): 51–52.

"Store of Knowledge." *Contract Design* (June 1997): 6.

Swiggett, Jeffrey. "Peel Me a Log." *Contract Design* (April 1999): 98.

Thomas, Vivian F. "The First Carnegie Library." *Wilson Library Bulletin* 9 (1995): 52–54.

Newspaper Articles

The Arizona Republic, "Latte-da! New Library Has a Café," August 30, 2000, from *The Washington Post.*

_____, "Library Turns Teens' Ideas into a Cool Learning Space," Valley and State, March 1, 2006, sec. B4.

_____, "Quiet, please! Robot Librarian Hard at Work: Book-retrieval Gear Cuts Costs, Time," November 4, 1991, A3.

Beard, Betty. "Libraries Start to Join the High Tech Revolution." *The Arizona Republic,* July 17, 2000, p. B5.

Gayle, Jacqueline Simone. "Library Space with a Teen Twist, Youth Panel, Architect Design 4th Floor Center," *The Arizona Republic,* June 30, 2000.

Graysue, Marcia. "Not Your Padre's Library." *The Arizona Republic,* Friday, January 6, 2006, p. 1.

O'Donnell, Jayne. "Designers buckle up whole line of seat belt fashions, furniture." *USA Today,* December 2, 2004, sec. 4B.

Weeks, Linton. The Library of Congress and the Future of the Book, *The Washington Post Magazine,* Sunday, May 26, 1991 p. 10–17 and 27–31

Young, Ty. "Centers (don't say senior) look to get hip to draw baby boomers." *The Arizona Republic,* December 5, 2005, sec. A14.

Reports, Codes and Catalogs

ALA/LAMA/BES APL Committee, Checklist of Library Building Design Considerations 7/88.

ANSI/BIFMA X5.4–1983 and GSA specification FNAE-80-214.

Creating Library Spaces: libraries 2040, Rob Bruijnzeels, available at http://www.ifla.org/IV/ifla68/papers/037-094e.pdf.

"Eco-Glossary "http://www.vivavi.com/materials.php.

Federal Register/V01.56, No 144/Friday, July 26, 1991/ Rules and Regulations 8.0, Libraries, p. 35668.

Federal Register/V01.56, No. 144/Friday, July 26, 1991/Rules and Regulations 4.2.1 Space Allowance and Reach Ranges; Wheelchair Passage Widths 4.30.1–8 Federal Building Signage Requirements

Flatow, Ira. National Public Radio interview with Josh Dorfman on *Talk of the Nation: Science Friday,* March 10, 2006 (new design-centric environmental movement).

Frankel, Arthur D., Mark D. Petersen, Charles S. Mueller, Kathleen M. Haller, Russell L. Wheeler, E.V. Leyendecker, Robert L. Wesson, Stephen C. Harmsen, Chris H. Cramer, David M. Perkins, and Kenneth S. Rukstales. 2005 Seismic-hazard maps for the conterminous United States: U.S. Geological Survey Scientific Investigations Map SIM-2883, 6 sheets, available at http://pubs.usgs.gov/sim/2005/2883.

Klein, F.W., A.D. Frankel, C.S. Mueller, R.L. Wesson, P.G. Okubo. 2000 Seismic-hazard maps for Hawaii: U.S. Geological Survey Geologic Investigations Series I-2724, 2 sheets, available at http://greenwood.cr.usgs.gov/pub/i-maps/i-2724/.

"L.B. Training School: Enthusiastic opening of eight weeks summer course for prospective salesmen." *Salesmen's Bulletin* 40 (22 July 1903).

"Libraries for the Future, Planning Libraries That Work," in *Papers from LAMA Library Buildings Pre-conference*, June 27–28, 1991, ALA, Ron G. Martin, ed. Chicago and London, 1992.

Library Bureau, *Classified Illustrated Catalog* (1902): 23, 43. and (1897): 5.138.

Library Technology Reports (November/December 1998): 848–852. "Test Reports on 15 Models of Bracket-type Steel Library Bookstacks."

MJ Industries Color Selector Card, 2005.

National Electrical Code, Article 605 — Office Furnishings, 70–576.

Wesson, Robert L, Arthur D. Frankel, Charles S. Mueller, Stephen C. Harmsen. 1998 Seismic-hazard maps for Alaska and the Aleutian Islands: U.S. Geological Survey Geologic Investigations Series I-2679, 2 sheets, available at http://greenwood.cr.usgs.gov/pub/i-maps/i-2679/.

Wilson 16.2M 6/86.

Websites

Helpful Websites and sources relevant to planning libraries will be updated periodically: www.libraryfurnishings.com.

ADA Compliance: ADA Website at http://www.ada.gov.

American Foundation for the Blind Facts About Aging and Vision, June 2002, http://www.afb.org/info_documents.asp?CollectionID=2 and http://www.

Access-oard.gov/adaag/html/adaag.htm#lib.

Consumer Price Index Conversion Factors, 1800–2005, to convert dollars to 2005 dollars, available at http://oregonstate.edu/Dept/pol_sci/fac/sahr/cv2005.pdf.

Feather, John, and Paul Sturges, eds. *International Encyclopedia of Information and Library Science*. New York: Routledge, 2003. *Questia*. 24 Feb. 2006, available at http://www.questia.com/PM.qst?a=o&d=107733853.

Green materials archive: http://www.treehugger.com.

http://www.Cryptonfabric.com/test_specifications.aspx.

http://www.disastercenter.com.

http://www.homepage.ntlworld.com/g.blaike/interiors.htm.

http://www.Kartoo.com and http://www.edfacilities.org/rl/libraries.cfm

http://www.visualizerset.com.

http://www.wes.army.mil/REMR/bulls/v0113/n03/text/voc.htmlhttp://www.libraryfurnishings.com.

"Inside the Libraries 1907," photographs of Langside Library contributed by Wilma Moore.

LEED certification: http://www.usgbc.org.

Left-handed persons, sources for: http://www.anthingleft-handed.co.uk/faq.html and http://www.intertek-etlsemko.com.

Library of Congress Website: http://www.loc.gov/about/history/.

Librisdesign.org/docs/furniturefinaltext_newdoc?bbatt=y.

Lightscape program @ Lightscape software: Publisher: Discreet, a division of Autodesk, Inc., available at http://www.autodesk.com.

OSHA Ergonomic Solutions: US Department of Labor Website includes a checklist guide and purchasing evaluation for computer workstations and chairs, available at http://www.osha.com; http://www.osha.gov/SLTC/etools/computer-workstations/index.html; and http://www.osha.gov/SLTC/etools/computer-workstations/wkstation_enviro.html#lighting

Power, Matthew. "From a Bamboo Crisis—Innovation," September 9, 2004, available at http://www.csmonitor.com/2004/0909/p14s01-sten.htmlArchive and conservation of materials, and http://www.lib.az.us/archives/conservation.cfm.

Seismic maps and information: http://www.seismo.unr.edu/htdocs/bldg.html.

Sign companies, national and local: http://www.signsearch.com.

Treehugger Archives, http://www.treehugger.com/files/materials/index.php and http://www.sustainabledesignguide.unm.edu/MSDG/materials_pi.html.

2040 conference: http://www.ifla.org/IV/ifla68/papers/037-094e.pdf.

UL Listing available at http://www.ul.com/consumers.

"Underwriters Laboratory," *Wikipedia: The Free Encyclopedia*, available at http://www.en.wikipedia.org/w/index.php?title=Underwriters_Laboratory&direction=next&oldid=35201366 (accessed March13, 2006).

Index

Aalto, Alvar 167
ADA: accessible 98; ADAAG Accessibility Guidelines 101; aisle spacing 96, 102; Area of Rescue Assistance 160; assembly areas 102; barrier 100; checkout lanes 102; compliance 94, 98; design 100; disability 99; exceptions 99; Federal Register, 1991 102; federal requirements 159; 5% per element 102; Links 194; "making a reasonable accommodation" 103; minimum requirements 97; RBK Consulting Services, Inc. 99; signs 158, 162, 163; survey 26 188 189; table clearance 102; wheelchair 108
Aisle spacing 96, 101
All Sign Systems 155, 163
Allegheny Public Library 158
Altman, Ellen vii
American Foundation for the Blind 103
American Libraries 35
American Library Association (ALA) 94, 99, 110, 139
American Sign Language 107
Amperage requirements 192
Anne Arundel County Library, MD 17
Architectural Review 3
Arizona Archives & Records 177
Armond, David 36
Association of Children's Librarians (ACL) 134

Bamboo 166
Barriers 100
Baruch College, NY 31
Beaverton City Library, OR 162
Bids versus contracts 70+
Billington, James H. 180
Book bins 91–92, 127–129
The Book on the Bookshelf 144
Book supports 87–88
Bookstore atmosphere 6, 27
Boomerang Project 35
Braille 164
Break rooms 24–25
Brigham Young University, UT 30
Bruder, Will 136
Buckstaff Company 62
Bunner, Henry Cuyler 74
Burnette, Wendell 139
Burton Barr Central Library, AZ 124, 137
Business & Institutional Manufacturers Association (BIFMA): performance testing 113
Byron vii

California Bureau of Home Furnishings Technical Bulletin 133 (CAL133) 117
California State University 178
California State University Library 145–146, 178
Camas, Washington 131
Canadian Standards Association (CSA) 42

Canopy tops: calculating dimensions 81–82, 93–94
Carnegie, Andrew 134, 149, 151
Carnegie Corporation 134, 151
Carnegie Formula 123
Carnegie libraries 121–122, 151
Cellular floor 48
Chairs *see* Seating
Chandler, AZ 35
Children's area 20, 124+, 127
Coffee shops 14, 28
Colorado State University, CO 49
Commons 4
Conan Doyle, Sir Arthur 53
Concession amenities/stores 6, 13–14, 27+
Construction time line 31–33
Creep 80, 82, 94
Critical measurement 79
Cummings, Nancy 36
Customer's Own Material (COM) 118

Danko, Peter 167
Defining tasks and responsibilities of the development team 183
Department of Justice vs. New Oxford Burrough, PA 101
Desert Broom Branch Library, AZ 156, 161, 170–172
Dewey Decimal 160
Dewey, Melvil 149–150
DiMattia, Susan 164

INDEX

Displays 13; multimedia 11
Dorfman, Josh 169
Droke, Steve 40
DVD collection 92

Eames, Charles 167
Eco-glossary 173–174
Edwards, Tyron 110
Electronic planning: amperage 192; electrical 40–41, 191
Eliot, T.S. 165
End panels 81, 93–94; calculating dimensions 81
Enoch Pratt Free Library, MD 172
Environmental Protection Agency (EPA) 84, 172

Fabric: American Society for Testing and Materials (ASTM) 117; Association for Contract Textiles 117; durability ratings 117
Farmington Public Library, NM 9, 10, 12, 15, 100, 136, 137, 139, 140
Farnham, Shera 138
Fayetteville Public Library, AR 170
Feng Shui 107
Finishes: paint 83; plastic laminate 65; types of 68+
FK Importation 165
Flammability 117
Flanagan, John 149
Flatow, Ira 169
Food and drink 28, 29
Foot-candles 29
Forest Stewardship Council (FSC) 172–173
Franklin, Benjamin 97
Friends of Phoenix Library, AZ 136
Fuqua, Johnathon Scott 155
Furniture, Fixtures & Equipment (FF&E) 32

Garlitz, Bill vii
Getty, Paul 178
Gibson, Charlie 124
Gilbert, Cass 151
Gilbert, AZ 9
Glendale Library, AZ 154
Glenwood Library, MD 28
Green, Bernard 177

Greenpeace 172
GSA Performance Test 114

Helikon Furniture Company 63
Heraclitus 1
Homer 148
Hoover, Jeffrey 160
How to Select Furniture for the Library 68
Howard County, MD 27
Hudson, Kelly 177

Institute of Business Designers (IBD) 67
Issigonis, Sir Alec 175

Jefferson, Thomas 147, 168
Joint/shared use 33
Joints (carpentry) 67

Kay, Dr. James 34
Ketchican, Alaska 9
Koolhaus, Rem 160

Las Vegas, NV 36
The Lazy Environmentalist 169
Leadership in Energy & Environmental Design (LEED) 169–170, 172
Library Bureau 149–150
Library of Congress 146–148, 153, 168, 177, 180
Library Technology Reports 83
Lighting 29, 89–90; foot-candles 29
Lockwood, Tina 155, 163
Lohrer, Nancy 68
Los Angeles Public Library, CA 136
Lumbercore 59+

Mace, Ronald 97
McColgin, Michael 177
McDonough, Kristin 154
McLachlan, Ross 52
Means, Keri vii
Media storage 90–92
Metcalf, Keyes 183
Miller, E. Ethelbert 136
MJ Industries 76
MJ Steel Shelving 79
Monticello 148
Morgan, Jake 139

Moses 148
Myller, Rolf 9

National Digital Library effort 180
National Electric Code (NEC) 192
National Particleboard Association (NPA) 62
National Public Radio (NPR) 169
National Recognized Testing Lab (NRTL) 42
Nevada, MO 151
New York Public Library 154
New York Science, Industry & Business Library (SIBL), NY 154

OPAC 51
Oviatt Library, CA 178
Oxfordshire, England 178
Oxon Hill Branch, Prince George County, MD 13

Paint finishes 83
Parenting 124
Particle board 60-63
Performance Testing: ANSI/BIFMA 68; Business & Institutional Manufacturers Association (BIFMA) 113; Canadian Standards Association (CSA) 42; flammability testing 117; GSA Performance Test 114; seating 110; Underwriters Laboratories (UL) 117
Peter Danko Designs 166–167
Peterhouse, Cambridge, England 146
Petroski, Henry 144, 145, 146
Phoenix Main Library, AZ 52, 137
Phoenix Public Libraries, AZ vii, 52, 104, 135, 137, 153
Plato 148
Plymouth State College, NH 68
Plywood 59+, 166
Poor Richard's Almanack 97
Power, Matthew 166

Public Libraries vii, 135
Puck 74

Radio Frequency Identification (RFI) 11, 14
Rayford, Merlene v
Register, Judy 35
Reupholstering 119–120
Request for Proposal (RFP) 58
Robertson, Merryman, Barnes, Architects, Inc., OR 19
Rules of Daily Conduct 135

Scottsdale Civic Center Library, AZ 136, 138, 177
Scottsdale Public Library, AZ 35, 136, 139, 177; Knowasis 138
Seating 110+; biomechanics 111; construction 166; design and testing 112; heights 127, 141; history of 122; lounge 120–121; performance and use 110–123; "plus size" 116, 131; reupholster 119; things to look for 114; two position 115; types of 114
Seattle Public Library 37, 160
Seismic requirements 85, 94
Service desk 14+
Shakespeare 148
Shelf Check Unit 98
Shelving 74+; stability 84+; *and see* Steel shelving
Sierra Club 172
Signage 11, 155+; ADA 158, 162–163; end panel 160
Slat wall 94
Sound 25-26
Special needs area 103+; adjustable work stations 106; Kurzweil machine 104; Toybrary 104–105
Steel shelving: accessories 87; book supports 87–88; canopy tops 93–94; case-type 75; critical measurement 79; deflection 85; depth of shelves 81; end panels 78, 93–94; installation 95–96; materials 92–93; media storage 90–92; newspaper display 88; nominal depth 78; range 75; Seismic zones 85; testing 94; volumes per linear foot 81
Storage 22
Stokes, Bill, Jr. 99
Study areas 22–24
Stuecker, Barry vii
Survey 26 188
Sustainable design 171
Swiggett, Jeffrey 63

Tables 127
Tasks & responsibilities 183
Teen areas 136+, 170
Teen Central 137
Telluride Wilkinson Public Library, CO 128
Thiele Busch, Jennifer 165
Thoreau, Henry David 143
Tigard Public Library, OR 29
Tropical Forest Foundation 165
Two-position chairs 115

Underwriters Laboratories (UL) 117
United States Geological Survey, Seismic Zone Map 86
United States Green Building Council 169, 172
Universal design 97, 99, 108
University of Nevada, Las Vegas, Lied Library 25, 31, 119
Upchurch, Jenny 143

Vajpayee, Atal Bihari 166
Van Slyek, Abigail 149–151
Veneer 59+
Vivavi 169, 173
Volatile organic compounds (VOC) 84, 169–170, 172

Warranties (manufacturers') 114
Weeks, Linton 147, 149
Wheelchair 101-102, 108
Widom, Rodeanne 154
Wiggers, John 173–174
Windows 29, 30, 36-37
Wireless fidelity (Wi-Fi) 139
Wood (kinds of) 165-167, 173–174
Wood joints 67
World Wildlife Fund (WWF) 172
Writing specifications 94, 112

Zick, Medina 136

DISCARDED